Provoking the Field

Provoking the Field

International Perspectives on Visual Arts PhDs in Education

Edited by Anita Sinner, Rita L. Irwin and Jeff Adams

intellect Bristol, UK / Chicago, USA

First published in the UK in 2019 by
Intellect, The Mill, Parnall Road, Fishponds, Bristol, BS16 3JG, UK

First published in the USA in 2019 by
Intellect, The University of Chicago Press, 1427 E. 60th Street,
Chicago, IL 60637, USA

A catalogue record for this book is available from the British Library.

Copy-editor: MPS Technologies
Cover designer: Alex Szumlas
Production managers: Katie Evans and Emma Berrill
Typesetting: Contentra Technologies

Print ISBN: 978-1-78320-991-0
ePDF ISBN: 978-1-78938-028-6
ePUB ISBN: 978-1-78938-027-9

This book was published with the support of a Partnership Development Grant from the Social Sciences and Humanities Research Council of Canada (890-2014-0065: The Pedagogic Turn to Art as Research: A Comparative International Study of Art Education). Grants were also received from Concordia University through the Office of Research.

This is a peer-reviewed publication.

Social Sciences and Humanities Research Council of Canada
Conseil de recherches en sciences humaines du Canada
Canada
Concordia

Contents

Introduction

The aim of this book is to open a *conversazione,* to invite debate on, and provide a resource for, arts researchers in education engaged in critical analysis and the articulation of such inquiry in doctoral studies. *Provoking the Field* encompasses creative acts and actions as part of the wider constellation of educational research, and advances pedagogical and experimental perspectives, reflective and evaluative assessments, methodological deliberations, and ethical issues and concerns in relation to a host of topic areas in visual arts education.

Across the chapters in this volume, we oscillate between intimate imaginative praxis and the tensions of academic protocols, doing so in ways that locate best practices in the negotiation of considerations, depictions and uniqueness of research processes as part of a growing body of exemplary inquiry. Such inquiry explores what constitutes the arts in educational research and how new frameworks are evolving in the academy (see for example Barrett and Bolt 2010; Biggs and Karlsson 2010; Elkins 2014; Leavy 2018; Tavin and Hiltunen 2017; Viadel and Roldán 2017). Braiding these strands of inquiry together provides the latitude to interrogate diverse forms of arts inquiry by bridging visual with literary, performative and digital methods, as well as the relationship of the arts with qualitative approaches.

As a survey of the pulse of current practices, authors guide us in reimagining the nature of dissertation research and scholarly inquiry in three knowledge clusters: Provoking Doctoral Processes that questions theoretical and methodological perspectives alongside emergent activities; Provoking Doctoral Practices where innovative inquiries and hybrid approaches develop as applied methods in the visual arts; and Provoking Doctoral Programmes, in which institutional climates and proprieties of programmes are inscribed in the concrete deliverables of scholarship, be that the thesis, exegesis or body of creative work. Areas of interest span from formal and informal learning environments, such as schools to post-secondary institutions, as well as community and adult education, placing pedagogy at the forefront of our inquiry with chapters from Australia, Brazil, Canada, Finland, Japan, Portugal, Spain, Taiwan, Turkey, the United Kingdom and the United States. We address questions including but not limited to: what is visual arts education and how does it take shape in doctoral research? How are visually oriented research methodologies being applied? What educational theories are widening debates concerning the visual arts in doctoral research? How might best practices be adapted cross-culturally?

Each section in the book offers compelling perspectives in which arts scholars and recent PhD graduates in the field of art education help inculcate deeper understandings of the interconnections among a growing international community of inquiry. In this way, arts dissertations as 'possibility spaces' (DeLanda 2016) move beyond the orthodox of standardized research practices, to open ways of thinking, doing and expressing the doctoral experience as unfolding, uncertain and potentially unexpected. Possibility spaces are active and flexible encounters, revealing the mediation of theory and practice as emotional, sensory and/or experiential knowledge, despite the existence of what has been described as a 'climate of extreme instrumentalism in higher education' (Macleod and Chapman 2014: 138). DeLanda's (2016) proposition 'lives' in why the arts as scholarly gestures are influencing this juncture in the academy, where deliberating on '*when* is a dissertation' underscores how discourse is being imagined beyond traditional models of what constitutes academic study. Broadening parameters of 'thinking-with', authors in this collection embrace a conjunctive space of *and*, bridging interpretive lenses to recognize the growing influences of post-humanism and new materiality. The following chapters evoke issues and priorities concerning the notion of researching in situ, with a wide spectrum of representational to nonrepresentational inquiry, as we pursue our educative prerogatives as intensities that are imaginative, rhythmic, organic engagements. Such degrees of difference embody the freedom to think in new ways within institutional parameters, as a kind of social cartography, where the arts are a catalyst for envisioning scholarship, and for making investigation, interpretation and evaluation more relational, conditional and contingent, while focusing on differentials within the research design and deliverables.

A compelling attribute of this collection is the breadth of terms invoked to articulate research design by individual authors, including diverse understandings of and hybrid mixing between practice-based, artistic research, arts-based, arts-informed, a/r/tography, as well as numerous customized methods shaped to meet the scope of inquiry in a given time and place. Michael Biggs and Henrik Karlsson, in their seminal text concerning research in the arts, note that such 'terminological differences indicate[d] an underlying common view that there was a new and problematic activity emerging in the creative and performing arts', and for us too, to move this conversation forward, it may be 'more important to find similarities' (2010: xiii). For visual art educators in this collection, our emphasis is on generative concept creation as a way into the contours of changing discourses of art education. It is the refinement and diversification of practice that arguably makes the arts as research a living, sustainable mode of inquiry. In this way the arts as research becomes an adaptive process, with multiplicity, subjectivity and relationality in the act and action of inquiry, unbound by the restrictions of conventional qualitative applications.

For instance, many authors in this collection have taken up forms of inquiry that are implicitly informed by the arts to studies that are explicitly defined as artistic, with a host of customized methods and perspectives informed by practice. In the case of a/r/tography for example, this may have begun as a localized approach in the early 2000s in Canada with renderings guiding inquiry (see Sinner et al. 2006), but it is now widely rearticulated in new and dynamic ways in transnational contexts, in relation to cultural, social, economic, political and educative activities. This is demonstrated in several chapters from geographically distributed locations, and among authors who have encountered a/r/tography as an alternate way of proceeding in relation to their research trajectories. Improvising approaches in this way destabilizes notions of methodology, and resists the impulse to solidify and concretize practice. Instead, moving from a/r/tography as part of arts-based orientations originally, to a/r/tography as practice-based, artistic and related forms of inquiry, suggests that as we move to greater innovation, we are at the same time charting uniquely situated events of knowledge creation and knowledge dissemination.

This referential approach to shaping research orientations maps shifting processes and practices from early studies concerning the arts as research, where defining practice was paramount, to a more discretionary construction of research design. We propose a disposition that as art educators we are always located between approaches, between different traditions and between different disciplines of education and art, much as Hofsess, Riddett and Siegesmund demonstrate in their adaptation of artistic research within educational associations, and in how Ravisankar embodies new materiality as an educator in ways that resonate with artistic research, even though the location of inquiry is not explicitly stated as such. It is in the cultivation of such proliferation, and provocation, that art education resides.

Art education has been and continues to be influenced in different measures across educative spaces and places, and across areas of inquiry, from the fine arts, social sciences and sciences, as this collection suggests. By drawing comparatively on related inquiries concerning the arts and doctoral research, our collection suggests movements are underway, informed by intellectual exchanges that have come to transcend set boundaries of thought. For example, in a survey of studio art dissertations (referred to as art education), Elkins (2014) characterized six regional doctoral cultures: the UK model (including former colonial countries), Continental European model, Nordic model, Japanese model, Chinese model, but notes a lack of a defined North American model (2014: 9–13). Historically, hotspots of arts research in the United Kingdom, Continental and Nordic orientations focused on artistic and practice-based approaches, while North America has been more strongly associated with arts-based and arts-informed perspectives. Although such assemblages are certainly evident in historic reviews, and at times have been at the heart of long-standing debates of disagreement within art education, these patterns of engagement are shifting as the circulation of approaches now takes on new forms, akin to 'diffractive entanglements' as innovation (see Barad 2012).

The conversation is moving beyond the intent of definition – what is practice-based, what is arts-based and so on – to attend to distinctiveness as a hallmark trait of quality and qualification in arts research. It may be that in the future, we will see a radical departure from such descriptors in research entirely, as the paradigmatic shift to post-qualitative orientations matures (St. Pierre 2013). In this way, *Provoking the Field* aligns with process ontology (Ulmer 2017), where our theories, methodologies and practices are always emerging through experimentation, rather than applying set approaches designed and defined in advance (Pedersen and Pini 2017).

As the authors demonstrate, the arts generate an enlargement of traditional dissertation evaluation, adding to baseline criteria of a substantial, original intellectual product that demonstrates the ability to conceive, plan and conduct a programme of study; complete a relevant and comprehensive survey of literature; document the skills required to critically analyse information; and finally, present the completed research in an oral exam. In this way, the arts add more complex expectations and an expansion of knowledge concerning practice-in-relation to what is already underway. In our triad of knowledge clusters, the strength of arts research resides in the diversity of modes of expression, the scope of issues relating to arts education and the implicit and explicit world-views as situated contexts from which research has materialized.

In Part 1, Provoking Doctoral Processes, the development of discerning theoretical and methodological innovations brings to the fore notions of transformational possibilities. The chapters in this section cohere around the issues of epistemology and methodology to which arts-based research methods give rise in doctoral education. These include the understandings and assumptions that underpin practices which might be assumed to be agreed upon or universally shared, but as these chapters demonstrate, this is often not so, and to suggest uniformity may well be problematic at a conceptual level.

Biggs opens the collection with a vision for the conceptualization of knowledge creation methods as a spectrum that has the effect of deterritorializing the field of power and authorizing minority communities to legitimize methods that are locally meaningful. Barrett advances the relationality of two paradigms of research: creative arts research and Indigenous research as modes of discovery that further challenge traditional approaches to inquiry. In two case studies, Adams and Arya-Manesh highlight the potential of creative interventions upon the professional practices of doctoral students who previously had little opportunity or experience with creativity in their research. Jokela, Huhmarniemi and Hiltunen discuss four exemplars of arts-based action research (ABAR) as an approach to developing professional methods for the artist-teacher-researcher seeking solutions and future visions at the nexus of the natural environment and communities. Working on the borders between fields, Hernández-Hernández draws on relationality and non-normative logic to demarcate alternate and/or resistant approaches to hegemonic languages that exist between research and art. With a position that the research question is not about a topic, but it is about living in a created personal, relational and ethical space, Hofsess, Riddett and Siegesmund make a case for visual art practice activated by theory to generate aesthetic spaces of inclusion and lacuna.

Provoking Doctoral Practices (Part 2) builds upon this conversation by provoking debate about embracing multiplicity within methods and the arts. Through a pair of red shoes, Bolt demonstrates how an object of investigation brings forward different questions, and serves as a means to tease out 'vexed' relationships between the conceptual framework and methodology in artistic research. Calderón promotes artistic research as a method to fold and unfold transitional disruptive social spaces, demonstrated through composing and editing a multiscreen video installation for her dissertation. Ravisankar poses the question: can matter, things and other non-human entities be considered as active agents in the artmaking process? This question evokes deliberations on subjectivity, agency, post-humanism and new materialism to reconsider the role of artmaking. By weaving notions of resistance-accommodation as intellectual gestures of exchange, Sinner, Sahagún Sánchez, Wicks and St. Georges contextualize dissertation journeys within a developing a/r/tographic community of practice. Shifting practices in Taiwan are the focus of Chen's chapter, where creating new rhythms for issues, reflections, writing and art practices are popular topics. Poietic learning objects (PLO) is an approach presented by Dias and Fernández that facilitates contiguity between theory, praxis and poiesis and the artist, researcher, teacher identities, in this case within the context of a continuing education course. The application of comparative visual research in Makemson's dissertation centres the research potential of structured symbolic objects, and outlines the practical application of comparative visual methodologies. Wren, Wright and Watkins offer an innovative practice-based approach to investigate how engagement with creative expression enables young children to explore, construct and express meaning through the arts. And finally, as a composition of artful engagement, White and Mandrona stage a dialogue on connective aesthetics from within their research locations of the university/museum and a rural community in South Africa, linking divergent contexts through values, ethics and democracy as potential forms of creativity in dissertations.

In the final section, Provoking Doctoral Programmes, authors broaden the definitions of artist, researcher and teacher, while fostering research communities engaged in inquiry as artwork scholarship. This section also addresses issues and tensions that arise when embedding arts practices in institutional programmes; these include ethical protocols, institutional orthodoxies of research practices and expectations for pedagogical practices, as well as institutional regulations that sometimes restrain or confound such approaches. The qualities of cultivation in artisan scholarship and the connoisseurship of a creative cluster within educational inquiry are inscribed between the lines of the individual immersed in institutional climates, the criteria for programme completion, and the interrelationships between student, supervisor and institution.

Turning to ethical issues, compliance with university protocols and practical steps to navigate this process are mapped by Blair in ways that focus on good mentorship and good scholarship. Site specific and regional cases of doctoral programmes then demonstrate arts research in action. Extending this discussion to digital e-learning, Grushka and Holbrook examine the legitimacy and transformative potential of artful participatory inquiry as an approach that constructs spatial complexity, reveals relational pedagogies and demonstrates the indeterminate nature of embodied learning. Eça and Saldanha survey arts-based and artistic research approaches in graduate courses in Portugal and

Spain. From Finland, Kallio-Tavin and Tavin offer examples of dissertation research that emphasize the interplay between art, education, research and its social function, and how the arts can be scholarly interventions. Naoe reviews the Japanese experience and his interest in cross-cultural and foreign language issues, contemplating whether they are barriers or catalysts. With structural shifts underway in what constitutes scholarship, similar concerns are expressed by Erişti, where in Turkey there is a need for further study on content development grounded in alternate methodologies, especially in the field of art and design. Shields and Irwin conclude Part 3 and the collection, bringing us back to the culminating ideas and possibilities articulated in the through-lines of the book by positing that arts-based research is uniquely situated, calling scholars to reflexively and reflectively consider their relations to artistic forms of inquiry, and to continue to provoke the boundaries of research leading to new forms of engagement and enhanced understandings of educational phenomena.

By undertaking this project, we are committed to making *Provoking the Field* a forum for dialogue that involves artful expression, innovative experimentation and critical propositions informed by aesthetic dispositions as well as tailored approaches for the advancement of the arts and education. Our goal is to encourage conversations dedicated to the development of discourses concerning visual arts education by offering a growing range of critical, reflective, speculative and evaluative standpoints concerning theoretical issues and visual practices. Our scholarly responsibility may be best vested in creating, nurturing and protecting creative spaces for arts research, and to continue to develop this area of study as part of mapping ideas, events and visual expression on a broad continuum from dissertations influenced by the arts to dissertations defined by art practice with infinite gradations.

This collection is not intended to be a definitive statement nor an exclusive review of arts dissertations, but a sampling of such work through an examination and reflection on the reciprocity of theory and practice and through ongoing questions of how we define expectations of new knowledge in educational research. The particularities of local perspectives provide insights into the ways emerging scholars, their supervisors and their institutions of learning embrace possibility spaces as a graduated reconceptualization of content, where the implicit – the commentary of the researcher – and the explicit – the sources of information – are a negotiated position of both the scholar (I) and the scholarship (object). The effectiveness of this work is then determined by characteristics of the imagination, accessibility and immediacy of the dissertation, resulting in a set of qualities that attend to the impetus of the provisional in arts research, with or even instead of conclusive findings.

Such an approach honours the methods of inquiry artists apply to art practice by extending the same orientation to a myriad of research designs surfacing through the arts in education. Guidelines for policies concerning arts dissertations may feature flexibility of standards, not strictly pre-set standards. As the doctoral student and supervisor are increasingly collaborative in the creation of possibility spaces, standards of validity and rigor may shift to focus on the suitability of the proposed work by way of embracing dislocation, unanswerable questions and/or experimentation with systems of thought. The process of thinking-with in this way, as well as the styles of writing and the modes of presentation that echo the supervisor-student exchange, can be deemed problematic within existing doctoral criteria and traditional research methods. Refining this approach places less emphasis on the artifice of research conventions, and brings our attention to the qualification of vibrancy concerning the significance of exchange, not as a utopic academic venture, but as a legitimate disposition of what can be described as the systematic inquiry of social and organizational contexts that produce artwork scholarship. Such traits, characteristic of art practice and consequential to the condition of art in a wider public forum, underscore the assembly of the arts dissertation, be that the written exposition, art installation and exhibition, or related activities. Therein lies a dilemma for the pedagogic turn to the arts in doctoral research as we move forward. When mediating steadfast expectations of institutional protocols, we need to find ways to advocate for greater autonomy in defining and evaluating creative dissertations. Though this debate has been ongoing for nearly two decades, a substantial body of rich, dynamic and analytical arts dissertations is to be found around the world, suggesting that arts research remains remarkably resilient to being classified in part because such work is conditional, and the conditions are seldom generic or normative. A potential outcome may be the recognition of specific practices as maturing localized knowledges at a given university. This may encourage future students to mobilize their interests in relation to institutional distinctiveness within visual arts research. The capacity of institutional communities of inquiry may prove a more important factor in doctoral recruitment than university rankings, attending more fully to what makes programmes unique as intensive thresholds of scholarship. By extension, the internationalization of art education may also place pressure upon existing protocols, such as the doctoral committee. While the institution hosts the emerging arts scholar and supervises the research, the required expertise of committee members – not just the external reviewer – may exist beyond the institution, rather than from within, as past practices have dictated, particularly in relation to arts research and the knowledge required to assess the nuance of thinking-with. Envisioning doctoral committees that are composed of transnational and transinstitutional members to support the development of, and resulting deliverables of arts dissertations, enlarges the parameters of the individual institution and arguably infuses discourse with multiplicity, furthering rigorous practice in the field. Such movements are already underway and may be traced in policies such as in Spain, where doctoral candidates are strongly recommended to complete a term internationally to receive a doctoral degree. In Canada, some institutions offer the option of a co-institutional doctoral degree between national and international universities and the implications for the potential of arts dissertation are significant in turn. Features of the arts dissertation are individualized and generative, yet destabilizing, and our authors problematize the politics of space within their institutions as an added layer in the growing sophistication of this creative potential.

A dissertation invoking arts research requires a degree of productive ambiguity, much like an open system where knowledge pathways are negotiated in ways that reshape the purpose, evolution, expectations and due diligence of the doctorate in the moment. By expanding theoretical and methodological constructs, the arts dissertation becomes increasingly adaptive, fostering greater specificity in linkages, networks of relations and geographies of self-in-relation, as suggested by a number of scholars in this collection where the alignment of arts research with the shift to post-post-paradigms offers another way forward. A new vernacular is beginning to take shape within educational inquiry concerning the form and content of the dissertation, attending to the idiosyncratic over thematic commonalities, singularity rather than generalizability, ambiguity as an expression of logic and immediacy instead of predictability.

This collection investigates the turn to the visual, with a companion text, *Visually Provoking: Dissertations in Art Education* (Sinner, Irwin and Jokela 2018), that embraces the advancement of scholarship as research creation, placing the visual essay at the forefront. As related volumes, these books may be read in tandem to demonstrate the array of textual and visual renderings, and how we can build upon the primary orientation of both modes of visual arts research in education. While the comparative qualities are important benchmarks to understand the arts in research from a genealogical perspective, it is equally important to recognize how arts research is a continuous streaming of intellectual engagement, where sustainable thinking-with arcs beyond the thesis, not as a conclusive document but as a trajectory of interest and expertise that continues to evolve as part of our ongoing pedagogic purpose. This collection, much as Macleod and Chapman (2014) suggest of artistic practice in the fine arts, demonstrates how arts research is indeed a new mode of artful writing, articulating research as an intervention of artistic agency, and serving as a hallmark of social pedagogy, or simply, art+education.

Anita Sinner
East Sooke
March 2018

References

Barad, K. (2012), 'Interview with Karen Barad', in R. Dolphijn and I. van der Tuin (eds), *New Materialism: Interviews and Cartographies*, Ann Arbor: Open Humanities Press, pp. 48–70.

Barrett, E. and Bolt, B. (eds) (2010), *Practice as Research: Approaches to Creative Arts Enquiry*, New York: I.B. Tauris.

Biggs, M. and Karlsson, H. (eds) (2010), *The Routledge Companion to Research in the Arts*, London: Routledge.

DeLanda, M. (2015), 'The new materiality', *Architectural Design*, 85:5, pp. 16–21.

——— (2016), *Assemblage Theory*, Edinburgh: University of Edinburgh Press.

Elkins, J. (ed.) (2014), *Artists with PhDs: On the New Doctoral Degree in Studio Art*, 2nd ed., Washington, DC: New Academia.

Leavy, P. (ed.) (2018), *Handbook of Arts-Based Research*, New York: Guilford.

Macleod, K. and Chapman, N. (2014), 'The absenting subject: Research notes on PhDs in fine art', *Journal of Visual Art Practice*, 13:2, pp. 138–49.

Pedersen, H. and Pini, B. (2017), 'Educational epistemologies and methods in a more-than-human world', *Educational Philosophy and Theory*, 49:11, pp. 1051–54.

Sinner, A., Irwin, R. L. and Jokela, T. (eds) (2018), *Visually Provoking: Dissertations in Art Education*, Rovaniemi: Lapland University Press.

Sinner, A., Leggo, C., Irwin, R. L., Grauer, K. and Gouzouasis, P. (2006), 'Arts-based dissertations: Reviewing the practices of new scholars', *Canadian Journal of Education*, 29:4, pp. 1223–70, https://files.eric.ed.gov/fulltext/EJ766913.pdf. Accessed 4 June 2018.

St. Pierre, E. (2013), 'The posts continue: Becoming', *International Journal of Qualitative Studies in Education*, 26:6, pp. 646–57.

Tavin, K. and Hiltunen, M. (eds) (2017), *Experimenting FADS: Finnish Art Education Doctoral Studies*, Helsinki: Aalto University Press.

Ulmer, J. (2017), 'Posthumanism as research methodology: Inquiry in the Anthropocene', *International Journal of Qualitative Studies in Education*, 30:9, pp. 832–48.

Viadel, R. and Roldán, J. (eds) (2017), *Visual Ideas: Arts-Based Research and Artistic Research*, Granada: University of Granada Press.

Part 1

Provoking Doctoral Processes

Chapter 1

The Knowledge Creation Spectrum

Michael Biggs

Latour begins his critique of laboratory life by noting that 'scientists often have an aversion to what non-scientists say about science' (Latour and Woolgar 1986: 11). This not only criticizes territorialism in science, but also reveals that knowledge creation is not just a univocal means-to-an-end but an activity that can be observed and critiqued in its own right. I have chosen the term 'knowledge creation' deliberately because I declare myself from the outset to be a constructivist: I believe that knowledge is principally constructed or made, rather than discovered or found. However, there is a spectrum between construction and discovery, and this chapter investigates this knowledge spectrum in order to ask what the present interest in practice-based research reveals about contemporary approaches to knowledge creation. Considering knowledge creation as a practical constructive activity has the advantage of integrating practice-based research and artistic approaches, and offers a new perspective on the activity of scientific knowledge creation too.

The scientific method

The Classical Model of scientific inquiry, which Latour had in his sights as something that is not as it seems, asserts that empirical science has developed a methodology, for example, a series of procedures, that when carefully followed can tell us what the external world is really like. It identifies both true facts about the world and generalized statements about relationships between those facts, such as causes and effects. These descriptions, or the ability to produce them, have been called 'naive realism' (Pronin et al. 2004), and are so culturally embedded that they correspond to what is often regarded simply as 'common sense' (Moore 1925). In everyday life we interact with objects as though they are really there and at an everyday level the laws of physics allow us to anticipate what is going to happen next. The apparent coincidence of the results of the scientific method with the common sense view has led to the basic laws of physics and other scientific principles being taught in school, and to it becoming fundamental to our western secular culture. However, over many centuries, there have been doubts about the legitimacy of some of the a priori logic of the scientific method and therefore doubts about the claims made by science. For example, Hume argued persuasively that we cannot conclude the existence of causes and effects from the repeated coincidence of events (Hume [1748] 2011: Section IV). These arguments have never been successfully refuted but in modern times they have been supplemented by additional procedures to keep the scientific method alive (Mill [1843] 2009; Boltzmann 1902; Popper [1959] 2002).

The unresolved problems with the underlying logic of the scientific method seem to be made irrelevant by the general usefulness of its findings, giving rise to what has been called the Pragmatic Model. Pragmatism (Mill [1843] 2009: Book III) sidesteps the issue of whether the claims of science are true, in favour of whether the claims of science are useful. According to this theory of knowledge creation, the scientific method enables us to interact with the world in effective ways, to predict and control in certain circumstances, and to create interventions that will achieve useful goals. Science, it turns out, is better described as a method of getting things done, than of finding out what the world is really like. Latour and Woolgar claim that the Pragmatic Model is the version of common sense that is generally held by contemporary scientists (1986: 19). Thus the principal benefits of the scientific method now rest on prediction and control rather than truth-claims. The shift from the Classical Model to the Pragmatic Model reveals that our concept of what we know can shift from Realism, in which we know the truth about the external world, to more hermeneutic claims that we know something about relationships within our model. This change of focus from extrinsic claims to intrinsic claims was finally brought into the foreground by Boltzmann who introduced Model Theory, in which scientific knowledge claims were further reduced from pragmatism. Model Theory merely claims that the outcome of scientific inquiry simulates behaviours that are analogous to what we observe happening in reality (Boltzmann 1902).

There are a few specific points to note from this brief history of several centuries of knowledge creation. First, I claimed that the naive realism of the Classical Model corresponds to the common sense view of the person in the street, but the common sense view of the practising scientist is more akin to the Pragmatic Model. The difference between these two models is that the Classical Model makes truth-claims about the nature of the external world whereas the Pragmatic Model makes utility-claims. This difference is significant for the cultural role that the scientific method, and science in general, has in society. Societally, scientists are held in high esteem because it is believed that they are finding out about what the world is really like. On the other hand, scientists themselves believe they are merely contributing to our ability to live in the world as we find it (Pew Research Center 2015), which perhaps merits less societal valorization than more practically beneficial activities such as psychoanalysis.

Second, it suggests that there is a scale or spectrum that is best viewed from outside both positions, for example, by adopting neither the view of popular common sense nor listening too much to the claims of scientists themselves. This perhaps explains Latour's observation regarding the aversion of scientists to what non-scientists say about science, that is, neither recognizes the descriptions of the other. But Latour's sociology of science goes a step further. It adopts neither the naive realist position nor the pragmatic position of scientists, but instead establishes a perspective from which the activities of knowledge creation amongst scientists is regarded as an activity undertaken by a community of like-minded individuals in pursuit of a common goal and set of beliefs.

Third, described in this way we start to see scientists as a community: establishing and reinforcing beliefs, identifying territory and behaving as a kinship group within the larger society (Cohen 1985). Science, according to Latour and using terminology that Cohen would recognize, is a social activity. Its principal function is neither to make truth-claims about reality nor to identify pragmatic ways in which we might cope with the world, but rather to reinforce the values and beliefs of the members of the group, to identify territory – in this case of the intellectual kind – and to fight border skirmishes with territorial invaders such as non-scientists and sociologists. This description shifts the emphasis away from the truth or benefit of the scientific method, towards seeing the activities of academic research and knowledge creation as a set of procedures almost like a choreography to which the participants conform (Bourdieu [1984] 1988). Nor can the pragmatist offer an overwhelming refutation of this sociological explanation. If one argues that science must be finding out something valid because technological and medical innovation have produced tangible benefits that must be related to reality in some way, one can also argue, conversely, that there are many issues in the world such as war, hunger, and oppression, etc., to which science does not seem to have made any contribution at all. This reveals a fourth point, which is that the measures of success are themselves selective and have been chosen to favour the apparent benefits of the system as perceived by the members of that system.

The historical shift from absolute to relative or relational claims is not something restricted to science. There has been a comparable shift in aesthetics from claims about intrinsic qualities (Baumgarten [1758] 2009; Kant [1790/93] 2015) to contextual claims (Collingwood [1923] 2013). Nowadays, the ideas of artistic research and collaborative meaning-making have replaced both Classical and Contextual aesthetic theories, lending 'more depth to discussions on quality, expanded concepts of knowledge, and forms of publication and communication' (Dyrssen 2015: 23).

It is not the objective of this chapter to either confirm or refute the claims of a single method or model. Its purpose is to reveal the scientific method as just one method of knowledge creation that sits on a spectrum of valid possibilities that extends to socially created and artistically created knowledge. It has both strengths and weaknesses, as do the other approaches to knowledge creation to be found on this spectrum. The hegemony of the scientific method, and the popular belief in its truth-claims, means that the scientific method appears to have a special authority in what Bourdieu calls 'the field of power' (Bourdieu and Wacquant 1992). This chapter discusses the alternatives that lie elsewhere on the spectrum and considers what they contribute to our understanding of the process of knowledge creation as a whole, and how the field of power will shift as these alternatives become more mainstream.

The critique of knowledge creation in science has tended to proceed from an explicit critique of the scientific method owing to the role it has in western culture as the principal means for the discovery of true knowledge. Bloor ([1976] 1991) chose to criticize the scientific method in terms of its discretionary emphasis on certain data and procedures. According to Bloor there are many irregularities and inconsistencies in scientific procedures, amongst the most apparent being the simplification and idealization of data. We have all encountered this at school where we were taught experimental procedures in the laboratory, along with some of the basic tricks of science. For example, we have probably had the experience of undertaking an experiment, recording data and plotting it on a graph. The trick is to draw a straight line that connects all of the points plotted on the graph. However there is never a straight line that connects these points because the exact position of the points has been influenced by practical features of the experimental apparatus and the conditions under which the experiment was undertaken. The line, we are told, represents what the result would have been like had the conditions been ideal. But of course there is no such thing in reality as ideal conditions. The purpose of making this idealized simplification is to enable us to form general rules and principles, a 'white lie' that can be used to understand the complexities of actual lived experience.

Bloor's purpose is to point out that at a fundamental level the procedures of knowledge creation that are employed in science have no greater claim to validity than many alternatives. His target is the perceived authority of the scientific method as a procedure, and in common with Latour he instead emphasizes the limited objectives of the method and the extent to which goals are set that the procedures are able to satisfy. In an activity theory of research such as Bloor and Latour share, despite their public disagreement about its motives (Bloor 1999; Latour 1999), the participants create knowledge through a series of shared activities based on common beliefs and attitudes about the benefits and purpose of the inquiry being undertaken. This diminishes the extrinsic claims for the activity in favour of the harmonization of the beliefs and activities within the group. Activity theory (Engeström et al. 1999) is a form of anthropology in Cohen's terms, and this diminution serves not to diminish the benefits of the outcome but instead to reposition our understanding of how knowledge creation works. In particular it diminishes our common sense assumption or desire for truth-claims and instead highlights the notion of satisfaction (Biggs and Büchler 2011), for example, questioning generally stops when participants are satisfied with an answer or response. It also recognizes that by setting the targets themselves, the group's claims for performance are based on self-selected criteria. As a member or participant in an activity, one is satisfied when the activities of the members are harmonious with the collective belief set, and this applies as much to feelings regarding knowledge creation as it does to any other kind of mutual reinforcement.

It is a claim of practice-based research that our shared beliefs can focus not only on belief sets about the external world or on notions of shared beliefs, but also on shared practices. Such practices include a shared societal valorization of the production of visual art, theatre performance and dance, music, etc. Such artistic activities were previously seen as distinct from the activities of science (Snow 1959). Under my proposed knowledge creation spectrum, they are part of a continuum of possible knowledge creation activities. Although the word 'knowledge' is not usually applied unmediated to the outcomes of artistic activity – where descriptions such as 'the advancement of creativity, insights, knowledge and understanding' are used instead (AHRC 2018) – I argue that this is pedantry based on an artificial division between technical and social knowledge of the kind described by Latour (Latour and Woolgar 1986: 23). If one accepts Latour's description of the scientific method as just one example of the practices that are legitimized by society, one can compare quantitative, qualitative, a/r/tographic, performative and other modes of inquiry as equally viable sites on the knowledge creation spectrum, generating discrete bodies of knowledge with the added possibility of knowledge exchange between them.

Biggs and Büchler (2008) proposed an intrinsic set of conditions in which knowledge and knowledge production, its evidence, methods and argumentation, all occur within the context of an audience of users and evaluators who are peers of the knowledge producers. However, they also proposed that the processes of legitimation and valorization occur within a more general audience who can perceive their relationship to other forms of knowledge in academia or in the arts. It is therefore clear that there is no significant difference between the description of practice-based research in the arts, and knowledge creation in other fields. The advantage of their analysis is that it avoids cultural prejudice that favours certain methods and procedures that arise from the hegemony of the scientific method in western culture, and replaces them with a meta-view of knowledge creation as a set of procedures undertaken by societally authorized groups, based in a range of activities including empirical observation, the pursuit of practical interventions, the reinforcement and development of shared understandings, and the reinforcement and development of shared practices.

Having identified a number of separate activity-based approaches to knowledge creation, we can now reflect upon the relationship between the characteristics of the activity and the characteristics of the knowledge produced. The main activities have been the observational approach that underpins the Classical and Pragmatic Models of science, the sociological approach that underpins Latour's and Bloor's models, and the practices and activity theory that underpin the model of Biggs and Büchler. Contemporary practice-based research in the arts highlights the possibility of activity or performance as a means of knowledge creation. This has been described elsewhere in terms of the fundamental performativity (Haseman 2006) and materiality (Carter 2004) of all types of research and knowing.

The observations of scientific inquiry are underpinned by practices in the form of experimentation. Experimentation is not merely the creation of certain real-world conditions, but a filtering process in which these conditions are abstracted with varying degrees of success from the surrounding complexity of the real world. The objective of these practices is to try to isolate the subject of scientific inquiry from its practical manifestation, or in terms of the present argument: to isolate the evidence that supports the interests of the field of power. The degree to which this cannot be achieved in practice is the degree to which certain simplifying and compensating activities must be included in the inquiry. It is these simplifications and idealizations that form the focus of Bloor's criticisms. The acceptability of these simplifications is an example of the kind of social cohesion and collusion that is criticized by Latour and constitutes the activity of belonging and kinship that would be recognized by Cohen. The results of scientific inquiry arise every bit as much as a consequence of a selective, choreographed performance, as they do in theatre or performance-based art. The principal difference, I claim, is merely a preference for the use of 'knowledge' in the case of the former and 'insight' or 'understanding' in the case of the latter. This, in turn, appeals to our cultural understanding that we have inherited from Plato, that knowledge should be something deeper, less contingent, more certain and therefore more meritorious, than insight, understanding and belief. Science is merely a series of performances in which physical experiments are staged and the data is analysed according to a selective choreography that highlights certain accounting practices. The process is stage-managed through the presentation of the activity as a research report (performance documentation) that exposes the insight and new understanding of the topic under investigation.

Knowledge creation, and the issue of 'what is research' in any field, can be answered by the concept of 'satisfaction' and not by appeal to truth-claims or productivity-claims. Productivity-claims are not satisfying in a world dominated by the Classical Model, just as truth-claims are viewed with suspicion in a world dominated by the Pragmatic Model. Satisfaction emerges as a unifying principle when one abandons the idea of a hegemonic model in favour of a spectrum of knowledge creation. Within any one domain, such as science, aesthetics or studio art, what validates a research methodology is that the community is satisfied that the research methods used have the capability to add meaningfully to the body of discipline-specific knowledge. Each domain uses its own methods, validated according to quite different criteria. For example, neither 'truth' nor 'utility' is normally criteria within art, whereas 'insight', 'understanding' and 'artistic ways of knowing and being research' (Springgay et al. 2005) are criteria that are used. By stepping outside all of these domains and observing what they have in common despite using different criteria, it becomes apparent that each is operating at a meta-level to satisfy the members that new knowledge has indeed been created.

In 2008, Biggs and Büchler already identified that the risk of such an approach is that individual communities could adopt completely idiosyncratic criteria that alienated their production from integration into the wider knowledge community. They therefore proposed that all academic knowledge creation occurs within a wider context of public scrutiny. These days one would describe this scrutiny in terms of 'stakeholder engagement' that ensures the potential for 'impact' by the research. The emerging popularity of relational aesthetics ensures that artistic research also meets this requirement. Indeed, art is often co-opted by science owing to its commitment to stakeholder engagement (e.g. Wellcome Trust 2018) leading to shared satisfaction by the communities of both knowledge creators and knowledge consumers.

What is changed by the replacement of hegemonic notions of knowledge creation based on criteria derived largely from the sciences, with the notion of 'satisfaction' based on regarding knowledge creation as an activity? Instead of having to reconcile or legitimize disparate knowledge paradigms, the knowledge creation spectrum reveals that knowledge creation methods do not have intrinsic worth, only worth in relation to satisfying broader community, societal or educational objectives. It also has the effect of 'deterritorializing' the field of power (Coessens et al. 2009) and authorizing minority communities to legitimize methods that are locally meaningful, and moderating the authority of the traditional academic gatekeepers to act outside their field of expertise. As a result, artistic research does not need to legitimize its activities using alien criteria but instead needs to demonstrate that not only is its own community satisfied, but also that producers elsewhere on the spectrum can be satisfied by it.

The curator Maria Lind once said to me that she would only be interested in artistic research when it produced good art. Perhaps the greater challenge is not to satisfy other knowledge-producing communities, who are already feeling the benefits, but to satisfy the field of art that artistic research methods have the capacity to produce knowledge.

References

AHRC (2018), 'Definition of research', https://ahrc.ukri.org/funding/research/researchfunding-guide/introduction/definitionofresearch/. Accessed 18 May 2018.

Baumgarten, A. G. ([1758] 2009), *Aesthetica,* Chicago: University of Michigan Library.

Biggs, M. A. R. and Büchler, D. (2008), 'Eight criteria for practice-based research in the creative and cultural industries', *Art, Design and Communication in Higher Education*, 7:1, pp. 5–18.

——— (2011), 'Communities, values, conventions and actions', in M. Biggs and H. Karlsson (eds), *The Routledge Companion to Research in the Arts,* London: Routledge, pp. 82–98.

Bloor, D. ([1976] 1991), *Knowledge and Social Imagery*, 2nd ed., Chicago: University of Chicago Press.

——— (1999), 'Anti-Latour', *Studies in History and Philosophy of Science,* 30:1, pp. 81–112.

Boltzmann, L. (1902), 'Models', *Encyclopædea Britannica*, 10th ed., vol. 30, pp. 788–91.

Bourdieu, P. ([1984] 1988), *Homo Academicus* (trans. P. Collier), Cambridge: Polity Press.

Bourdieu, P. and Wacquant, L. J. D. (1992), *An Invitation to Reflexive Sociology*, Cambridge: Polity Press.

Carter, P. (2004), *Material Thinking: The Theory and Practice of Creative Research*, Carlton: Melbourne University Publishing.

Coessens, K., Crispin, D. and Douglas, A. (2009), *The Artistic Turn: A Manifesto*, Leuven: Leuven University Press.

Cohen, A. P. (1985), *Symbolic Construction of Community*, London: Routledge.

Collingwood, R. G. ([1923] 2013), *The Principles of Art*, London: Case Press.

Dyrssen, C. (2015), 'Artistic research – A subject overview 2014', in T. Lind (ed.), *Artistic Research Yearbook 2015*, Stockholm: Swedish Research Council, pp. 20–32.

Engeström, Y., Miettinen, R. and Punamäki, R.-L. (1999), *Perspectives on Activity Theory*, Cambridge: Cambridge University Press.

Haseman, B. (2006), 'Rupture and recognition: Identifying the performative research paradigm', in E. Barrett and B. Bolt (eds), *Practice as Research: Approaches to Creative Arts Enquiry*, London: I.B. Tauris, pp. 147–57.

Hume, D. ([1748] 2011), *An Enquiry Concerning Human Understanding*, http://www.gutenberg.org/ebooks/9662. Accessed 28 March 2017.

Kant, I. ([1790/93] 2015), *The Critique of Judgement*, http://www.gutenberg.org/ebooks/48433. Accessed 28 March 2017.

Latour, B. (1999), 'For David Bloor… and beyond: A reply to David Bloor's "Anti-Latour"', *Studies in History and Philosophy of Science*, 30:1, pp. 113–29.

Latour, B. and Woolgar, S. (1986), *Laboratory Life: The Construction of Scientific Facts*, Princeton: Princeton University Press.

Mill, J. S. ([1843] 2009), *A System of Logic, Ratiocinative and Inductive*, New York: Harper & Brothers, https://www.gutenberg.org/files/27942/. Accessed 28 March 2017.

Moore, G. E. (1925), 'A defense of common sense', in J. H. Muirhead (ed.), *Contemporary British Philosophy*, London: Allen & Unwin, pp. 193–223.

Pew Research Center (2015), *Public and Scientists' Views on Science and Society*, http://www.pewinternet.org/files/2015/01/PI_ScienceandSociety_Report_012915.pdf. Accessed 28 March 2017.

Popper, K. ([1959] 2002), *The Logic of Scientific Discovery*, London: Routledge.

Pronin, E., Gilovich, T. and Ross, L. (2004), 'Objectivity in the eye of the beholder: Divergent perceptions of bias in self versus others', *Psychological Review*, 111:3, pp. 781–99.

Snow, C. P. (1959), *The Two Cultures and the Scientific Revolution*, London: Cambridge University Press.

Springgay, S., Irwin, R. L. and Kind, S. W. (2005), 'A/r/tography as living inquiry through art and text', *Qualitative Inquiry*, 11:6, pp. 897–912.

Wellcome Trust (2018), 'Public engagement fund', https://wellcome.ac.uk/what-we-do/directories/public-engagement-fund-people-weve-funded. Accessed 18 May 2018.

Chapter 2

Interpolation and Relationality: Extending the Field through Creative Arts and Indigenous Research Approaches

Estelle Barrett

In this chapter, I point out some of the similarities and distinctions between two relatively 'new' paradigms of research: creative arts research and Indigenous research conducted from a 'decolonizing' perspective. Both these approaches pose questions and problems that distinguish them as emerging paradigms that are nevertheless being positioned by doctoral and other researchers within the broader field of more traditional research methods. I suggest that a *critical positioning* of such revolutionary approaches in relation to the broader field of research is extending the general field of research; further that an acknowledgement of *relationality* that exists between paradigms can lead to innovative and generative approaches to research across the disciplines. This view is supported by philosophers of science, who have not only exposed some of the limitations of traditional scientific modes of inquiry, but also the ways in which the discourses of science fail to fully reflect its modes of operation. Hence, before considering the particularities of the two 'new' paradigms to be discussed here, it is necessary to examine the critical ideas of some philosophers of science that challenge traditionalist views of the scientific approach and the hierarchical separation of science and the arts. Central to my discussion is the contention that all research has an aesthetic dimension and that the boundaries between different approaches to research are not as rigid as is commonly thought. Also underpinning this discussion is the concept 'interpolation' that can be viewed as both method and as a mode of analysis and interpretation in research. As such, interpolation illuminates the active and processual nature of knowledge as well as *relationality* and *partial objectivity* as an ineluctable aspect of meaning-making.

The limits of science

In commenting about the limits of science, Bruno Latour observes that there was no sudden shift in modes of thinking that emerged in the sixteenth century and there are no specific differences between so-called enlightenment thinking and pre-scientific cultures, minds or methods. Moreover, today there are no 'mutants with larger brains working inside modern laboratories that can think differently from the rest of us' (Latour 1986: 2). Hence, the divides between science and other modes of inquiry and thought are arbitrary. These emerged partly as a process of differentiating cultural spheres into the 'scientific, the practico-moral and the artistic' and which 'also gave birth to our modern concept of art as the narrower practice of fine art' (Shusterman 1992: 48); rather than maintain rigid boundaries, we need to seek verifiable causes that can account for the differences in effects of the various approaches to knowledge production and also the ways in which they may be related. Latour points out that, as new technologies of reproduction of the formulae and data (what he calls inscriptions) produced by science increase, the volume and rate of circulation of inscriptions also increase the spread of errors or inaccuracies that are carried by them. Latour refers to 'cascades' of secondary data used in research, that become more and more removed from primary sources and with each new iteration move further away from the realities to which they refer. This is compounded because of constant evolution and change in natural, physical and social environments. Hence, the circulation of inscriptions results in the displacement of experience in favour of representation and discourse because the process of displacement and circulation of knowledge becomes less and less tied to real conditions. The approaches of artistic and Indigenous research, on the other hand, draw predominantly on lived experience and more direct engagement with materials and objects, providing alternatives that may help to overcome the limitations of more traditional modes of inquiry.

Disruptive paradigms and revolution

Thomas Kuhn (1970) puts forward some radical ideas that overturn many long-held beliefs that underpin the scientific approach. Kuhn's thinking contains a 'decolonizing' and disruptive dimension that can be aligned with aspects of artistic and Indigenous research paradigms. He does this by examining the mechanisms involved in promoting crises of paradigms and transformations that lead to new ones. Hence his account of science or research provides a good starting point and rationale for elaborating Indigenous, and artistic, approaches to research as disruptive paradigms that have the capacity to expand human knowledge and understanding.

So what are some of the elements that bring about crisis in paradigms? Kuhn suggests that there are alternating phases in the progress of (western) science: phases that relate to the practice of 'normal science' and revolution. Practitioners of normal science, described by Kuhn as working within the rules, processes and procedures of established paradigms, have a predetermined view of what constitutes data, instruments that are appropriate to be employed in research and what concepts are relevant to the interpretation of data. Normal science tries to ignore anomalous data and phenomena and only looks for what can 'refine, extend and articulate a paradigm that is already in existence' (Kuhn 1970: 122). Kuhn's ideas about paradigms were initially founded on the idea that research was the domain of scientists alone and evolved at a time of rapid expansion and diversification of scientific knowledge in the first half of the twentieth century. However, as Kuhn points out, the developments of ideas in disciplines such as psychology, philosophy, linguistics and even art history have thrown up crises by articulating different conceptions of data that expose the inadequacies of the scientific mode of research. Through linguistics, for example, we have come to know that words cannot fully capture reality and that the language we use mediates what we can know about the world. Thus, the idea of observing and then presenting the ultimate truth about objects in the world no longer holds. For these and other reasons, normal science inevitably gives rise to anomalies and crises that lead the researcher to look in different places and use different instruments of research (Kuhn 1970: 122).

Kuhn tells us that the rational rules of science cannot account for creative dimensions of discovery. He points to the role of experiential, non-rational and intuitive dimensions of inquiry: the 'lightning flash' that inundates a previously obscure puzzle and that allows its components to be seen in a new way. This does not come about by rational interpretation alone, but through flashes of intuition and the gathering up of large portions of experience that can be bundled up and then 'linked piecemeal to the new paradigm and not the old' (Kuhn 1970: 123).

More radically, Kuhn tells us that the research environment and the world are not fixed or static, but are themselves subject to change. This becomes evident in times of revolutionary science. He refers to examples of the theories of motion (of a falling stone) held by Galileo – who focused on motion as 'process' as opposed to Aristotle, whose focus was on the 'state' of the object – to demonstrate that, with a change in paradigm, the scientist will afterward work in a different world (Kuhn 1970: 121). Just as Galileo's experience of falling stones was different to that of Aristotle, so the experience of and approach to the world of Indigenous and artistic researchers is different to that of science researchers. Kuhn's observations allow researchers working through disruptive paradigms and in different worlds not only to position their experiences and methodologies, but also to justify this positioning.

Science and falsification

In his work *Conjectures and Refutations* (1963), Karl Popper asserts that scientific theories are not absolute truth, but rather they are conjectures that are subject to falsification. This is because theories may not hold for all time and in all conditions and must therefore undergo continual testing for their validity. Popper, therefore, views the notion of unfalsifiable theory as unscientific. Like that of Kuhn, his theory of refutation was firmly grounded in and contextualized by approaches to research within the field of science. The role of the researcher then is not so much to look for evidence that will support established theories and laws, but to be on a constant lookout for evidence that might overturn them. In Popper's view scientific theory can be distinguished from myth or pseudo-science on the basis that a scientific theory can ultimately be refuted. I would argue that the underlying principles of his theory of refutations can be extended to other fields. Indeed, Popper concedes that so-called pseudo-sciences, which he likens to 'primitive myths', can produce legitimate and verifiable 'knowledge' in a scientific sense of the term. He states that he wished to distinguish between science and pseudo-science, 'knowing very well that science often errs, and that pseudo-science may happen to stumble on the truth' (Popper 1963: 4). What can be deduced from the above discussion is that scholars from within the field of science itself have also challenged its hegemony by pointing out limitations in its assumptions and approaches.

Interpolation

The etymology of the term 'interpolation' is useful for extending critiques of science and for reframing the process of creation and discovery as knowledge-in-process. Various definitions and the etymology of the term, taken from the Latin '*interpolāre* to give a new appearance to', from inter- + *polīre* 'to polish' (*Collins Dictionary* 2016), also provide a scaffold for the positioning of new paradigms in relation to more traditional forms, as the following explanations illuminate: 'to put (something) between other things or parts; especially to put (words) into a piece of writing or a conversation' (*Collins Dictionary* 2016). The term can operate not only as a noun, but also as a transitive and intransitive verb; it encapsulates the notion of making and doing as well as that of interpretation and analysis. This idea is extended in further definitions: 'to alter or corrupt (as a text) by inserting new or foreign matter' (*Collins Dictionary* 2016); also 'to insert (words) into a text or into a conversation' (*Collins Dictionary* 2016). Unpacked within the context of this chapter, 'interpolation' can be seen to correspond with the creative practice, as a process of the expansion of language that occurs in art making. This is demonstrated in, for example, improvisation in music, innovations in chorography and various forms of poetic language (both verbal and visual), where usually incommensurate categories are brought together to create new images, metaphors and other tropes – the aesthetic images from which the new and the unexpected is revealed.

Interpolation, interpolative reasoning and fuzzy logic

Interpolation can broadly be defined as 'an informed estimate of the unknown' (Thévenaz et al. 2017). There are many forms of interpolation in science and other areas where mathematics, computer and other technological means are used to capture or extend data. Underpinning all of these procedures is an acknowledgement of the need to harness approximation and intuitive and inferential logic. Linear interpolation in mathematics involves using algebraic formulae to estimate or predict data points. In a sense, these formulae operate as language allowing researchers not only to express what is not yet known, but also to predict and articulate a value or function that may hitherto have been inexpressible. This can be seen in an example of linear interpolation formulas to find unknown values:

To find y_2,

$$y_2=(x_2-x_1)*(y_3-y_1)/(x_3-x_1)+y_1$$

To find x_2,

$$x_2=(y_2-y_1)*(x_3-x_1)/(y_3-y_1)+x_1$$

To find out the value of x_2 we must know the value of y_2; to find y_2 we must know the value of x_2 (ncalculators.com 2017).

In portraiture, on the other hand, the placement of marks or lines (visual language) that make up a coherent image involves sensory and aesthetic responsiveness or the artist's intuitive interpolation and transposition of marks ('data points') on to the surface of the paper so that the visual image or form can emerge. Likewise, the realization of colour beyond those that are given in the colour wheel *emerges* from artistic experimentation and estimations or *subjective* interpolations by the artist through experience-in-practice from what is available in his or her palette. Computer algorithms in programs such as the one used by David Hockney called Brushes Redux developed by designer Christoffer Hoel are built on mathematical interpolations. Whilst they model human intuitive processes, I would argue they can never capture infinite mind/body possibilities inherent in experiential practice and meaning-making.

In engineering and science, a set of data points can be obtained by sampling or experimentation that also involves inferential modes and estimation. Interpolation begins with experimentation, the problem of finding out what happens, or finding of the values that occur between isolated points particularly in vague environments. Once new modes of modelling and predication are found and applied, they are incorporated into rational logic and procedures *after the fact*. Where interpolation methods are used, there is an acknowledgement and acceptance of margins of error, and because the outcomes of estimations and inferences cannot be known in advance, they remain hypothetical until after the value or function has been applied or enters into relations with other values or functions as realized *effects*. In describing interpolation as an art, meteorologist Jeff Habby explains that, despite being an imprecise and subjective process, interpolation is central to predicting weather patterns (Habby 2017).

Luc Anselin comments that various forms of interpolation are used in applied research in the fields of environmental and resource economics where there is a need to combine data obtained from different sources using different sample designs and methodologies (Anselin 2001: 705). Extrapolating from Anselin, we can conceive of an example of research on market values of real estate that relies on integrating data obtained for house and land values collected through quantitative surveys; the use of satellite imagery to provide spatial modelling of land use and land coverage and through the use of sensors alongside socio-metric data to express air and water quality. Interpolation involves the search for a language or *form* through which such complex information can be made intelligible. An example of this approach to modelling knowledge spatially involves interpolative and extrapolative reasoning, which is illustrated in research that models data on consumer tastes and music genres. In both cases, rule-based knowledge is augmented with knowledge about geometric representation of labels in a conceptual space (Schockaert and Prade 2011).

In Australian Indigenous societies, the primary mode of making, preserving and transmitting knowledge is through verbal and visual storytelling, including dance. The process is communal, and both the storyteller and audience are involved in rearticulating knowledge passed down from previous generations in processes that can be understood as *interpolation*: the insertion of situated knowledge or new understanding of current states of affairs and conditions into established narratives as a dynamic and evolving mode of cultural production. This communal and egalitarian co-production of knowledge has led to the adaptation of western methods of interviewing into the concept of 'yarning' as a distinctly Indigenous and valid mode of engagement and communication in research (Bessarab and Ng'Andu 2010). Through yarning, *relationality* is established and the researcher and the participant become co-producers of knowledge. Again, this involves processes of interpolation by both the researcher and participants involved in cycles of 'storytelling' and reflection that allows the insertion of data derived from multiple perspectives.

As I have discussed above, the notion of 'interpolation' is not confined to articulating aesthetic processes. In certain fields of science, interpolation is understood as a process used to estimate the values of an item of data, or a function, between two known values and to make assertions of estimated values. In the field of mathematics and of numerical analysis, 'interpolation' is described as a method of constructing new data points within the range of a discrete set of known data points. Notably, the definitions of interpolation as a research instrument from the fields of science and mathematics indicate that the processes involved are neither precise not strictly rational, but involve largely intuitive predictions or extrapolation of intermediate or unknown values from an array of available data in order to simplify or establish serviceable patterns and trends not hitherto available. Often the process of estimation is a subjective one that is done for the purpose of simplifying intractably complex data (Hon and Wu 2000).

Refiguring 'data'

I would like to return now to my earlier discussion regarding the need to refigure normal conceptions of 'data' in order to better appreciate the capacity of artistic research to produce alternative forms of representation that can overcome the limitations of what numerical symbols, formulae and prepositional statements cannot reveal (Barrett 2014).

Elliott Eisner suggests that art objects have the capacity to go beyond propositional limits by 'giving rise to multiple perspectives, creating productive ambiguity and engendering empathetic participation' (Eisner 1997: 4). In artistic research, the ambiguity of the aesthetic image increases the number of questions that can be asked about the phenomena being presented and allows the transformation of the personal (what is inside of consciousness) or the private to enter the public sphere through the viewing experience. I suggest that this involves a process of interpolation through which the viewers or audiences become co-producers of new understandings and insights through the insertion of material related to individual experiences and perspectives. In order to better appreciate this and go beyond the approaches of traditional paradigms, we need to move away from the notion of data as representation toward an understanding of both the research method *and* the experiencing of artefact as ongoing processes of production. Whilst artworks may be symbolic, in that they allow us to name certain ideas or objects, language cannot fully capture the referent or stand in for it. Moreover, as Latour has taught us, objects are neither static nor immutable, nor waiting to be captured or frozen representations. What we can know about them always involves *relationality* – a process that in viewing and reflection, by artists themselves or by viewers/audiences, involves interpolation. Hence interpretation and analysis can be understood as a process of *production of production*. Interpolation and relationality as aspects intrinsic to both artistic and Indigenous research helps us to reconfigure understandings of *how* knowledge is produced. Praxical knowledge is not a priori there to be discovered, but is knowledge as *action* or 'knowing' that emerges from both thought and biological or sensory interaction, or as I have previously noted, from aesthetic experience (Barrett 2007: 2). One of the strengths of artistic research is its capacity to uncover or reveal the aesthetic dimension of *all* forms of discovery.

Shawn Wilson (1999, 2008) observes that this aesthetic dimension is true of Indigenous research. Ritual and the ceremonial aspects of artmaking, storytelling and engagement with others underpin this view. In Indigenous research, relation building is paramount and occurs through reiterative talking circles that occur even before the research can commence. Also throughout the research, ongoing development of strategies is required to respond to changing and unpredictable situations that arise during the research process (Wilson 2008: 38). Part of this involves negotiating related shared and tacit knowledge belonging to participants from diverse cultural groups.

Michael Polanyi tells us that tacit knowledge is a fundamental aspect of human activity and learning (Polanyi 1969). It refers to embodied knowledge or 'skill' developed and applied in practice and apprehended intuitively – a process that is readily understood by Indigenous and artistic researchers who recognize those oppositions between explicit and tacit knowledge, the imaginary and the real, and the spiritual and the worldly are false.

Researchers from within these paradigms recognize that we cannot separate knowledge to be learned, from situations in which it is used. They engage in situated inquiry that demonstrates a unity between problem, context and solution. A general feature of practice-based research is that personal interest and experience, rather than objective 'disinterestedness' motivates the research process. This is an advantage to be embraced since in terms of the acquisition of knowledge, artistic research provides a more profound model of learning. 'Praxical knowledge' or what can be understood as the material basis of knowledge provides a framework for understanding the acquisition of human knowledge as emerging from real-life experiences as well as the partial and provisional nature of all knowledge claims. This view is in accordance with Kuhn's contention that the gaining of knowledge is *experiential* and the approaches and outcomes of research are dependent on cultural and social factors that influence the researcher (Kuhn 1970: 112–14).

Donald Schön's notion of 'knowing-in-practice' adds to our understanding of the process of experiential discovery that is central to creative practice as research. It involves reflection-in-action and reflection-on-action, processes through which the researcher is able to 'make new sense of the situations of uncertainty or uniqueness which he may allow himself to experience' (Schön 1983: 62). Schön's description resonates with Karen Martin and other

Indigenous scholars' accounts of Indigenous ways of knowing that involve reiterative cycles of storytelling and reflection (Martin 2003; Smith 2004; Wilson 1999).

Indigenous knowledge systems

Alongside the discourses on artistic research, the growing influence of literature on Indigenous knowledge systems and research by scholars in Canada, the United States, New Zealand and Australia (amongst others) is presenting further challenges to assumptions held in the west about what constitutes research, its instruments, approaches and outcomes. Linda Tuhiwai Smith (2004) views research as sites of struggle between ways of knowing in the west and Indigenous ways of knowing, and points out how science and western disciplines of knowledge are implicated in imperialism. Western knowledge systems construct non-European peoples in ways that justify scrutiny, colonization and exploitation of the other for economic, social and political gain. Indigenous research allows stories to be told that question the nature of western ideals and lenses (Smith 2004: 2–4). Moreover, unlike positivist approaches that demand distanced observation, Indigenous research is grounded within social and political conditions and realities that are expressed through personal narratives. Like the productions of artistic research, these stories are emergent, subjective and interactive – changing according to the context of the narration and who is doing the telling. The knowledge that emerges thus moves from the personal and particular to the general through audience participation, and because of this participation, like knowledge produced through artistic research, is necessarily relational. Margaret Kovach comments on the active and interactive nature of Indigenous language, which is predominantly oral and grows out of Indigenous epistemology that is fluid, non-linear and relational (Kovach 2005: 27). Indigenous ways of knowing are also *experiential* and derived from teachings that have been passed down from generation to generation. This can involve 'non-rational' ways of knowing derived from subconscious processes including dreams (Kovach 2005: 28). Such knowledge is nevertheless sustaining. I suggest that though they emerge from quite different traditions and histories, some similarities can be seen in the approaches of these two paradigms.

Parallels between paradigms

Notwithstanding very clear differences between the two paradigms I have discussed here, I argued in this chapter that parallels cannot only be drawn between the two, but also between these paradigms of research (Kovach 2005; Botha 2011; Martin 2013) and approaches based on the assumptions and premises of science-based inquiry (Ihlein 2010; Armstrong 2014). I suggest further that scholars and researchers from within the field of science have recognized the need to critique and overcome the limitation of traditional approaches and my examination of these critiques also reveals that many of the procedures and features of research in these fields correspond with those that are embraced in artistic and Indigenous research. Finally, I have suggested that a reconfiguration of what is understood as 'data' in research, and an application of the concept 'interpolation' as an intrinsic mode of research brings seemingly discrete disciplines of research closer together. An informed positioning of these approaches is not only necessary for validating emerging paradigms, but may help doctoral students from the fields of creative arts and Indigenous research to articulate how their own methodologies can reframe and extend the broader field of research.

References

Anselin, L. (2001), 'Spatial effects in econometric practice in environmental and resource economics', *American Journal of Agricultural Economics*, 83:3, pp. 705–10, http://www.jstor.org/stable/1245103?seq=1#page_scan_tab_contents. Accessed 20 September 2017.

Armstrong, K. (2014), '"Conversations before the end of time": Re-futuring applications of a new media arts praxis', in E. Barrett and B. Bolt (eds), *Material Inventions: Applying Creative Arts Research*, London: I. B. Tauris, pp. 67–83.

Barrett, E. (2007), 'Experiential learning in practice as research: Context, method, knowledge', *Journal of Visual Art Practice*, 6:2, pp. 115–24.

——— (2014), 'Extending the field: Invention, application and innovation in creative arts enquiry', in E. Barrett and B. Bolt (eds), *Material Inventions: Applying Creative Arts Research*, London: I.B Tauris, pp. 1–21.

Bessarab, D. and Ng'Andu, B. (2010), 'Yarning about yarning as a legitimate method in Indigenous research', *International Journal of Critical Indigenous Studies*, 3:1, pp. 37–50.

Botha, L. (2011), 'Mixing methods as a process towards Indigenous methodologies', *International Journal of Social Research Methodology*, 14:4, pp. 313–25.

Collins Dictionary (2016), 'interpolate', http://www.collinsdictionary.com/dictionary/english/interpolate. Accessed 4 February 2016.

Eisner, E. W. (1997), 'The promise and perils of alternative forms of data representation', *Educational Researcher*, 26:4, pp. 4–10.

Habby, J. (n.d.), 'The art of interpolation', http://www.theweatherprediction.com/habyhints/81/. Accessed 30 October 2017.

Hon, Y. C. and Wu, Z. (2000), 'A quasi interpolation method for solving stiff ordinary differential equations', *International Journal for Numerical Methods in Engineering*, 48:8, pp. 1187–97, http://onlinelibrary.wiley.com/doi/10.1002/%28SICI%291097-0207%2820000720%2948:8%3C1187::AID-NME942%3E3.0.CO;2-K/full. Accessed 15 June 2016.

Ihlein, L. (2010), 'To follow things as I encounter them: Blogging, art and attention', 127Prince, 14 May, http://127prince.wordpress.com/2010/05/14/to-follow-things-as-i-encounter-them-blogging-art-and-attention-lucas-ihlein. Accessed 9 August 2016.

Kovach, M. (2005), 'Emerging from the margins', in L. Brown and S. Strega (eds), *Research as Resistance*, Toronto: Canadian Scholars' Press, pp. 19–36.

Kuhn, T. S. (1970), *The Structure of Scientific Revolutions,* Chicago: Chicago University Press.
Latour, B. (1986), 'Visualization and cognition: Thinking with eyes and hands', *Knowledge and Society: Studies in the Sociology of Culture Past and Present*, 6:6, pp. 1–40.
Martin, B. (2013), 'Immaterial land and Indigenous ideology: Refiguring Australian art and culture', PhD thesis, Melbourne: Deakin University.
Martin, K. (2003), 'Ways of knowing, ways of being and ways of doing: A theoretical framework and methods for Indigenous re-search and Indigenist research', *Journal of Australian Studies*, 76, pp. 203–13.
ncalculators.com (2017), 'Linear interpolation worksheet with example', http://ncalculators.com/math-worksheets/linear-interpolation-worksheet-example.html. Accessed 1 August 2017.
Polanyi, M. (1969), *Knowing and Being: Essays by Michael Polanyi*, M. Greene (ed.), London: Routledge and Kegan Paul.
Popper, K. (1963), *Science: Conjectures and Refutations: The Growth of Scientific Knowledge*, London and New York: Routledge.
Schockaert, S. and Prade, H. (2011), 'Interpolation and extrapolation in conceptual spaces: A case study in the music domain', in S. Rudolph and C. Gutierrez (eds), *Web Reasoning and Rule Systems,* RR 2011, Lecture Notes in Computer Science, vol. 6902, Berlin: Springer, pp. 217–31.
Schön, D. A. (1983), *The Reflective Practitioner: How Professionals Think in Action*, New York: Basic Books.
Shusterman, R. (1992), *Pragmatist Aesthetics*, Cambridge: Blackwell.
Smith, L. T. (2004), *Decolonizing Methodologies: Research and Indigenous People,* London and New York: Zed Books.
Thévenaz, P., Blu, T. and Unser, M. (2017), 'Image interpolation and resampling', http://bigwww.epfl.ch/publications/thevenaz9901.pdf. Accessed 1 August 2017.
Wilson, S. (1999), 'Recognising the importance of spirituality in Indigenous learning', https://acea.org.au/wp-content/uploads/2015/04/Shaun-Wilson-paper.pdf. Accessed 3 March 2014.
——— (2008), *Research Is Ceremony: Indigenous Research Methods,* Halifax and Winnipeg: Fernwood.

Chapter 3

Transformative Interventions: Creative Practices in an Education Doctorate Programme

Jeff Adams and Emma Arya-Manesh

Non-arts students

Through our research into arts-based practices as research in education we have, over the years, become increasingly interested in those students from non-arts backgrounds who encounter these practices for the first time but who nonetheless go on to appropriate them into their research methodologies (Adams 2010, 2012). They are interesting precisely because their unfamiliarity and inexperience sometimes leads them into rethinking their ideas through fresh and innovative research methods. This is not an argument for abandoning orthodox research methods, nor is it making the case for intentionally assumed naivety or deliberate incompetence; rather it is asserting the place for arts-based practices alongside more conventional approaches to research, even for those from other disciplines.

This research stems from a university in the north-west of England with doctoral students who are largely based in a faculty of education. The university is relatively young; although it has existed as a training college for teachers since the mid-nineteenth century, it has only acquired postgraduate research degree awarding powers relatively recently. Hence most of the doctoral students who have participated in this research are either still studying or have only recently graduated with their doctorate. All of the participants are part-time students who are also professionals – teachers, lecturers, councillors, trainers – in the broad field of education. Most do not come from an arts background, but all those studying for an EdD have to complete a creative practice module as part of their study, and it is their experience of undertaking this that is the focus of this study. From this group our discussion here focuses on two case studies to illustrate the diverse complexity of research practice that emerged.

The idea that arts-based research methods were largely gratuitous since they could not be expected to yield any worthwhile or reliable data was a common assumption amongst the participants. It was with some reluctance and not a small amount of trepidation that students participated in the module, feelings that seemed to be exacerbated by the staging of some of the workshops in a large public contemporary art gallery, the Tate Modern. Interaction and dialogue were the main features of the sessions, characteristics that understandably generated personal anxieties about the notion of revealing their uncertainties publicly. However, the very experienced gallery staff who managed the workshops were quickly able to dissipate their anxieties by providing affirming and positive experiences that ensured the participants' contributions were respected and engaged with seriously. Activities included making connections in the gallery between works on display and personal experiences as derived from significant possessions, or making collaborative interpretations in the gallery as a response to selected works, or debating the relational, polysemic characteristics of some works and the diverse meanings that might be generated.

From these very intensive arts-based experiences the students were then expected to engage in research through creative practices, accompanied by a short conventional text-based essay. The diversity of their research approaches is itself interesting and has in recent years comprised street dance, spoken voice and song, poetry, painting, collage, sculpture, installation, relational events, film, photography, role play and storytelling. Paradoxically, the variety of media appeared to be correlated inversely to the arts experience of the participants: in other words, the less prior experience that the students had, the more likely they seemed to be willing to explore novel (to them) means of carrying out research, perhaps bearing out Cropley and Cropley's thesis on the contradictions inherent in creative practices (2008).

The dynamic that occurred between student and medium was redolent of the concept of research encapsulated by a/r/tography (Irwin 2013), where the process is charged with the energy of novelty in combination with the constantly transforming conception of what it means to carry out research. The encounters between student, practice and research were fluid renegotiations of an engagement that is not normally seen in more orthodox research methodology training. The 'failures' that inevitably emerged seem to be less disabling for researchers unfamiliar with the arts, once they were assimilated into the broader learning process that all research students have to undergo, rethinking failures as necessary events in the experimental practice of the novice undergoing the development of expertise (Adams and Owens 2015; Lindstrom 2006).

Doctoral students exploring creative methodologies

Karen: A health practitioner

Karen is a health practitioner and manager who works with dementia patients. Like the other students, she undertook the creativity module in the second year of her studies. For her, arts-based practice was unknown territory. Not only was the paradigm unfamiliar, she also felt that it was likely to be an unsettling experience, largely unnecessary for her studies. Karen had never been to a contemporary art gallery nor ever seen the need to go to one, and consequently reacted negatively, and not without a small amount of hostility, towards the works to which she was expected to respond. In common with many people encountering contemporary art for the first time, Karen was at first perplexed and unwilling to engage with the possibilities that the methods employed in their production might be transferable to other types of research like her own. However, one work did capture her attention and subsequently led to a revaluation on her part of the nature of some of the works that she encountered. The work in question was a video installation in which the images had a predictive narrative imposed upon them, as if anticipating what the characters in the film were going to do. According to Karen the disconcerting effect of the out-of-sync installation struck a chord with her because of her own work with dementia sufferers, the idea that the characters and personal histories that are masked by the disease are occasionally revealed in similarly disconcerting moments. This led Karen to produce an installation piece centred around a decoupage chair that she made and upon which participants would sit; inspired by the poem 'Crabbit Old Woman' (Anon. 1966), which was pasted underneath the seat of the chair, Karen invited the participants to engage with unsettling experiences derived from direct experience of care for dementia sufferers.

The construction of the chair, with its metaphorical meanings that grew and developed as a project progressed, had unexpected consequences in terms of the authority with which Karen was able to speak in her thesis. She shifted from third person 'academic' speak to first person, which was a measure of her growing confidence as a doctoral researcher. The recognition that an artist can appropriate and fashion an object, and in doing so generate a plethora of meanings, some of which could not be anticipated but which offer new and unique insights into the field of study, was something of a revelation for Karen. This new understanding spilled over into her more conventional academic research methods, manifest in her new-found confidence in the handling of new juxtapositions of ideas. As Karen put it:

> It has made me do a different thesis to the one I would have done, because I was going to do apprenticeships, and that's very quantifiable [...] whereas this way it's more uncomfortable for me because I'm going in [to work] and saying: 'what's your favourite time of day? Why is that?' and looking for things that come out of it.

In Karen's case the striking thing about her involvement with arts-based practices is that it has liberated her research methods yet at the same time maintained or even improved her confidence as a doctoral researcher. This is despite her self-confessed ignorance of creative methodologies prior to beginning her doctorate. The exposure to these practices did not turn her into an artist as such, but gave further confidence to apply artistic means to investigate topics that she might hitherto have thought were beyond the scope of such practices.

It is important to recognize the significance of Karen's sense of 'otherness' prior to her experience of arts-based practices in her research:

> To be honest before I did this [the creativity module] I would have thought that I was the least creative person going and it worried me to death doing the creative bit. However, by doing that module and the assignment that came alongside it [a supporting essay], I realised, actually, how creative I was without realising that I was being creative [...].

Karen had conceptualized working with dementia patients and managing staff as beyond the realm of creativity, and so when preparing her research proposal similarly did not think that creative practices would be appropriate. Once exposed to the catalyst of the creative workshops she not only reconsidered her position about her approach to research, but also reconceptualized her own working practices, recognizing the creative impulses driving her everyday experience as a worker. This convergence seems to have enabled her to make sense of creativity as embedded in her working practice, and therefore also as intrinsic to her research through practice.

Susan: A mathematics teacher

Susan is a maths teacher who moved into higher education and teacher training in mathematics. She had always had an interest in the conceptual aspects of mathematics education, rather than its instrumental application in schools (from her work on Skemp [1976] amongst others). As a consequence, her thesis was based on a comparison between transmission methods of mathematics education compared to conceptual models. As part of her methodology, she incorporated practical creative means to facilitate conceptual understanding for training teachers to develop their pedagogy.

Susan had worked with images drawn from contemporary art for a considerable period prior to her doctorate, and this experience consequently informed her research. She described using an image as acting in a twofold way when teaching mathematics to children:

> The images allow conceptual development, so the pupils are seeing connections between the concepts [...] the image is a stimulus for the conversation as well as being a way of representing the concept that they are actually supposed to be learning.

For Susan the input from the creativity workshops helped to rationalize the work that she had already been doing to develop conceptual understanding by arts-based means, rather than providing new methods per se; that said, she did develop new methods, but these were augmenting her existing research rather than being completely new additions. As she explained when discussing applying her understanding of creativity when teaching maths to children:

> The creative elements were all, as they had been before, about making connections [...] and I think that's where the creativity seeps into everything if you're learning; [...] it would be very rare to be novel in maths; maths is built on agreed truths but the way that they made sense of it, and the way they connected it to what they knew already, would be unique and in a lot of cases novel if they are in an environment where they are allowed to articulate how they made sense of a problem rather than just seeking answers.

Part of the creative process to which Susan had been introduced was rooted in the idea of narrative expression, and this became an important methodological device in the capturing of data (utilizing the work of Clough and Nutbrown 2009). Reflecting on her earlier work of data gathering through interviews, she noted that her former technique of interviewing participants using a semi-structured framework with minimal input from herself resulted in an over-emphasis on her interpretations of the participants' responses. Subsequently, and as a result of her experiments in narrative storytelling, her later interviews were much more dialogical, allowing her to engage in a more dynamic manner with her participants. She felt this was both more honest – she was more openly interpreting as she engaged more fully in the conversation – and also yielded richer data, since the participants were continually prompted and provoked during the interview, and therefore more likely to disclose and articulate their experiences as practitioners.

As part of the creative practices to which she was exposed – a combination of visual arts, performance and narrative – Susan became increasingly sensitive to, and interested in, the idea of metaphor and allegory. These became dominant features in the organization of her thesis, to the point where, for instance, if a participant were to describe a work of contemporary visual art, upon which she had been invited to comment, as 'rubbish', then this metaphor would be explored and exploited for its potential as structuring concept within the thesis. As a consequence the whole thesis then became organized allegorically, with 'menu' titles like 'Souvlakia and Turkey Twizzlers' and 'Gateaux and one of your five-a-day' (both ideas arising from the participants during the data collection), or issue-based ones like 'Divorcing Parents and Authentic Voices'. The latter resulted from a participant (a beginning teacher of mathematics) complaining, as Susan explained, that the divide between the philosophies of the university and those of the school (conceptual vs. transmission models) meant that the student was caught like a child between divorcing parents: under tension, torn, and with loyalties to both sides. Rather than be left as an anecdote, Susan worked this metaphor into a theme to classify and analyse data, in much the same way that an author of fiction or a narrative painter would pursue a theme in order to compose a work.

When reflecting on her approach to research after completing her thesis, Susan observed that the creative, arts-based methodologies that she was now accustomed to applying had significant advantages when it came to researching 'difficult' problems. By this she meant that researching the effectiveness of a particular model of education by means of behaviour or outcomes was relatively straightforward when compared to researching changes in ways of thinking about learning, for example, conceptual understanding in maths. One of the objections that Susan encountered posed by established teachers to her research was, ironically, that the deployment of arts-based methods in mathematics in the classroom was 'trivializing' learning. Nonetheless, one of the enduring legacies of the creative practice elements of the taught doctorate in Susan's research is her confidence and willingness to research through practice, with a more sophisticated understanding of the complementarity of research and practice, and less hierarchical conception of theory and practice.

New insights

In both of these cases the new methods of research in which Karen and Susan had been willing to engage yielded new insights into their field of study; this in itself was not that surprising, since those of us who are familiar with researching through arts practice would probably anticipate that this would happen, and indeed often adopt such practices in order to create opportunities for new meanings to arise. What was surprising, however, was the way that the methods gave rise to a new found confidence as researchers per se, even when engaging in more orthodox means of research. They both seemed more willing to recognize the limitations of conventional research methodologies, as well as those of arts-based means, and how each can complement – and compensate for – the other.

The metaphorical dimension that was developed to quite a high degree in both cases has remained with both Karen and Susan as permanent features of their approach to research. Since arts-based practices are intrinsically metaphorical, since they employ one means of representation to stand in for another, their adaptation to research seems to have raised profound questions about the nature of research itself, and what it means to be a researcher. This is not disabling, as both Karen and Susan may have thought it might be when they were presented with the task of adapting unfamiliar methods to their research, but on the contrary seemed to have engendered a deeper sensitivity to the research process itself. A critical consciousness seemed to have been achieved in both cases, initially by displacement into another realm of research followed by an enduring legacy of a renewed engagement with research, this time as a creative practice.

Acknowledgement

We would like to thank the Social Sciences and Humanities Research Council of Canada for funding our research.

References

Adams, J. (2010), 'Risky choices: The dilemmas of introducing contemporary art practices into schools', *British Journal of Sociology of Education*, 31:6, pp. 683–701.

——— (2012), 'Art practice as education research', in J. Adams, M. Cochrane and L. Dunne (eds), *Applying Theory to Educational Research: An Introductory Approach with Case Studies*, Oxford: Wiley-Blackwell, pp. 203–17.

Adams, J. and Owens, A. (2015), *Creativity and Democracy in Education: Practices and Politics of Learning through the Arts*, London and New York: Routledge.

Anon. (1966), 'Crabbit Old Woman', http://mrmom.amaonline.com/stories/CrabbitOldWoman.htm. Accessed 29 February 2016.

Clough, P. and Nutbrown, C. (2009), *A Students' Guide to Methodology: Justifying Enquiry*, London: Sage.

Cropley, A. and Cropley, D. (2008), 'Resolving the paradoxes of creativity: An extended phase model', *Cambridge Journal of Education*, 38:3, pp. 355–73.

Irwin, R. L. (2013), 'Becoming a/r/tography', *Studies in Art Education*, 54:3, pp. 198–211.

Lindstrom, L. (2006), 'Creativity: What is it? Can you assess it? Can it be taught?', *International Journal of Art and Design Education*, 25:1, pp. 53–66.

Skemp, R. (1976), 'Relational understanding and instrumental understanding', *Mathematics Teaching*, 77, pp. 20–26.

Chapter 4

Art-Based Action Research: Participatory Art Education Research for the North

Timo Jokela, Maria Huhmarniemi and Mirja Hiltunen

The organization of doctoral education in art education

Master's level teacher training in visual art began in Lapland in 1990, and doctoral research in the field became possible in Finland around the same time. The first PhD in visual art education was awarded at the University of Lapland in 2005 when only a few had been completed in the field in the whole of Finland. Notably, doctoral studies at the University of Lapland were guided by academic models derived mainly from pedagogy, and from art history and cultural history. The beginning was marked by a lack of structured curricula and doctoral programmes. Each doctoral candidate, to some extent, had to create their own path. At present, 10 doctors have graduated from the University of Lapland in the field of visual arts education and today there are currently 15 active doctoral candidates. Working models are emerging and the interaction between art and research is becoming clearer. The university's research strategy now guides doctoral studies in art education. Research on change in the Arctic and northern areas is central, and art education is expected to make a contribution. Many research projects have met this expectation (see Jokela et al. 2015b). The university's joint multidisciplinary Graduate School has three thematic doctoral programmes that support the strategy: culture-centred service design; northern cultures and sustainable natural resource politics; and communities and changing work. It is hoped that students will be attached primarily to these programmes.

The service design doctoral programme is based on wide-ranging, multidisciplinary research related to service design, guided by a human-centred perspective. The programme emphasizes the meaning of the societal and cultural and natural environments as contexts of design-oriented, practice-based research. The fields featured within the programme include, for example, applied art and design, tourism and mobilities, social work, marketing, media, multimodal communication, learning and education. The aim is to equip the students with the theoretical and practical know-how of the concepts, methods and processes of practice-based service design. Service design also offers a forum for research in arts education to consider the field as a developer of art, culture and education services, especially in sparsely populated areas (see Jokela 2013).

The themes of the doctoral programme in northern cultures and sustainable natural resource politics relate to the use of natural resources and more generally to natural resource policy and its means of control. A wide range of values are linked to nature per se, from anthropocentric values, such as mythological and aesthetic values, to the intrinsic value of nature. The aim is that doctoral candidates should become fully oriented in the phenomenological field of northern cultures and sustainable natural resource politics, acquire the capacity to apply multidisciplinary methods and understand the complexity affecting northern cultures and sustainable natural resource politics. The themes of the Graduate School have close links with art education's strong research in art-based environmental education, environmental art and Indigenous art and pedagogy (see Jokela et al. 2015b).

The doctoral programme in communities and changing work is based on social changes and their communal impact in various fields of science and art. The themes covered by the programme relate to various changes in private and public communities, work and operational environments, focusing on specific features of the northern region. This thematic doctoral programme at the University of Lapland is linked in many ways to strong collaborative art education and its research interests, infusing critical social science perspectives with the arts (see Hiltunen and Rantala 2015).

The multidisciplinary doctoral programmes include courses and seminars relating to their subject area, combine researchers from scientific and artistic fields, and thus support the multidisciplinary nature of doctoral degrees. In each educational field, doctoral programmes operate alongside research groups involving doctoral candidates, which are dedicated to the key issues and methods of their respective disciplines.

Northern Art, Community and Environment Research Group

Northern Art, Community, Environment Research (NACER) is a research group led by professors Timo Jokela and Mirja Hiltunen, in which visual art education and applied visual art are researched and developed in a northern context. Group members combine an understanding of visual art education as a social activity with a strong vision of the innovative potential of contemporary art. Methodologically, the groups share an interest in the development and application of art-based action research (ABAR). The key question is how well artistic products meet the research questions, what role they play in defending a dissertation and how they can be assessed in a way that does justice to the art and especially to the art of art education.

Doctoral thesis models used in the University of Lapland offer very flexible opportunities to apply the ABAR method. It is possible to write either a monograph or an article-based doctoral thesis, either of which can contain one or more individually assessed artistic productions. The artistic productions relate to the same research task or research question as the written scientific section. Instead of a traditional monograph, a doctoral dissertation can thus be composed of, for instance, articles and exhibitions or other separately evaluated artistic productions.

The position of art-based action research in relation to other artistic research and action research

The starting point for the development of ABAR has been contemporary art, which is by nature, context-linked, process-oriented, interactive and dialogical. While critical contemporary art and artistic research usually try to bring matters into the open and to stimulate discussion, the objective of ABAR is to identify and distinguish problems and find solutions. The method is strongly attached to environments and to communities. It takes into account, inter alia, the creation of spaces for encounters, the environment, the history of the community and the performative nature of art (Jokela et al. 2015a).

Artistic research, in which practice is understood in terms of research or research methodology (practice as research and practice-led research), and action research share many equivalent principles. Artistic research and action research share, among other things, the aim of changing and developing practices. The cyclical progress of research, alternating between planning, practical action, reflection and evaluation, unites the starting points for research. The objective of artistic research is often the development of artistic expression or method and the research subject is often a creative process or a concrete practice with technical-material dimensions (Borgdorff 2011). Instead, ABAR draws upon the social sciences, in which action research is often associated with communities and organizations. According to Hiltunen (2009), communal thinking in art education and action research at the University of Lapland combines active operational objectives with audience or community participation and increasing understanding of self and the world. Action research focuses on the objective of influence and change, while community art focuses on the creation of interaction by means of art. In ABAR the objectives are mutually supportive and it shares the intentions of participatory action research (PAR).

ABAR has parallels in the a/r/tography method. The starting points for both lie in artistic research and action research. Practical and theoretical research run in parallel and research topics are situated in the middle ground of teaching, art and communities. While phenomenology, feminist theory and theories of contemporary art have contributed to a/r/tography (Irwin and Springgay 2008; Springgay et al. 2008), ABAR adheres to the working methods of environmental and community art, project-based action and community-based art education. It has been influenced by, inter alia, social pedagogy, in particular sociocultural inspiration and critical pedagogy. Action research trends in ABAR have features in common with design research (see Figure 1). Design research influenced by action research is a cyclic research process based on planned interventions, which aims to solve practical problems and to develop functional theory (Heikkinen et al. 2006). ABAR also shares similarities with service design processes in which artist-designers seek to solve the problems of environments and communities using communal and interactive methods (Jokela 2013).

The key goal of ABAR is not to develop the artist-teacher-researcher's own artistic expression, but rather the interaction between other cooperating artists, researchers,

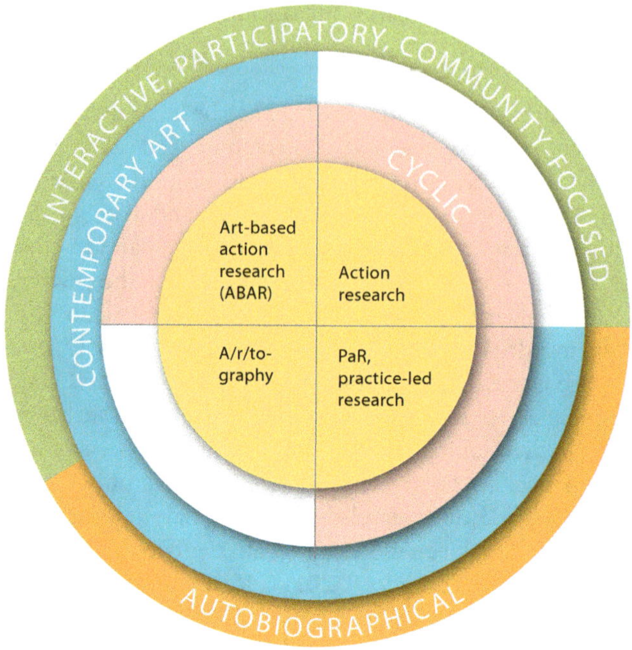

Figure 1: ABAR, action research, a/r/tography and practice-led artistic research emphasize in different ways the auto-biographical researcher, interactivity, cyclicality and the phenomena of contemporary art. Huhmarniemi, 2016.

communities and participants. Objectives also address community empowerment, social change, and an increase in environmental responsibility and sense of community (Jokela et al. 2015b). ABAR highlights involvement with the community instead of the scholar-artist's personality and personal history.

ABAR is more a methodological approach than a complete method. Therefore, its definition is always changing and becoming more precise with each study. In the manuscript of her own thesis, doctoral candidate Maria Huhmarniemi defined artistic action research, based on the NACER research group, as follows:

> Art-based action research is a research-based approach that aims to develop methods and approaches for the artist-researcher or artist-teacher, and to seek solutions for problems and future visions identified in environments and communities. Art-based action research starts from research questions that are relevant to visual art education, to applied visual art, or from the viewpoint of the target environments and communities. The research proceeds in cycles that include planning, theoretical background work, artistic work or similar interventions, reflective analysis, conceptualisation, and specification of objectives. The research process and its results are documented. The data for the process of analysis includes completed artistic productions, and observations and documents from activities and experiences. The research is published for the scientific

community, the art world, and the general public. The research is evaluated, in part, on the basis of functionality.

(2016: 44–45)

The role of artistic productions in the doctoral thesis

It is the central role of artistic productions that distinguishes art-based action research most clearly from other forms of action research. First of all, the nature of artistic work in ABAR differs from traditional academic research. As Jokela (2008) explains, in artistic work, the process is partly intuitive and based on experience and tacit knowledge. In artistic work, the objective and the chosen method are usually not very clear at the beginning of the process. According to Borgdorff (2011) artistic research proceeds intuitively, through trial and error, and leads to unexpected results and surprising insights. The research topic and questions become clearer as the research progresses. McNiff (2013) wrote that artist-researchers experience a need for space and freedom in order to find their own methods. This may be due to the nature of artistic knowledge and the research questions typical of artistic research.

However, ABAR places more emphasis on the relevance of design and the theoretical background to practical intervention than on artistic knowledge, intuition and tacit knowledge. Alongside the background work and artistic outputs, the research data includes participant perceptions and experiences, gathered, for example, by participant observation, photographic documentation, interviews and feedback discussions. The artistic productions of ABAR, therefore, are not normally representations of research results, as is often the case in artistic research. In contrast, artistic productions are spatial and time-related processes, the documentation of which produces research material, and in turn may be represented as a contemporary art exhibition. The researcher analyses the material, often in partnership with the participating community. The results of the analysis may be presented as an artistic production, such as installation art, exhibition and environmental art (Jokela 2009).

A special feature of ABAR is the place of art productions in the evaluation of the research, along with the functionality of the method or validation of the quality of the research. Together with the text of the research, they demonstrate how effective, successful and empowering the art process has been. The evaluation criteria for effectiveness include the ability of the work and the research to generate ideas, feelings and mental images, as well as a sense of empowerment, increasing participants' confidence in their own capabilities and skills (Jokela 2009, 2012).

Four examples illustrating ABAR

Next, we present four doctoral theses, in which art and art education have had a functional yet, in terms of ABAR methodology, distinct purpose.

Tuula Vanhatapio's (2010) doctoral dissertation was based on boys' requirements for visual art education. The aim was to create more egalitarian visual art education.

Vanhatapio used a mixed-method approach and combined case study research with action research. The purpose of the case studies was to reveal self-evident truths and stereotypes relating to boys' leisure activities. In the second part of the study, the boys' perspective on art education was developed, using action research, from the content of art education and the methods of adventure education, creating an experience-based approach to teaching. Sociability among friends, kinaesthetic learning and the boys' learning strengths were at the centre of the planning work. Art educational activities were used as a development method, but the process did not produce independent art productions, to be subjected by means of exhibitions to peer review and further development. Vanhatapio's research included ABAR features, but owing to the limited role of art, we do not consider it ABAR activity.

Seija Ulkuniemi's (2005) doctoral thesis, in turn, is an example in which artistic productions were carried out for data collection, but not assessed as artistic sections for the doctoral thesis. Ulkuniemi's subject was the family photograph. In her research, she used literature to provide a background to the emergence and development of the genre of family photographs, as well as the typical features of the images. She compiled her research material from four spatial works based upon a theoretical framework, each of which reflected on family photograph albums. The spatial works were visual-pedagogical productions. Ulkuniemi placed them in dialogue with the viewers so that viewers could comment on them and share their own experiences. On the basis of open feedback, Ulkuniemi investigated the kind of dialogue created with the themes of the works when the work and the viewer encountered each other. The results were presented in a monograph doctoral thesis, but the effectiveness of the process was not evaluated on the basis of the artistic productions so we do not consider this research to be ABAR.

In her article-based doctoral thesis, Mirja Hiltunen (2009) examined community-based art education in a northern sociocultural environment. This research developed a theory and practice of community-based art education in sparsely populated northern areas in Finnish Lapland, using the methods of art-based action research in interaction with interdisciplinary projects and the education of visual art teachers. The research relates to a socio-constructivist and phenomenological-hermeneutic paradigm, and the tradition of pragmatic and critical study by means of an action research approach. Many voices and interpretations from the development process behind art events were brought out by means of mixed-methods of participation in community art as well as collected material, such as surveys and interviews, student reports, practice diaries and official documents.

The performative and participatory art of art education produced in Hiltunen's research, using ABAR methods, was publicly displayed in communities (Figure 2). In the projects, the works, performances and annual celebrations operated as condensed communalities, concrete awakeners that caused people to see, think, feel and share matters in a new way. However, the art events in Hiltunen's doctoral thesis were not subjected to evaluation by outside experts. Instead, the researcher made them available for international assessment in the form of peer-reviewed articles published as part of her article-based doctoral thesis.

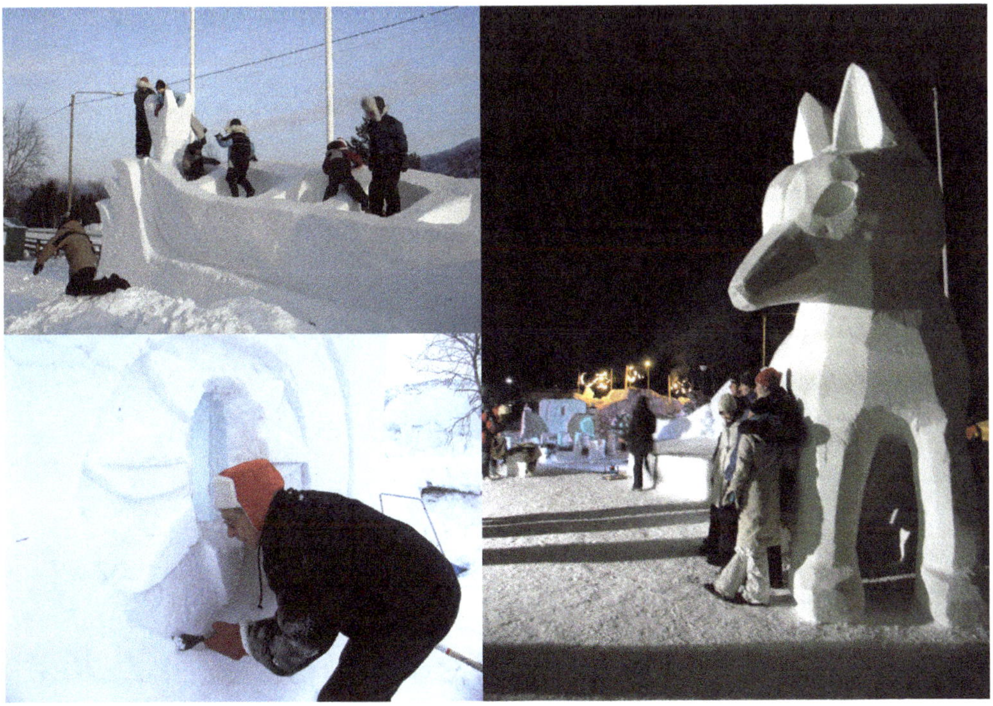

Figure 2: Firefox event in Utsjoki in 2015 and 2016. Photos Mirja Hiltunen.

One reason for this was that it is almost impossible to halt the processual, performative art of art education for assessment in a particular time and place. Although Hiltunen's doctoral thesis consisted of a series of articles dealing with community-based art education, with a related theoretical analysis and conclusions, art developed by means of artistic action research and the embeddedness of the actors was closely bound up with her research.

The purpose of Maria Huhmarniemi's (2016) research was to take part in discussions on environmental conflicts through art. Huhmarniemi used ABAR methodology to prepare three separately assessed exhibitions, in which she dealt with local environmental conflicts in Lapland (Figure 3).

She analysed them in research articles, and published an article-based doctoral thesis. In her first artistic production *Fragile*, an installation at the university's Valo Gallery, Huhmarniemi tackled the adverse effects of hydropower construction by drawing attention to the habitat of the protected butterfly species, *Capricornia boisduvaliana*. The installation produced a perspective on biodiversity within a reference framework of environmental ethics and aesthetics. In an article relating to the exhibition, Huhmarniemi compared contemporary art with opinion pieces as discussions on environmental policy. Another artistic production, the *Berry Tours* exhibition, was concerned with conflicts between

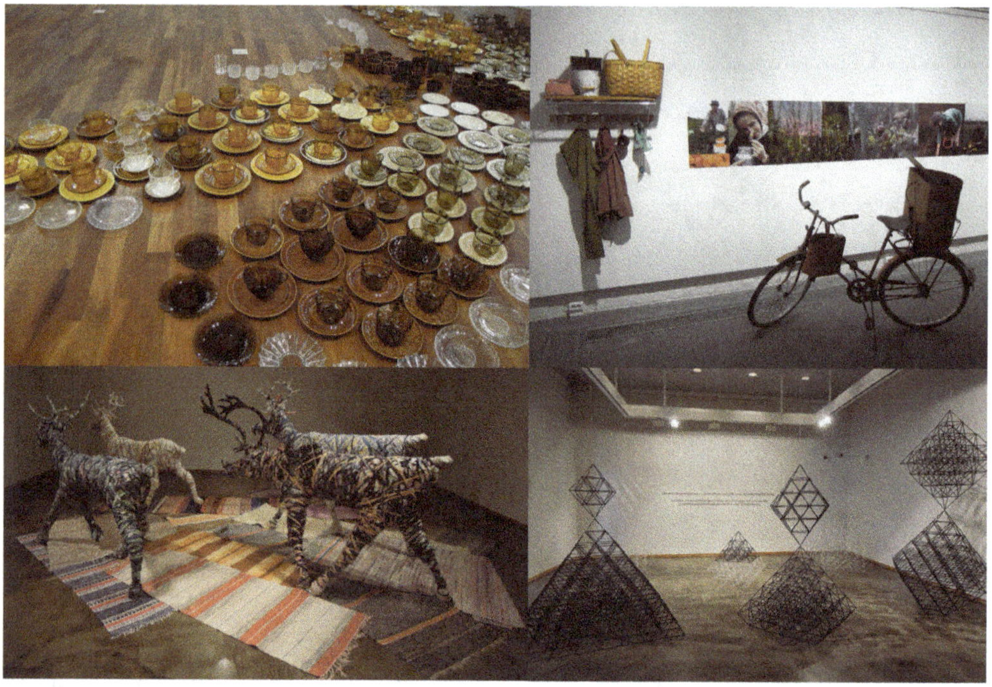

Figure 3: Exhibition views from the dissertation by Maria Huhmarniemi. Photos Maria Huhmarniemi.

foreign and local berrypickers caused by increased commercial berry picking in Lapland. Huhmarniemi cooperated on the project with researchers in environmental sociology and policy and produced the *Berry Pickers* installation, in which she explains the reactions of berry pickers in Lapland to foreign berry pickers and changes in the berry industry. Picking berries relates to cultural habits that are partly tacit knowledge and partly the background to conflict. Huhmarniemi conducted interviews with berry picking hobbyists and borrowed photographs from home albums, as well as artefacts relating to berry picking (Huhmarniemi 2012). As is typical of action research, research questions were reoriented and became more precise with each research cycle. The aim of the *Reindeer Husbandry in the Arctic* exhibition at the Aine Art Museum, Tornio, was to interpret and present research data in contemporary art. The preparation of the exhibition involved cooperation with two researchers: reindeer researcher Mauri Nieminen, and shamanism researcher Francis Joy. In the exhibition, Huhmarniemi dealt with contradictions between the mining industry, tourism industry and reindeer herding.

The conclusion to Huhmarniemi's research was that contemporary art can convey research information to the public in a symbolic, multi-sensory and multi-level format. ABAR can bring out side-lined viewpoints that justify the protection of land and natural resources. The meaning of the research is associated with the development of visual art teacher training, environmental education that integrates art and science studies and art-based environmental research (Huhmarniemi 2016).

ABAR as a method

The aim of this chapter has been to introduce the background and ideology for the development of the ABAR method as a part of Art Education graduate school at the University of Lapland. Development work is a research process that itself takes time. The method is collaboratively developed by a small group of artists, educators and researchers with the participation of the students of art education. The aim has also been to explain the interaction between artistic, scientific and educational orientation in the art education profession. The developers' personal artistic activities in the field of participatory and engaged art have been seen as an important tool in constructing ABAR methods. Creating art does not exclude research, and vice versa. In ABAR the focus is not on developing one's own personal artistic expression but on the interaction between co-artists, co-researchers and participants. The result of this sharing and empowering process can also be called 'the art of art education'.

References

Borgdorff, H. (2011), 'Knowledge in artistic research', in M. Biggs and H. Karlsson (eds), *The Routledge Companion to Research in the Arts*, London: Routledge, pp. 44–63.

Heikkinen, H. L. T., Konttinen, T. and Häkkinen, P. (2006), 'Toiminnan tutkimisen suuntaukset' ('Trends in action research'), in H. L. T. Heikkinen, E. Rovio and L. Syrjälä (eds), *Toiminnasta tietoon: Toimintatutkimuksen menetelmät ja lähestymistavat* ('From action to knowledge: Methods and approaches in action research'), Helsinki: Kansanvalistusseura, pp. 39–76.

Hiltunen, M. (2009), 'Yhteisöllinen taidekasvatus: Performatiivisesti pohjoisen sosiokulttuurisissa ympäristöissä' ('Community based art education: Through performativity in northern sociocultural environments'), PhD thesis, Rovaniemi: Acta Universitatis Lapponiensis A160.

Hiltunen, M. and Rantala, P. (2015), 'Creating art-based approaches in working life development: The shift from success to significance', *International Journal of Education Through Art*, 11:2, pp. 245–60.

Huhmarniemi, M. (2012), 'Berry wars: A science centre as a forum for a dialogical, interdisciplinary art project', *International Journal of Education Through Art*, 8:3, pp. 287–303.

——— (2016), 'Marjamatkoilla ja kotipalkisilla: Nykytaiteilija ympäristöpoliittisten keskustelujen osallistujana pohjoisessa' ('Artists in the landscape of berry wars and reindeer husbandry: Contemporary art as a forum for environmental politics'), PhD thesis, Rovaniemi: Acta Universitatis Lapponiensis 324.

Irwin, R. L. and Springgay, S. (2008), 'A/r/tography as practice-based research', in M. Cahnmann-Taylor and R. Siegesmund (eds), *Arts-Based Research in Education: Foundations for Practice*, New York: Routledge, pp. 103–24.

Jokela, T. (2008), 'A wanderer in the landscape', in G. Coutts and T. Jokela (eds), *Art, Community and Environment: Educational Perspectives*, Bristol: Intellect, pp. 217–40.

——— (2009), 'Kollaborative, projekkorientierte Studien in der Kunstpädagogenausbildung' ('Collaborative project-based studies in art teacher education'), in C.-P. Buschkühle, J. Kettel and M. Urlaβ (eds), *Horizonte: Internationale Kunstpädagogik* ('Horizon: International art education'), Oberhausen: Athena, pp. 137–50.

——— (2012), 'The art of art education and the status of creative dialogue', in C.-P. Buschkühle (ed.), *Ein Diskurs zur kunstlerische Bildung* ('Conversation on artistic education'), Oberhausen: Athena, pp. 359–76.

——— (2013), 'Engaged art in the North: Aims, methods, contexts', in T. Jokela, G. Coutts, M. Huhmarniemi and E. Härkönen (eds), *Cool: Applied Visual Arts in the North*, Rovaniemi: Erweko, pp. 10–21.

Jokela, T., Hiltunen, M. and Härkönen, E. (2015a), 'Art-based action research – Participatory art for the North', *International Journal of Education Through Art*, 11:3, pp. 433–48.

——— (2015b), 'Contemporary art education meets the international North', in M. Kallio-Tavin and J. Pullinen (eds), *Conversations on Finnish Art Education*, Aalto University Series: Art + Design + Architecture, Helsinki: Aalto ARTS Books, pp. 260–79.

McNiff, S. (2013), 'A critical focus on art-based research', in S. McNiff (ed.), *Art as Research, Opportunities and Challenges*, Bristol: Intellect, pp. 109–16.

Springgay, S., Irwin, R. L. and Kind, S. (2008), 'A/r/tographers and living inquiry', in C. J. Knowles and A. L. Cole (eds), *Handbook of the Arts in Qualitative Research: Perspectives, Methodologies, Examples, and Issues*, Thousand Oaks: Sage, pp. 83–92.

Ulkuniemi, S. (2005), 'Valotetut elämät: Perhevalokuvan lajityyppiä pohtivat tilateokset dialogissa katsojien kanssa' ('Exposed lives: Dialogues between viewers and installations examining the genre of family photography'), PhD thesis, Rovaniemi: Acta Universitatis Lapponiensis.

Vanhatapio, T. (2010), 'Poikavoimaa kuvataideharrastukseen: Pohjoinen näkökulma poikien ja lasten vanhempien näkemyksiin kuvataideharrastuksesta ja kuvataideopetuksesta' ('Boy power for visual arts hobbies: Northern aspect of boys' and parents' visions of visual arts hobbies and art education'), PhD thesis, Rovaniemi: Acta Universitatis Lapponiensis.

Chapter 5

Researching the Unknown through Arts-Based Research to Promote Pedagogical Imagination

Fernando Hernández-Hernández

Introductory scene

June 2015: A member of a PhD dissertation board starts his review by saying: 'When Fernando invites you to assess a doctoral thesis you know that this research will not follow the normal rules'. Some of my colleagues know or maybe suspect that, in our arts and education doctoral programme at the University of Barcelona, as in contemporary art, the approach to research we try to follow 'is concerned with the production of the new, which in some cases has transformative effects upon practice and understanding' (Atkinson 2012: 8). This is something doctoral candidates interiorize very early, as Lilian said in her doctoral defence: 'In this doctoral program you are invited, not to reproduce existent methodologies, but to create new ones' (Ucker-Perott 2015).

The context of the doctorate in Spain

In Spain, doctoral studies are regulated by the central government and doctoral programmes are approved by a central agency. Universities adapt this legislation to their idiosyncrasies and traditions. Hundreds of PhD dissertations have been 'defended' around Spain. In the arts and education doctoral programme at Barcelona, ten theses have been presented as of 11 February 2016. Topics of these researchers included the following issues: cosplay identities (Castelán García 2016); women clowns as feminist performers (Lima Caminha 2016); Mexican women's transitions in South California (Garcia-Crispin 2016); art community projects in Colombian rural areas (Falla Rodríguez 2016); museum educators in Spain under the pedagogical turn (Soria-Ibarra 2016); art teachers' life histories in Argentina (Giambelluca 2016); inclusive art education in Brazil (Caira Githay 2016); relationships with otherness in contemporary visualities (Bernardo Rangel 2016); and youth imaginaries on the post-memory of Chilean dictatorship (Bello Navarro 2016). In this chapter I will try to interrogate the last two of these dissertations through the following questions:

- What are the ontological, epistemological, methodological and political assumptions of these academic productions?
- How do arts-based research approaches articulate these research topics?
- What approach to art education is circulating among these dissertations?

The reason I take up these two cases is because they make possible a conversation about their assumptions and research strategies.

Introducing the arts and education doctoral programme

Since the year 2000, in the Unit of Cultural Pedagogies of the Fine Arts Faculty at the University of Barcelona, we have offered a doctoral programme on Arts and Education. In this context our approach to research tries to promote a pedagogical imagination that 'allows us to invent, experiment and create, isolated from routines and trends' (Hernández-Hernández 2008: 56). This positionality relates to the notion of the 'pedagogical event' presented by Atkinson (2012), to whom 'an event' is a situation in which 'a disruption of established ways of knowing, through learning events' emerges (Atkinson 2012: 10). In the doctoral programme, doctoral candidates are encouraged to be involved in an experience of participating in an inquiry research project, which 'produces a new alignment of thinking and action' (Atkinson 2012: 9). We invite emerging researchers to be part of a community of practice, in which we constantly challenge our comfort zone by trying to do research on topics involving authentic learning. Authentic learning affects, involves and transforms the learner and brings him or her to new perspectives.

Valeska's research (Bernardo Rangel 2016) starts from the central idea of thinking about otherness in a contemporary visuality, when the other is represented in situations geographically distant from ours. The approach of her inquiry lies in two key concepts: looking and otherness, guided by a visual culture studies epistemological frame. María José (Bello Navarro 2016) researches how images may generate knowledge about a Chilean dictatorship, based on an educational-artistic project carried out with youth in the Museum for Memory and Human Rights, Santiago, Chile. In this project she tries to give an account of how visual memories of the past draw out young people's experience of when they were affected by post-memory narratives displayed in the exhibition space. Both research approaches acknowledge that doing research as an experience of coping with the unknown escapes from a pre-established epistemological and methodological norm. It is during the process of inquiry, through its movements, when what is researched is articulated and made meaningful. This process creates and maintains the desire to dig deeply into research topics and confronts doctoral students with complex problems and challenges to solve (Laur 2013).

From narrative research to arts-based research

For over a decade, within the consolidated research group ESBRINA – Contemporary Subjectivities, Visualities and Educational Environments (http://esbrina.eu/en/home/), we have been using narrative inquiry, not as a trend but as a necessity that responds to the work we endeavour to carry out. This brings us to taking naturalist and narrative methodologies such as ethnography, arts-based research and biographical narrative forms of inquiry as ways of holding the complexity of human experiences and to using non-totalitarian narrative strategies (Conle 2000) that enable reflecting on the different sources and references collected through different research methods to configure narrative accounts (Kincheloe and Berry 2004).

My aim is to give an account of how narratives derived from the experiences of subjects who participate in a research project can generate new knowledge and promote greater understanding (Sancho and Hernández-Hernández 2013). In addition, I assume that the researcher cannot remain external to the phenomenon that s/he is investigating. Inquiry and research are two processes that can converge (Eisner 1991), but which can also follow autonomous paths in our attempt to shed light on the complexity of the actions, stories and representations that we generate.

Working with Juana Sancho-Gil, our ontological, epistemological and methodological positionings (Hernández-Hernández and Sancho-Gil 2015) within the research group and in the doctoral programme are scaffolded by a constructionist approach (Gergen and Gergen 2004; Holstein and Gubrium 2008) that guides us in the analysis and understanding of 'the social bases of knowledge and the symbolic origins of reality' (Ema López and Sandoval Moya 2003: 7–8); hermeneutic phenomenology, as foundational to the notion of educational and artistic experience (Dewey 1934; van Manen 1990; Shusterman 1991); narratives of experience (Clandinin and Connelly 2000); and narrative research methods as ways of catching and giving account of these experiences (Conle 2000; Clandinin 2007). These are the bases where research is anchored in interconnected relationships.

We pay attention to research questions, and how to raise them for their power to shape the very nature of the phenomena studied; and in deciding the methodological approach and the research methods, we look for coherent ways to undertake the type of research where 'subjects' (women clowns, cosplay performers, Mexican emigrants, art teachers, museum educators, Colombian farmers, Chilean youth and so on) are not reduced to the category of data. This positionality sustains a research ethic founded on a reciprocal relationship with the 'Other' who gives us their time and experience 'without recourse to arrogance but with openness and humility' (Back 2007: 4). Further, to the extent that our academic tradition, working conditions and educational culture permit, we seek to evolve from the notion of participatory research as 'a research process which involves those being researched in the decision-making and conduct of the research' (Bourke 2009: 458), to a more inclusive perspective (Nind 2014) in which research problems are owned by people and participants. In this way, there is a collective ability to exert some kind of control over the process and outcomes, thus making the research process – from questions to reports – accessible to participants (Nind 2014: 4).

This brings me to narrative methodologies such as ethnography (Troman et al. 2005), arts-based research (Barone and Eisner 2011) and biographical narrative forms of inquiry (Kincheloe and Berry 2004) as ways of holding the complexity of human experiences; and to using non-totalitarian narrative strategies (Conle 2000) that enable reflecting on different sources and references collected through various research methods to configure the narrative accounts (Kincheloe and Berry 2004).

This kind of research sustains the tension of limits as the distance between who does the research – the researcher – and on (or with) whom the research is done – the 'subjects' (Sancho and Hernández-Hernández 2013). A consequence of considering the fragility of these limits is the need to make visible the network of relationships taking place during the research process (Clandinin and Connelly 2000; Porres 2012).

Our research group and the doctoral programme also sustain a political position that leads us to permanently discuss the continuum: researching to (academically) succeed versus researching to understand and transform. The phenomena we study are highly contextualized and shaped by a combination of human actions and discourses. From this positionality the turn to ABR was a 'natural' development for our work; by incorporating artistic research approaches (artistic research, arts-based educational research) and methods (visual, performative and literary), we gained tools that allowed us to reveal that which would remain unseen. In addition, some members are professors in the Fine Arts Faculty, where the debate on and interest in research (beyond what takes place during the creative process) has grown in recent years (Hernández-Hernández 2006, 2008, 2013a, 2013b).

The approach to arts-based research

We are primarily concerned with the various approaches to link arts and research. We differentiate, based on our seven years of experience of doing arts-based and artistic research (Fendler and Hernández-Hernández 2012) four approaches: creative research (research implicit in artistic practice); artistic research (where the process of researching is made explicit by written or/and visual forms of narrating); image-based research that goes beyond the arts and represents a rich debate in social sciences 'that combines the practices, theories and ideas of different disciplines to produce novel outcomes and contributions to knowledge, theory and applied interventions' (Pink 2012: 8); and arts-based research. From our approach, we understand that using images or developing artistic practice is not enough to label an educational activity or an artistic practice as research (Calderón-García 2015; Onsès-Segarra and Servalls Munar 2013). In this sense, we think that ABR has to do with the use of artistic media in social, educational and artistic research. This means 'making new worlds; enabling others to re-experience vicariously the world' (Barone and Eisner 2011: 20).

This entanglement of positionalities and displacements is reflected in the research by Valeska. She started with a question: how might we disturb our gazes beyond the symbolic devices of exceptionality and distance? To explore this issue, she developed three 'Gazes Workshops'. These were configured as a series of meetings with three different groups of participants. The dynamic revolved around some key questions, some images, small texts and pieces of films.

The workshops were designed to compile the narratives of each participant, collected in their 'Gaze Diaries', around the experience of looking at images from artists such as Martha Rosle, Alfredo Jaar and Thomas Hirschhorn and the photographers Ghaith Abdul-Ahad and Rogerio Ferraz. These images acted as activators of resonances for those people in vulnerable situations. In the case of Valeska ABR was, at the same time, an opportunity for expanding the semiotic power of images, to create a space of encounter with participants in the workshops and to give an account of their resonances and wonderings generating new images.

In this context, the concept of living inquiry is an effective framework for opening-up ABR, by acknowledging that everyone is an expert of her/his own lived experience. This notion comes from Merleau-Ponty (1962) who conceives research as an enactive space of living inquiry. In a/r/tography, for example, 'living inquiry is an aesthetic encounter, where the process of meaning-making and being are inextricably connected to an awareness and understanding of art' (Springgay et al. 2005: 902). From this perspective, 'living inquiry is an embodied encounter constituted through visual and textual *understandings and experiences* rather than mere visual and textual *representations*. One cannot separate, through abstract means, visual and textual interpretations of lived experiences' (Springgay et al.: 902). In addition to democratizing the notion of who can carry out research, this position then also recognizes that the research process cannot be fully controlled or contained. It is a term that places value on the journey of a research process and on the transition that inquirers (and the inquiry itself) go through (Fendler 2013). This idea of the entanglement between experience and understanding was visible in the ABR praxis developed in María José's process of inquiry. She assumed that images play a fundamental role in comprising the territory of memory that approaches the past. The portrayal in the media of the historical trauma that led to political violence was based on the use of documentary material: photographs, reports, newspapers, videos, documentaries, posters and so on. But how were these images communicated? Is it possible to think of a way of seeing that which distances itself from an objective-documentary logic? What is the role of images within a pedagogical memory? She explored these questions with the young people who participated in the first stage of her research. Images displayed at the museum were analysed in terms of visual culture (what imaginaries they mediated) and the notion of memory that the museum was producing. At the same time, they developed a process of inquiry to make visible the museum's pedagogic discourse. After this initial contact and inquiry, the theoretical framework, methodological approach and artistic methods to be used during the project with youth were established.

In María José's case, the concept of *living inquiry* (Meyer 2010), with its ties to action research, was an effective framework for recognizing that the ABR process cannot be fully controlled or contained. We find that within this process, our goal as supervisor is not to direct the doctoral students in their research process, but to guide the group towards developing an 'attitude of inquiry' (Marshall and Reason 2007), which will allow us to cast a quizzical and critical gaze on our/their own research practices (Fendler and Hernández-Hernández 2015).

The approach to art education

The meaning of art education in this doctoral programme has to do with those experiences that generate disruptions, surprise us, question us and invite us to escape from our comfort zone. Art education opens spaces for a dialogue placing artistic practices and pedagogical practices as elements of the construction of a common world. Art education is presented as an aperture to the pedagogical imagination that 'allows us to invent, experiment and create, isolated from routines and trends' (Hernández-Hernández 2008: 56).

Both Valeska and María José are committed to a praxis of artistic education and invite others to discover not what is seen, but what articulates the gaze of those who see. In Valeska's case, the experiences of relationship with images made it possible not only to recognize modes of relationship with otherness, but an openness to realize that the other is also in the viewers' way of looking. Something similar happened with the young people that María José accompanied. They related to the images of the memory of the dictatorship in Chile, not only by generating forms of appropriation that were reflected in the photographs they created, but also by identifying the pedagogical strategies that the museum uses to fix a particular meaning of memory through images. Through this art education process, there is an opportunity to be part of a real learning experience that 'involves a movement into a new ontological state; it defines a problem of existence, in contrast to more normative learning in its everyday norms and competences' (Atkinson 2012: 9).

On limits and possibilities

The permanent ontological, epistemological and methodological debate linked to the practice of research based on the doctoral programme and exemplified in the cases of Valeska and María José has brought us to specify the following characteristics to guide our ABR approach:

1. Any artistic process is not necessarily research. Research always has a specific paradigm or approach from which it is formulated. It is not an epiphenomenon but an ontological, epistemological and methodological frame.
2. All ABR has a context that is different from other areas of research. The purpose of research in art-therapy or artistic research will not be the same as that of educational arts-based research or the use of arts in a collaborative research with youth.
3. Any inquiry process using images does not constitute ABR per se. The use of images (as evidence or as creative objects), the roles they play in research and the meaning we give them determines whether we are developing a research or an artistic process. An image can illustrate, document or mediate in a research process, and could be (or not) considered as part of an art-based research process.

4. Artefacts and art devices are not reduced to images. Body gestures, actions, words, texts and music are manifestations that can help us expand our knowledge of the problem of study.
5. The notion of art (and artist responsibility) has been expanded in current times. The artistic references given by some examples of ABR seem linked to a territory and visual expressiveness that contemporary art has long since crossed. The notion of artist linked to these references has been answered by collaborative and community artistic practices that blur the notion of authorship and can provide meaningful strategies for ABR.

From these foundations in the Arts and Education doctoral programme, ABR becomes a space for acting, resisting and reinventing. It follows a non-normative logic, in an effort to think and construct our gaze critically, in our particular space and time. The ontological, epistemological and methodological resources provided by ABR allowed us to connect, and above all understand, bridging between the personal and the political, the artistic and the social, and the intimate and what we share with others.

ABR introduces an alternative to other ways of researching the experiential and subjective. In the doctoral research frame, we understand artistic processes as a critical apparatus for dialoguing with the images, art practices and representations that surround us. We understand that we are working from the border between fields, demarcating an alternative, or a resistance, to hegemonic languages, both within research and the arts.

References

Atkinson, D. (2012), 'Contemporary art in education: The new, emancipation and truth', *The International Journal of Art & Design Education,* 31:1, pp. 5–18.

Back, L. (2007), *The Art of Listening*, Oxford and New York: Berg.

Barone, T. and Eisner, E. (2011), *Arts Based Research*, London: Sage.

Bello Navarro, M. J. (2016), 'Imagen-tiempoy pedagogías transaccionales: Reconfigurando la postmemoria de la dictadura con los jóvenes a través de un proyecto de investigación visual', PhD thesis, Barcelona: University of Barcelona.

Bernardo Rangel, V. (2016), '(Des)ubicar las miradas, más allá de la compasión y la lejanía: Percepciones de la alteridad en la visualidad contemporánea', PhD thesis, Barcelona: University of Barcelona.

Bourke, L. (2009), 'Reflections on doing participatory research on health: Participation, method and power', *International Journal of Social Research Methodology*, 12:5, pp. 457–74.

Caira Githay, A. M. (2016), 'La articulación y el tránsito de las concepciones de inclusión/exclusión y de enseñanza de las artes visuales en las prácticas de un Instituto de Artes', PhD thesis, Barcelona: University of Barcelona.

Calderón-García, N. (2015), 'Irrumpir lo artístico, perturbar lo pedagógico: La Investigación Artística como espacio social de producción de conocimiento', PhD thesis, Barcelona: University of Barcelona.

Castelán García, C. A. (2016), 'Tecnologias performativas en el disfraz: Recodificacion corporal en el cosplay', PhD thesis, Barcelona: University of Barcelona.

Clandinin, D. J. (ed.) (2007), *Handbook of Narrative Inquiry: Mapping a Methodology*, Thousand Oaks: Sage.

Clandinin, D. J. and Connelly, M. (2000), *Narrative Inquiry: Experience and Story in Qualitative Research*, San Francisco: Jossey-Bass.

Conle, C. (2000), 'Thesis as narrative or "what is the inquiry in narrative inquiry?"', *Curriculum Inquiry*, 30:2, pp. 189–214.

Dewey, J. ([1938] 1997), *Experience & Education*, New York: Free Press.

——— ([1934] 2005), *Art as Experience*, New York: TarcherPerigee.

Eisner, E. (1991), *The Enlightened Eye: Qualitative Inquiry and the Enhancement of Educational Practice,* New York: Macmillan.

Ema López, E. and Sandoval Moya, J. (2003), 'Presentación: Mirada caleidoscópica al construccionismo social' ('Introduction: Kaleidoscopic approach to social constructionism'), *Política y Sociedad* ('Policy and society'), 40:1, pp. 5–14.

Falla Rodríguez, M. P. (2016), 'La Fraternidad*:* Conflictos, posibilidades y divergencias de una práctica agrícola, artística y comunitaria en el municipio de Soracá, Colombia', PhD thesis, Barcelona: University of Barcelona.

Fendler, R. (2013), 'Visual culture as living inquiry: Looking at how young people reflect on, share and narrate their learning practices in and outside school', *Mapping and Evaluating Research on Young People as Visual Culture Producers*, UPNA, Pamplona, 22–23 November.

Fendler, R. and Hernández-Hernández, F. (2012), 'The role of the virtual campus in the undergraduate course "arts-based research": A site for student experimentation and authorization', *Proceedings of the 11th International Society for Education through Art (InSEA) European Congress*, Cyprus: Limassol, pp. 361–70.

——— (2015), 'Visual culture as living inquiry: Looking at how young people reflect on, share and narrate their learning practices in and outside school', *+ q knsmidrs d imgns: Mapeando y evaluando la investigación sobre Jóvenes Productores de Cultura Visual* ('Mor thN img cnsmrs: Mapping and evaluating research on young people as visual culture producers'), Pamplona: Universidad Pública de Navarra, pp. 281–99.

García-Crispín, G. (2016), 'Trazando líneas y contando historias: Investigación biográfico narrativa en torno a experiencias femininas de migración México-California', PhD thesis, Barcelona: University of Barcelona.

Gergen, K. and Gergen, M. (2004), *Social Construction: Entering the Dialogue*, Chagrin Falls: Taos Institute.

Giambelluca, G. (2016), 'Cambios sociales y profesionales en las historias de vida de docentes de educación artística', PhD thesis, Barcelona: University of Barcelona.

Hernandez, F. (2008), 'Após a aventura, persiguiendo uma utopia' ('Following an adventure, chasing a utopia'), *Pátio: Revista Pedagógica*, 49, pp. 56–59.

Hernández-Hernández, F. (2006), 'Campos, temas y metodologías para la investigación relacionada con las artes', in M. Gómez-Muntané, F. Hernández-Hernández and H. Pérez-López (eds), *Bases para un debate sobre investigación artística*, Madrid: Ministerio de Educación y Ciencia, pp. 9–49.

——— (2008), 'La investigación basada en las artes: Propuestas para repensar la investigación en educación', *Educatio Siglo*, XXI:26, pp. 85–118.

——— (2013a), 'Investigar con imágenes, investigar sobre imágenes: Desvelar aquello que permanece invisible en la relación pedagógica', in R. Martins and I. Tourinho (eds), *Processos e Práticas de Pesquisa na Educação da Cultura Visual*, Santa María: Universidade de Santa Maria, pp. 77–95.

——— (2013b), 'Artistic research and arts-based research can be many things, but not everything', in F. Hernández-Hernández and R. Fendler (eds), *Proceedings of the First Conference on Arts-Based and Artistic Research: Critical Reflections on the Intersection of Art and Research*, Barcelona: University of Barcelona, pp. viii–xi, http://hdl.handle.net/2445/45264. Accessed 29 March 2017.

Hernández-Hernández, F. and Sancho-Gil, J. M. (2015), 'A learning process within an education research group: An approach to learning qualitative research methods', *International Journal of Social Research Methodology*, 18:2, pp. 651–67.

Holstein, J. and Gubrium, J. (eds) (2008), *Handbook of Constructionist Research*, New York and London: The Guilford Press.

Kincheloe, J. and Berry, K. (2004), *Rigour and Complexity in Educational Research: Conceptualizing the Bricolage*, Berkshire: Open University Press.

Laur, D. (2013), *Authentic Learning Experiences: A Real-World Approach to Project-Based Learning*, New York: Routledge.

Lima Caminha, M. (2016), 'Payasas: Historias, cuerpos y formas de representar la comicidad desde una perspectiva de género', PhD thesis, Barcelona: University of Barcelona.

van Manen, M. (1990), *Researching Lived Experience: Human Science for an Action Sensitive Pedagogy*, New York: State University of New York Press.

Marshall, J. and Reason, P. (2007), 'Quality in research as "taking an attitude of inquiry"', *Management Research News*, 30:5, pp. 368–80.

Merleau-Ponty, M. ([1945] 1962), *Phenomenology of Perception*, New York: Routledge.

Meyer, K. (2010), 'Living inquiry: Me, myself, other', *Journal of Curriculum Theorizing*, 26:1, pp. 85–96.

Nind, M. (2014), *What Is Inclusive Research?*, London and New York: Bloomsbury.

Onsès-Segarra, J. and Servalls Munar, R. (2013), 'Learning arts-based research starting from a shared inquiry: The experience of silence in university classes', in F. Hernández-Hernández and R. Fendler (eds), *Proceedings of the 1st Conference on Arts-Based and Artistic Research: Critical Reflections on the Intersection of Art and Research*, Barcelona: University of Barcelona, pp. 223–26, http://hdl.handle.net/2445/45264. Accessed 29 March 2017.

Pink, S. (ed.) (2012), *Advances in Visual Methodology*, Thousand Oaks: Sage.

Porres, A. (2012), 'Subjetividades en tránsito: La relación pedagógica como un encuentro conversacional entre sujetos en torno a la cultura visual', PhD thesis, Barcelona: University of Barcelona.

Sancho, J. M. and Hernández-Hernández, F. (2013), 'Developing autobiographical accounts as a starting point in research', *European Educational Research Journal*, 12:3, pp. 342–53, http://dx.doi.org/10.2304/eerj.2013.12.3.342. Accessed 29 March 2017.

Shusterman, R. (1992), *Pragmatist Aesthetics*, Cambridge: Blackwell.

Soria-Ibarra, F. (2016), 'El giro educativo y su relación con las políticas institucionales tres museos y centros de arte del contexto español', PhD thesis, Barcelona: University of Barcelona.

Springgay, S., Irwin, R. L. and Kind, S. (2005), 'A/r/tography as living inquiry through art and text', *Qualitative Inquiry*, 11, pp. 897–912.

Troman, G., Jeffrey, B. and Walford, G. (eds) (2005), *Methodological Issues and Practices in Ethnography,* Studies in Educational Ethnography, vol. 11, Amsterdam: Elsevier JAI, pp. 227–30.

Ucker-Perott, L. (2015), 'De ida y vuelta: Una investigación biográfico-narrativa en torno a las experiencias de ser estudiante internacional en la universidad', PhD thesis, Barcelona: University of Barcelona, diposit.ub.edu/dspace/bitstream/2445/66263/1/LUP_TESIS.pdf. Accessed 29 March 2017.

Chapter 6

Taking Shape: Visual Appearance and Theory

Brooke Hofsess, Karinna Riddett and Richard Siegesmund

Introduction: Richard

In educational research, a sage piece of advice is that the research question should drive the selection of research methodology. Even if the researcher has training as a visual artist, and the site of search is a visual classroom or art studio, predetermining that one will use visual methods is inappropriate. Such a perspective is akin to getting the cart before the horse. The research question, formed with an educational concern grounded in social science (Mertens 2010), must always remain primary. What is being studied? Why is it being studied? The question needs to be educationally significant. Then the researcher needs to explain how incorporating the visual provides a substantive insight beyond what other analytic tools allow.

In the twentieth century – and spilling into the twenty-first – iterations of German philosophy and French theory have provided multiple lenses for considering the limitations and insufficiency of language and symbolic thinking. They offer lenses through which to rethink perception. These theories are multifaceted and densely complex. One theory does not fit all. The thought of a single philosopher may significantly shift over time. For us, as with the selection of research methodology, the question drives a search for theory. We find that the compulsion to inquiry often arises in our first encounter with the unexplainable. It is the view into the void – our first awareness that there is a void – that prompts us to explore theory. Inquiry becomes a messy grappling with heretofore unconceptualized gaps of knowledge – the unperceived – which includes a panicked realization that one does not know what it is that one does not know. Thus, one moves forward – cautiously, circumspectly, forging inferential and abductive pathways. Theory helps give form to that which is first sensed in visual appearance.

The research question

In our view, the research question may either suggest a methodology and a theoretical lens for framing the inquiry, or may suggest a theoretical lens that invites a particular methodology. In both approaches, the research question remains primary. This is a place of beginning: understanding alignment, driven by the research question. This is a minimum requirement for a dissertation proposal.

Although this may be the place of beginning, it does not guarantee the final structure of the research. Questions and means frequently shift during the study. Insisting on this initial orientation for commencing arguably demonstrates that the candidate understands the structure that guides inquiry. If the research question should change in the course of the study, if the study should evolve in unexpected ways in the doing, this initial alignment provides a template to the candidate of how to adapt on-the-fly. This base understanding allows the candidate to not become wedded to a style of research, but to be prepared to risk an unexpected path of adventurous inquiry.

The visual is not an end in itself. In our experience, it is a tool, and that tool may help structure symbolic thinking. It may invite the exploration of qualitative materiality. It can create aesthetic spaces of inclusion and lacuna: of time and tempo. It can be an entry to what we somatically sense – what we know in our bones before we find the words to say it. It is a tool for entering into what has been sensed but not been said before – to explore the unarticulated.

The following two authors, Brooke Hofsess and Karinna Riddett, each a winner of the annual dissertation award of the Arts-Based Educational Research Special Interest Group of the American Educational Research Association, as well as the Elliot Eisner Dissertation Award of the National Art Education Association, explain how their research demonstrates that the visual, rooted in materiality and guided by theory, embodies pre-linguistic concepts and a site for language to coalesce. Hofsess draws on phenomenological theory of Gadamer, Merleau-Ponty and Deleuze through letterpress printing. Riddett employs deconstructive theories of Foucault through fabric.

Embodied intensities in aesthetic experiential play: Brooke

The questions that coalesced, building momentum in my doctoral process, came from a braided river delta of experience. Salient encounters across our lives carve ribbons into earthy banks, becoming enfleshed as questions we find ourselves compelled to pursue (Gadamer [1975] 2004). For me, what cut deep and wide were questions like: how do I make time for my creative practice as a K–12 artist-teacher? And, how do I continue to teach when my energy, my fervour has gone still and quiet? How do art teachers sustain their creative presence in a classroom? The wonderings that flow from this inquiry drive my educational research. These questions led me to find resonance with literature on professional development and renewal, where my entangled questions and experiences intersected with the lives of other teachers as they, too, wearily traversed the terrain of an American educational system worn down by our collective racing to the top and scrambling, breathlessly leaving no child behind (see Hourigan 2011).

As Richard expressed, everything hinges upon the question: Not just what you seek, but how and why you are seeking. In this way, a research question becomes an invitation allowing research methodology to body forth, and (in my case) to demand something unpredictable at the start. As a doctoral student, I found that my research question only became eloquent and generative with time – the time it takes to live in the ambiguity of our seeking (Rilke

[1929] 2011). My interest in aesthetic experiential play (Dewey 1934, 1938; Gadamer 1986, [1975] 2004; Greene 1978, 1988, 1995, 2001), which I often abbreviate as A~E~P, arose from what I had sensed as an artist, teacher and researcher – that to play in and through aesthetic experience builds resistance against standardized education (see Hofsess 2013, 2016). From there, I wondered: what might A~E~P bring to bear in the professional development and renewal of artist-teachers, and in the practices of my life?

These questions led me to play as a beginner in the letterpress studio, where I was released and renewed as I manoeuvred dense trays of lead type, worked stiff ink into a buttery-soft pile and cranked the cylinder of a stately Vandercook IV proofing press as it hummed and clicked. It was in the studio where I envisioned gifting my students/research participants with printed stationery sets with blind debossing that traced the words of William James: 'we learn to skate in summer after having commenced in winter' (Dewey 1934: 24) at the end of our course based on A~E~P. What ensued was a year of exchanging correspondence art through the mail with my students as they earned graduate degrees and carried on with their work in K–12 art classrooms. What ensued was swell upon swell of embodied intensities made manifest.

As necessary as living the questions was in leading me to the visual as an inquisitive tool, alone it was not enough. I also needed to explore theories that would provoke my thinking. As my deeper readings of Deleuze and Guattari's ([1980] 1987) intensities and Merleau-Ponty's ([1945] 2005) embodiment permeated my research process, I found myself becoming less and less concerned with articulating A~E~P (so I could grasp it), and more intrigued by what A~E~P might do and become (so I could set it in motion). In this sense, my initial theoretical framework collapsed as it yielded to the demands of the theories I was putting to work methodologically.

I followed Deleuze's urging 'we have to take things and find visibilities in them' ([1990] 1995: 96). In doing so, I found A~E~P makes visible a becoming-different through movements: an aesthetic swell and an afterglow. I theorized the swell as a movement that unmoors and sets one adrift towards unanticipated, surprising possibilities, and afterglow as an illuminated space that unfolds with our commitment and openness to move in swell towards the ever expanding new. I found that as my students and I exchanged correspondence, we were unfolding together my primary research question: what is it to find oneself (or selves) in afterglow? Month by month, postcard by postcard, reply by reply – new and different visibilities were revealed: becoming less bent on perfection, becoming trusting of the process, becoming more visually expressive, becoming freer to fail.

All this led me to move methodologically in swell with the embodied intensities of afterglow along the doctoral process. Moreover, I was able to construct a text – a poetic cartography – drawn of the many subtle and distinct ways afterglow becomes visible in and through movement: mulling, waiting, receiving, mailing, journaling, printing, writing, making, pausing, conversing, and, and, and.... Moreover, such a mapping would be unthinkable, unimaginable without the body, which constantly, qualitatively cues sensations of movement and difference (Merleau-Ponty [1945] 2005). By embodying theory, I found a way to what is now described as post-qualitative, post-intentional phenomenological research (Vagle 2014).

To close, theory demanded more from me – inviting me to listen, fold and acquiesce into an exploration of the visual and material. Perhaps the most significant way theory took shape in my dissertation was in the crafting of the text in epistolary form. The research story is reimagined through letters addressed to a 'dear reader', and through visual-verbal excerpts of postcards and letters exchanged between my participants and I. Aesthetic experiential play, and its afterglow, illuminates becoming-different to new possibilities for living, inquiry, teaching and moving in and through the world: a becoming-different that I hope might connect to the possibility of also becoming-renewed in my teaching and creative practices – to a mode of seeking that might be captured this way:

> One will be continuously engaged in interpreting a reality forever new; one will feel more alive than one ever has before. Seeking the communicative gesture and the expressive word, such a teacher will try consciously to move among and reflect together with her students. Coexisting with them, opening up perspectival possibilities along with them, the teacher and the students may journey toward some important truths as the days go on. 'Sometimes one starts to dream,' Merleau-Ponty writes, 'about what culture, literary life, and teaching could be if all those who participate [...] would give themselves up to the happiness of reflecting together.'
>
> (Greene 1973: 96)

To risk the unexpected: Developing an arts of living: Karinna

As Brooke's writing so eloquently portrays the formation and transformation of research questions, so my journey into the nature of caring began as one question and transformed into another. While Brooke's work breathes delicate subtleties that resemble the swell and afterglow theorized in its pages, my work resembled a collapse and then a rebuilding. My dissertation, 'Developing an arts of living', was composed narratively of all the intricate severed pieces of research – photographic journaling, student work, scholarly writing and my own process and product of fabric arts – in an effort to invite the reader to linger and trouble the nature of caring by engaging with text and image, oftentimes with tension and deliberate unclarity.

My original research question asked: what kinds of art experiences lead to deeper aesthetic engagement with objects, people and environment and how might these experiences encourage students to develop an arts of living? Informed through the writing of Michel Foucault, I operationalized this as perceiving the quality and qualities of things and developing practices that help shift our perspective, in order to deepen our understanding of others and create ourselves as ethical subjects. Simply put, I wanted to know how we learn to care for others in the process of making art.

It was not something I could study by simply analysing the work of my middle school students. It was something I had to embody with them, a being-in-relationship, an empathetic journey that risked the unexpected. In order to do that, I needed a methodology and a theory that would allow for a redefining of ethics and aesthetics as a philosophy of relation (Riddett-Moore 2013). I found that framework in a/r/tography, a methodology that recognizes ethics as 'participating in a network of relations' (LaJevic and Springgay 2008: 68). Through this methodology, ethics can be formulated as how one encounters others, a shift from knowing another through knowledge about them to 'an inquiry that creates bodied encounters' (LaJevic and Springgay 2008: 69).

When I first began exploring the question of how one might learn to care for others in the process of artmaking, I conducted a semester-long pilot study teaching empathy as a one-to-one correlation. All the art projects were based on explicitly teaching caring. This approach only seemed to skim the surface of the topic of caring and empathy. Students' artworks, as well as my own, were portrayals about caring, but not in caring. They shared our ideas, but not our experiences. I began a three-semester study developing a curriculum that would set up experiences for students to explore their deeply held values and meanings by opening up multiple definitions through their artmaking. This shift from explicitly teaching caring to exploring personal truths reflected the deeper philosophical shift in my research informed by the philosophy of Michel Foucault. Learning to care was not about copying how others demonstrate caring, but rather in creating the self, and making personal, relational and ethical choices (Foucault [1984] 1997).

This shift stemmed from my personal experiences into the nature of caring as well as my frustration with students resisting artmaking. That is when the collapse occurred. While deeply enfolded in the research work of caring, I was hurled into a situation where caring was causing me pain. My marriage was in ruins, my heart had been broken and betrayed. I was desperate for a new way to care. My research question changed. I needed to re/discover what developing the arts of living meant for me. My study now became my journey to this new question, which I hoped might eventually return me to my original question. So pulled by desire and a bit of desperation, I began to create artwork with a twofold purpose: to work through the darkness of caring personally and to learn to empathize with my students who were asked to share their lives through artmaking, even though they were not competent in the materials of art. I, too, had to feel uncomfortable with my media, so I chose fabric arts, an area in which my knowledge was minimal.

My first project was making a bib. It came out of necessity and interest in the simple design. My youngest son's daycare needed new bibs; the old ones were extremely frayed and threadbare. Just my selection of a project helped me reposition my curriculum. It came from necessity and interest. My middle school students did not see their artmaking as a necessity, or an interest. I needed to begin there. I also had to physically take apart the bib in order to create a new one. I had to deconstruct to re/create.

The process of making the bibs was also an act of caring. I had to be delicate with the fabric, precise and gentle. I was also creating them out of care for my son and his nursery mates. I wanted to improve their daily life, just by having a clean, sturdy bib, with colourful patterns. There was an artistic decision in each step of making the bibs. Just as I cut away from a pattern to make a clear shape of the bib, I needed to cut away my curriculum to make the clear shape of what my students needed from me as their art teacher. My question shifted: what causes students to have moments of disruption/deconstruction?

Exploring caring experiences in the classroom was now not so much about learning about caring as they were about developing ourselves as ethical people (Foucault [1984] 1997). Foucault's care of the self is a forming of the ethical self, not a search for a hidden self, but of a transformation, a becoming (Flynn 2005). Foucault also theorizes that:

> We cannot transform ourselves through the simple act of knowing, through critical reason or reflection alone, but only by risking who we are, by voluntarily seeking out and testing ourselves in situations that illuminate the contours of our subjectivity, that destabilize our certainties.
>
> (Ambrosio 2008: 255)

I began to apply the work of deconstruction to my re/creation of caring. I had to move beyond a simple 'learn the task' project in fabric arts and make a work of art as a transformation. I deconstructed my wedding dress as an altered fabric art. Not all artmaking deconstructs, but I advocate for an art practice and pedagogy that disrupts.

The presentation of the study then presented deconstruction as a praxis experienced through the process of artmaking. Deconstruction 'is not an act or operation' (Derrida 1988: 3), but it does 'take place, it is an event that deconstructs it-self' (Derrida 1988: 4). One cannot point to a moment in a lesson plan when deconstruction happens, but the practice of creation in the arts is very much a way to collect and assemble what one hears, sees, feels and knows for the purpose of shaping the self. The research did not answer a question, it did not present. It became a way to invite; invite discussing, invite troubling, invite another perspective on the intricacies of caring, specifically of caring in art education.

Closing provocations: Richard

In these arts-based studies, both Brooke and Karinna demonstrate a pragmatic questing of reaching into the future. Both lines of inquiry begin in a sense of absence, of a not-knowing – even desolation – and a quest to make sense. In their intuition of the presence of something more, they seek to articulate what up until this moment has not been seen. This leads to new lines of inquiry into both physical making through art and the investigation of theory with a deliberate intent to try to break pre-existing frames of perception that will permit each researcher to see the world anew. The research studies display strategies for manifesting new possibilities. Both dissertations display Dewey's concept of flexible purposing – the ability to sense new possibilities and move towards a new horizon (Eisner

2002). In both cases, close attention to the materiality of artmaking – the qualitative relationship that arts media set in play – form a critical lens to their respective new becomings.

References

Ambrosio, J. (2008), 'Writing the self: Ethical self-formation and the undefined work of freedom', *Educational Theory*, 58:3, pp. 251–67.

Deleuze, G. ([1990] 1995), *Negotiations* (trans. M. Joughin), New York: Columbia University Press.

Deleuze, G. and Guattari, F. ([1980] 1987), *A Thousand Plateaus: Capitalism and Schizophrenia* (trans. B. Massumi), Minneapolis: University of Minnesota Press.

——— (1938), *Experience and Education*, New York: Simon & Schuster.

Derrida, J. (1988), 'Letter to a Japanese friend', in D. Wood and R. Bernasconi (eds), *Derrida and Différance*, Evanston: Northwestern University Press, pp. 1–5.

Dewey, J. (1934), *Art as Experience*, New York: Perigee.

Eisner, E. (2002), *Arts and the Creation of Mind*, New Haven: Yale University Press.

Flynn, T. (2005), 'Philosophy as a way of life: Foucault and Hadot', *Philosophy and Social Criticism*, 31:5&6, pp. 609–22.

Foucault, M. ([1984] 1997), 'The ethics of concern of the self as a practice in freedom', in P. Rainbow (ed.), *Ethics: Subjectivity and Truth*, New York: New Press, pp. 281–301.

Gadamer, H. (1986), *The Relevance of the Beautiful and Other Essays* (trans. N. Walker), Cambridge: Cambridge University Press.

——— ([1975] 2004), *Truth and Method* (trans. J. Weinsheimer and D. G. Marshall), London: Continuum.

Greene, M. (1973), *Teacher as Stranger: Educational Philosophy for the Modern Age*, Belmont: Wadsworth.

——— (1978), *Landscapes of Learning*, New York: Teachers College Press.

——— (1988), *The Dialectic of Freedom*, New York: Teachers College Press.

——— (1995), *Releasing the Imagination: Essays on Education, the Arts, and Social Change*, San Francisco: Jossey-Bass.

——— (2001), *Variations on a Blue Guitar: The Lincoln Center Institute Lectures on Aesthetic Education*, New York: Teachers College Press.

Hofsess, B. (2013), 'Methodology in the afterglow', *International Journal of Education & the Arts*, 14:1.8, pp. 1–21, http://www.ijea.org/v14si1/v14si1-8.pdf. Accessed 30 January 2013.

——— (2016), *Unfolding Afterglow: Letters and Conversations on Teacher Renewal*, Rotterdam: Sense.

Hourigan, R. (2011), 'Race to the top: Implications for professional development in arts education', *Arts Education Policy Review*, 112:2, pp. 60–64.

LaJevic, L. and Springgay, S. (2008), 'A/r/tography as an ethics of embodiment: Visual journals in preservice education', *Qualitative Inquiry*, 14:1, pp. 67–89.

Merleau-Ponty, M. ([1945] 2005), *Phenomenology of Perception* (trans. D. Landes), London: Routledge.

Mertens, D. (2010), *Research and Evaluation in Education and Psychology: Integrating Diversity with Quantitative, Qualitative, and Mixed Methods,* 3rd ed., Thousand Oaks: Sage.

Riddett-Moore, K. (2013), 'Developing an arts of living', *Visual Arts Research*, 39:2, pp. 116–25.

Rilke, R. ([1929] 2011), *Letters to a Young Poet* (trans. M. Harman), Cambridge: Harvard University Press.

Vagle, M. (2014), *Crafting Phenomenological Research*, Walnut Creek: Left Coast Press.

Part 2

Provoking Doctoral Practices

Chapter 7

When Is a Red Shoe not a Red Shoe? Conceptual Framing and the Consequences for the 'Object' in Visual Research

Barbara Bolt

This essay investigates the vexed relationship between conceptual framework, method and methodology in artistic research. It addresses the question of how different methodological approaches within artistic research produce very different 'experiences' of 'an object' of research: some focus on and magnify the aesthetic experience, some reveal the conceptual richness that emerges from this engagement, whilst other methodologies take our attention elsewhere – to the sociocultural and/or political realm so that the shoes in themselves disappear altogether. Through the interrogation of a pair of red patent leather high heel shoes, the essay will unpack the dynamic relationship between the researcher, the method and the conceptual framing to demonstrate how the conceptual framing affects the questions asked of an 'object' of research. Through this very practical example, the essay identifies how the choice of conceptual framing impacts on the method and methodological framework of the research design in artistic research and affects the understandings that emerge from the research.

Staging a workshop

I have between 7 and 35 people in an ordinary classroom for a two-hour workshop session. They are all artists who have established art practices and are sitting in this research methods workshop because they are undertaking a research degree or are in some way engaged with practice-led research. They have very different practices and different levels of experience – visual artists working across a variety of media and approaches, community-based art practitioners, queer and documentary film-makers, choreographers and dancers, dramaturgs, jazz musicians, sound artists and even the occasional opera singer. We are all here to 'talk' about methodology, or at least to set the stage for talking about methodology. How to do this in one two-hour session?[1]

I request that everyone bring their electronic devices for some 'speed research' – iPhones, iPads, tablets or connected laptops. I rearrange the tables and form small working parties across the different disciplines. I place a pair of red patent leather high heels in the middle of the room on a plinth. Each group receives a worksheet that asks them to address these red shoes from a particular conceptual framing of the shoes – animism, auteur theory, constructionism, constructivism, conceptualism, formalism, feminism, Indigenous onto-epistemologies, Marxism, narrative theory, new materialism, phenomenology, postmodernism, psychoanalysis, relational aesthetics, Zen, etc.[2] Their task is, on the surface,

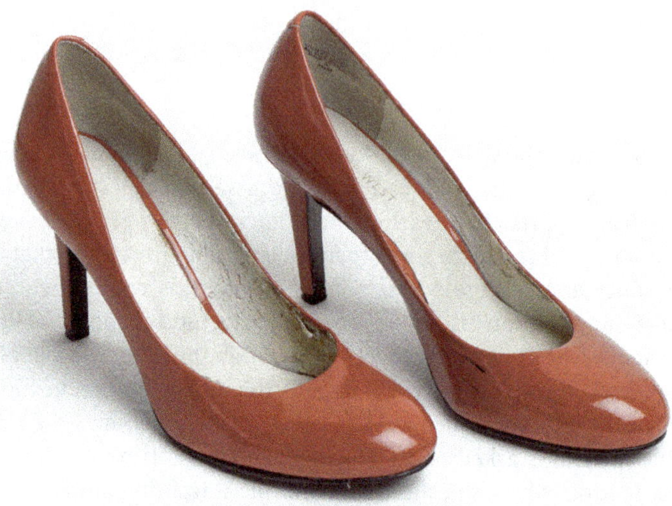

Figure 1: Barbara Bolt, *A Pair of Red Shoes*, 2015. Photography by Christo Crocker.

quite simple: how does a (formalist/feminist/Marxist/psychoanalytic, etc.) conceptual lens affect the questions that you ask of an 'object' of research? They are offered four focus points to help in the task:

1. Provide a brief working definition and an overview of the basic premise of the framework or theory, its assumptions and basic postulates.
2. What are the questions that arise from this conceptual framework that may direct your inquiry in relation to the 'object'?
3. Apply those questions to the red shoes and offer a 'reading' through the conceptual lens that you have adopted.
4. What happens to the pair of shoes through this analysis?

The groups have an hour to work together with their technology in order to offer an overview of the framework and to formulate their questions for the shoes. At the conclusion of that time, I ask each group to identify a spokesperson who speaks to the shoes and offers a reading/interpretation/analysis of its being as shoes, using the conceptual framing that they have worked with.[3]

Methodology: A working definition

The workshop does not attempt to establish the participant's methodological framework. Nor does it even begin to address the participant's method. Rather, it is a first step in thinking about the critical role that the conceptual framework plays in a research methodology. Its aim is to begin to tease out the difference between method and methodology and identify how our conceptual framing of the research influences what we might look for and what we might find.

However, before we commence any close engagement with a pair of red patent leather shoes, it is important to remind ourselves of some basic terminology. What is method, what is methodology and how does conceptual framework become entangled in that? In their discussion of methodology, Savin-Baden and Howell Major (2013) prise apart the terms 'method' and 'methodology', noting that in qualitative research, at least, there is often a conflation of the two terms. They observe that some researchers use the term 'methodology' as a 'substitute for the term method (what they are actually planning to do during the study, such as methods of data collection)' or else 'as a substitution for the philosophical traditions and frameworks that undergird their work' (Savin-Baden and Howell Major 2013: 40). Thus, their definition of methodology is 'a theoretical analysis of the methods and principles appropriate to a field of study or other branch of knowledge'. Methods 'are the particular steps or processes taken during the study' (Savin-Baden and Howell Major 2013: 41). In their definition of methodology, they propose a dialogue between methods and principles in interaction.

How does this dialogue proceed? Methodology is not an abstract framework imposed upon our 'object of investigation'. It is a living, breathing material-semiotic complex that involves the researcher's body, the materials and processes of art practice in interaction with the conceptual and philosophical ideas adopted in and through the research.[4] It is the identification and unpacking of those ideas in practice that becomes central to articulating the methodology that underpins the research design. In this conception, the conceptual and theoretical framework provides a means through which *to locate the researcher and the inquiry* within the context of the historical, sociopolitical and contemporary. It also requires that the researcher position themselves and their research in the field.

The shoes

How do the red shoes figure in this investigation of methodology? We have in front of us a pair of red patent leather high heel shoes (see Figure 1). The shoes were brought at the Salvation Army store on Sydney Road in Coburg, Victoria for AUD $12.00. The brand is Nine West, a shoe brand originally founded in 1973 in New York in the Solow building at 9 West 57th Street. They are a mid-range priced shoe now primarily manufactured in China as well as in smaller East Asian countries and India. Brand new they sell for US $59.99 online.

The left shoe is slightly scuffed on both sides and the interior man-made lining on the interior of the shoes is breaking away suggesting that the shoes are of some age. The Nine West brand name is worn away much more on the right shoe than the left, suggesting that the wearer placed more weight on their right leg than their left. The spiky heels of the shoes show very little wear. They are slightly too small for me and although I can squeeze into them, I am unable to walk in them. They retain an almost imperceptible whiff of the feet that have inhabited them. This clings to my fingers when I handle them. These are the basic facts about these red shoes as I know them.

How might we understand these red shoes differently and differentially? Even with this small amount of information, a number of different narratives emerge. There are the objective 'facts' of the shoes in themselves, their character as mass produced products sold in an increasingly global market; there are the facts of their purchase in an opportunity shop in Victoria; and finally there is the experience that I have in wearing or trying to wear these shoes. This specific information about these particular red shoes can be set off against the symbolism of 'the red shoes' that is transmitted to us through literature, film and song, for example: Hans Christian Andersen's fairy tale 'The Red Shoes' (1845) and its film adaptation *The Red Shoes* (1948) directed by Michael Power and Emeric Pressburger; the ruby red shoes worn by Judy Garland as Dorothy Gale in *The Wizard of Oz* (1939); Kate Bush's album *The Red Shoes*; or even Jerry Butler's song 'Little Red Shoes'. Each 'interpretation' is imbued with rich symbolism. However, what of the shoes in themselves and how might these particular red shoes enable us to tease out a question about the conceptual framing of artistic research?

What can the exercise of subjecting the 'red shoes' to different conceptual frameworks reveal about an object of investigation? How might this be valuable for thinking about visually oriented research methodologies being used across doctoral programmes? Does it collapse artistic research into the broader realm of visual methodologies or are some specific and unique lessons here for practice-led research?

Contrasting 'readings' and what they reveal or conceal about the shoes

In the workshop, the first question – provide a brief working definition and an overview of the basic premise of the framework or theory, its assumptions and basic postulates – identifies the complex task of selecting a conceptual framework for the research. Even before the groups could address the red shoes, they were required to locate or position themselves within the field of inquiry. For example: the 'feminist' team had to decide 'which' feminist perspective they wanted to work with – second wave feminism, socialist feminism, radical feminism or perhaps post-feminism; the phenomenologists had to consider which phenomenologist's writings they wanted to draw on for their analysis – Edmund Husserl, Maurice Merleau Ponty, Martin Heidegger, Hannah Arendt or the 'new phenomenologists', perhaps Francisco Varela or Hubert Dreyfus; the Marxists could draw directly from Marxist materialism and the development of capitalism to analyse the relations of labour embodied in the production of the shoes, or look to the Frankfurt school theorists such as Theodor

Adorno, Herbert Marcuse or Jürgen Habermas; whilst the psychoanalysts could draw on Sigmund Freud, Jacques Lacan or Julia Kristeva for their analysis of the shoes.

How a formalist theorist might engage with the shoes

The formalists recognized at the outset that their 'approach is qualitative and arguably takes a reductive position within the greater possible range of lenses' (Ananda 2015). With this qualification, being firmly grounded in modernism, they adopted a manifesto-type approach to the exercise:

> For the purposes of this research we are going to be formalists. As such, we are constructing a lens to remove associative or historical context. We are most concerned with physical and material attributes discernible from primary, perceptual experience. We are interested in how artists achieve an aesthetic order and balance and how this brings us to elemental truths through the use of colour, composition, etc.
>
> (Ananda 2015)

The group began their questioning of the shoes by a close examination of the actual shoes, asking questions such as: how shiny are they? What are they made from? What does scale contribute to this composition? How do the red objects stand up on the plinth? What is the relationship between negative spaces and positive forms? Are its proportions successful? Does the object embody an elemental/formal truth? Would the composition be better without the plastic interface between the red objects and the plinth? Would the work be better served by a clean plinth? How well do the symmetrical elements work? What is the quality of dialogue between the multiple forms? Is this an assemblage or are there three separate objects on a plinth? And, is the elevating (propping) element of each red object thrusting upward or downward? In addressing these questions, they made the following observations:

> The formal composition, excluding the plastic surface between the two red objects and the plinth, is very successful. The variety of forms, colours and surfaces creates a rewarding aesthetic experience. The elevation of each form provides an interesting tension between the plinth surface and the greater body of the red forms. The dynamic range of material finishing and positive and negative form creates successful tension. The black underside provides a weight and framing of the negative space against which the polished surface has visual lift.
>
> (Ananda 2015)

In this interpretation, the social and cultural were bracketed out completely. There was no questioning of the modes of production and relations of power, nor was there any investigation of the personal, psychological or psychic. They were not interested in the history of the shoes or with its social value as shoes to be worn.

'The Red Shoes' as a postcolonial theorist might see them

The postcolonial investigators' task was a very different one. Postcolonial theory deals with the aftermath of colonialism and its impact on relations of power between colonizer and colonized. With its genesis in the writings of such theorists as Edward Said and Gayatri Spivak, postcolonial theory emerged as a hybrid theory during the 1970s and 1980s as a critical social theory that aims to interrogate and works to transform iniquitous power relations. Its intellectual history, as Leela Gandhi notes 'is marked by a dialectic between Marxism, on the one hand, and post-structuralism/postmodernism, on the other' (Gandhi 1998: 7).[5] With this background, the group began with a series of questions that reflected this critical social criticism: who were they made for? Who made them? What is their purpose/function? What is the alternative to these? How does the form operate as a carrier of meaning? Heels, colour, material…? In order to begin to address these questions, they turned to the Nine West website:

> Nine West is a world-renowned fashion leader. Today the brand is beloved by women around the world […] Nine West seeks to satisfy women's ongoing desire to achieve their personal sense of style by delivering diverse, sexy fashion that is on trend and at attainable prices […] Smart and sophisticated, she is elegant with a chic modern look. She loves fashion and uses it to develop her own sense of personal style, while still appreciating good quality without compromising on price.
>
> (Nine West 2017)

The group's analysis proceeded in the following way:

> According to Nine West's website, the shoes were made for a smart, sophisticated, elegant, sexy and stylish woman. The shoes would originally have retailed for over $100. The fact they have been given away to an Op Shop, still in very good condition, attest to the fact their original owner may have been more interested in style than practicality. Were we looking from a feminist perspective we may query the structures of power and patriarchy that induce women to buy these sorts of products. From a postcolonial framework, [however] we ask what do the shoes tell us about dominant power structures, in relation to the West, who outsourced the manufacture of consumer products to countries where labour is cheaper?
>
> (Freney 2015)

Their discussion ranged from production of the shoes, the global flow of raw materials and manufactured goods, the poor working conditions of the workers, the inequities in the pay scale for the workers and the profits of multinational corporations, to considerations of consumption concluding that:

> From a postcolonial perspective then, the form of these shoes – high heels, shiny red leather, and so on, become significant carriers of meaning. They are artefacts of the dominant culture, and in fact, we conclude, they represent the insidiousness of contemporary cultural imperialism. They represent the power of the capitalist West over those countries to which we outsource our unethical and environmentally destructive means of production, in order to satiate our desire for cheap luxury goods.
>
> (Freney 2015)

This postcolonial critique had no need to address the shoes directly. Rather, as an object of research, the 'one pair of patent red Nine West high heeled shoes' took the group away from the shoes and into an analysis of the cultural and political conditions of production and consumption that operate within a globalized economy.

Key concerns

Two key issues were identified through the workshop that has implications for the selection of a conceptual framework for a research design. First, the alignment or non-alignment of the researcher's world-view with the conceptual frame adopted. As Savin-Baden and Howell Major have noted, researchers adopt research methods or rather methodologies that are compatible with their own world-view (2013: 3, see also pp. 68–70). This makes logical sense, but only comes into focus when researchers are asked to 'view' an object through the lens of a theoretical or philosophical model that diverges or is incompatible with their own world-view.

Second, through identifying the questions that the different conceptual lenses ask of an object of investigation, it became apparent that each has its particular focus as to what is critically important in understanding/revealing/reading/interpreting the shoes. Other aspects of the shoes' existence tend to be 'bracketed out' as unimportant or of lesser importance for the framework. In other words, to use a specifically visual metaphor, some aspects are brought into view whilst others remain out of focus. For example, modernist formalism, championed by the American art critic Clement Greenberg focused on what was specific to an art form. What was specific to painting, he claimed, was the flatness of the surface, the shape of the support and the properties of the pigment. Thus for Greenberg each art form had to be pared back to its 'pure' and unique qualities (Greenberg 1992: 755). In the focus on the purity and independence of the art form, the 'social' became bracketed out. On the other hand, Marx was only interested in the object as it related to the relations of labour and the use and exchange value of the shoes as commodity (Marx 1977).

This 'bracketing' out affected how the groups interacted with the shoes during the session. Some groups stood up and came close to the shoes, picked them up, asked questions of them (formalists and new materialists) and even tried to wear them (phenomenologists), while other groups showed very little or no interest in the *actual* shoes. Their attention circled the shoes without addressing them directly. They focused on the social and gender relations (feminists), or modes of production and use value and exchange value of the shoes as a commodity (Marxists) and/or the relations of power that surrounded the production and distribution of goods and services in a neo-liberal, post-capitalist global network (postcolonial group and feminists). Meanwhile the psychoanalysts became obsessed with desire, the unconscious and shoe fetishism.

Negotiated dialogues

The contrasting readings/interpretation/analysis/understandings revealed through such a workshop returns us to the question of methodology and the definition that I introduced at the beginning of this essay. Methodology is a complex material-semiotic process that brings the methods into *dialogue* with conceptual frameworks and paradigms of knowledge that provide a means through which to discuss the research and to locate the inquiry within the context of the historical, sociopolitical and contemporary. The selection of a conceptual framework does not proceed in advance of the practice, but rather emerges through this negotiated dialogue. It is through this complex questioning that we may come to be able to forge a robust and critical research design as arts researchers.

Acknowledgement

I would like to make two acknowledgements. Firstly, I would like to thank Estelle Barrett for providing the initial impetus for this essay. I also wish to thank the staff at the Adelaide Central School of Art for their generous and enthusiastic engagement in 'testing' out the shoes in the workshop. In particular, I would like to thank Roy Ananda and Zoe Freney and their teams for sharing their notes from this workshop.

References

Ananda, R. (2015), 'Formalism', unpublished notes from Research Methodologies workshop 'The Red Shoes' with Barbara Bolt, 25 May.

Andersen, H. C. (1845), 'The Red Shoes', *New Fairy Tales: First Volume*, Denmark: Rietzel.

Bush, K. (1993), *The Red Shoes*, CD-ROM, USA: EMI and Columbia Records.

Butler, J. (1997), 'Little Red Shoes', *Ichiban Blues at Christmas, Volume 4*, CD-ROM, Atlanta: Ichiban Records.

Dilthey, W. (2002), *Selected Works, Vol. 3: The Formation of the Historical World in the Human Sciences* (eds R. A. Makkreel and F. Rodi), Princeton: Princeton University Press.

Fleming, V. (1988), *The Wizard of Oz*, video recording, New York: Janus Films and Voyager Press.

Freney, Z. (2015), unpublished notes from Research Methodologies workshop 'The Red Shoes' with Barbara Bolt, 25 May.

Freud, S. (1986), *The Essentials of Psycho-Analysis* (trans. J. Strachey), London: Hogarth Press and the Institute of Psycho-Analysis.

Gandhi, L. (1998), *Postcolonial Theory: A Critical Introduction*, New York: Columbia University Press.

Greenberg, C. (1992), 'Modernist painting', in C. Harrison and P. Wood (eds), *Art in Theory 1900–1990*, Oxford: Blackwell, pp. 754–60.

Haraway, D. (1988), 'Situated knowledges: The science question in feminism and the privilege of partial perspective', *Feminist Studies*, 14:3, pp. 575–99.

——— (1991), *Simions, Cyborgs and Women*, New York: Free Association Books.

'Hermeneutics' (2014), *The Stanford Encyclopedia of Philosophy* (ed. E. N. Zalta), Winter ed., Palo Alto: Stanford University.

Marx, K. (1977), *Capital: A Critique of Political Economy* (introduced by Ernest Mandel, trans. Ben Fowkes), New York: Vintage Books.

Nine West (2017), http://www.ninewest.com.au. Accessed 29 March 2017.

Savin-Baden, M. and Howell Major, C. (2013), *Qualitative Research: The Essential Guide to Theory and Practice*, Oxon and New York: Routledge.

Notes

1 In May 2015, I conducted a research methodology workshop with lecturers from the Adelaide Central School of Art. The observations appearing in this essay are derived from this workshop.

2 See Chapter 2 'Research Choices and Lenses' and Chapter 3 'Philosophical Stance' in Savin-Baden and Howell Major (2013).

3 The choice of the different terms 'reading' and 'interpretation' and 'analysis' in this essay reveals certain unquestioned or unattributed assumptions about the world, and these terms are associated with particular conceptual frameworks. To offer a 'reading' is consistent with post-structuralist ideas that everything can be considered to be a text and that we look to the subtext, the underlying biases that structure reality. An 'interpretation', on the other hand, draws from Hermeneutics and is concerned with the understanding and interpretation of discursive and non-discursive forms (see 'Hermeneutics' 2014).

4 This understanding of methodology is informed by Donna Haraway's elaboration of the material-semiotic actor that grew out of her engagement with writer Katie King's 'apparatus of literary production'. In King's schema, the apparatus of literary production is the matrix that spawns 'literature'. Literature emerges at the intersection of bodies, materials, ideas and technology (Haraway 1991: 200). What is critical to Haraway's position is that the 'object of knowledge' is no longer a resource, ground, matrix, object, material or instrument to be used by humans as a means to an end. Rather an object of knowledge or object of investigation is an 'active, meaning-generating axis of the apparatus of bodily production' (Haraway 1991: 200).

5 The indebtedness of postcolonial theory to Marxist, post-structuralist and postmodern theories points to the need to identify and define the difference between a paradigm, a philosophy and a theory and to be able to articulate the intersections and differences between them.

Chapter 8

How Can Artistic Research (Still) Be Disruptive?

Natalia Calderón

Artistic research has been debated for more than 25 years,[1] a milestone that should be celebrated by raising questions about this practice, rather than merely continuing to repeat ourselves until we establish artistic research as a stable and fixed field. This call for critique responds to the fact that artistic research is sought to be 'context responsive', and therefore led by inquiry, while recognizing that it has traditionally been the artists, theorists and academics who developed the concept of *artistic research* through practice.

Slager (2012) warns us about the academization of artistic research and its consequences. He argues that artistic research should not become a stable field or a fixed discourse immersed in the academy, which would impede it from generating real knowledge. Instead, artistic research should be a convulsion, a destabilizer of reality, a question in itself: a question that needs to be interrogated. This change is reflected not only in how artworks and exhibitions aim to show the process and documentation supporting the projects, but also in the curricula design of art education as it shifts art in the direction of research-based practices. Therefore, we must confront the immanent risk of perceiving artistic research as a pre-existing method. We can draw on the urge for *reflexivity* in the research process to question what its own representation means and the positionality of the (artistic) researcher. The actual creation of new epistemological relations should not seek to fix methodologies but to create (social) spaces that introduce disruption and surprise.

The question is thus: how can artistic research still be disruptive? How can we pick away at the hardening margins that discursive logic imposes in an effort to normalize this strategy of knowledge production? How can we maintain a space of disruption and surprise?

For my doctoral dissertation (Calderón García 2015) I worked through artistic and pedagogical frameworks, problematizing both assumed notions. One research experience was analysed through these two gazes. When different conceptual frameworks overlap a normalized situation or context, fractures and gaps become visible, unveiling the *unknown* (Atkinson 2011). Here the unknown is not assumed to be a step behind in the progressive transition towards knowledge. The unknown is a situation where different understanding frameworks clash and something new and surprising emerges, something that cannot be signified. It is these gaps between diverse representations where the unknown is found.

It is in the process of seeking the unknown when artistic research is able to turn a situation into an *event*. An event disturbs what is expected or stable (Badiou 1999). Therefore, a pedagogical relation as an event can be understood as that which transforms subjects into something else. In a pedagogical relation we all are *subjects-yet-to-come* (Atkinson 2011) because the event exceeds meaning and knowledge production, and a pedagogical subject is ultimately generated. It was in the process of developing my dissertation that I *became a researcher*. Together with the produced knowledge and the social/epistemological relations, we, the research agents (the research collaborators, the literature used and I), emerged as subjects-yet-to-come. In other words, in the case of my dissertation, the artistic research (text, videos and drawings) was the event of becoming-subjects and researcher-yet-to-come.

But, how to tend to the unknown to generate disruption? Perceiving the production of knowledge as a pedagogical event entails the creation of social (epistemological) spaces. Artistic research is able to fold and unfold structured fields into transitional disruptive (social) spaces. By questioning its own representational means, artistic research can produce transitional knowledge. That is, transitional in the sense that it is not fixed, that it will continue to change once and again, folding and unfolding, questioning the context and conditions.

Elizabeth Ellsworth introduces a metaphor, the hinge, which disrupts the inside and outside duality and proposes relationships (2005: 46). A hinge illustrates the transitional pedagogical relation. In my research the figure of the hinge was key to show how different conceptual frameworks could fold, activate and become a productive relationship. Ellsworth uses the hinge when explaining her theory of *pivot spaces* that turns pedagogy towards a destabilizing dynamic.

Artistic research is not disruptive as avant garde art once was, in the sense of novelty. Based on a contemporary art context, artistic research recognizes its own structures and limits to open up small fissures through which to glimpse new epistemological and ontological landscapes. Thinking in new epistemological and ontological landscapes does not mean to obviate the existing structures. I am not calling for a binary old/new. Nicolas Bourriaud (2004) explains it in a very simple way. He defends how contemporary art does not work with raw material, but with cultured material: ideas and even objects that have been used or made by other artists and theorists. The artist, then, is positioned as a post-producer. Bourriaud illustrates his argument by using a DJ: a cultural producer that remixes and intervenes in (scratches) already existing products. Hence, this is not a call to abandon previous existing structures; it is not a matter of valuing novelty over the old. Separating this binary would mean being in an eternal race chasing after the new. Instead, working towards transitional disruptive knowledge is a call for instability, and artistic research to be in continued doubt.

During my doctoral research, I explored these limits by overlapping pedagogical and artistic conceptual frameworks throughout the composition and editing of a multiscreen video installation. These videos document a reflexive-drawing encounter where an artist – Núria Güell –, a curator – Oriol Fontdevila – and an artistic researcher – me – rendered visible and reflected on the disruptive (social) spaces of knowledge production that artistic research made possible. My research aimed to make visible the processes through which Núria and Oriol, and later myself, produced knowledge. There were conceptual details I had to sharpen along the way: what kind of knowledge was I looking for? Rather than a progressive, technical or informative knowledge, I realized my research was seeking disruptive knowledge. And, for my dissertation, looking for disruptive knowledge meant working towards a destabilizing dynamic: the unknown. By activating different perspectives and methods – drawing, video, text – the artistic and pedagogical tools helped me avoid the panoptical view of a single author in the research (Marrero Guillamón 2008: 25). I used videos, and the unconventional viewpoints that the different cameras allowed, in addition to a series of multiple and changing diagrams, and a long-term text to question and denaturalize the situation we were experiencing. In other words, it was necessary to generate an event. Together with a video team, we made an installation with four cameras. We used a blackboard drawing table as a focal point for my interviews with both the curator and the artist. It became clear that an account of the artistic process would not be enough to unveil how they produced knowledge in artmaking. It was not the production by itself but the total of the process of reflection, representation and presentation.

It took me three months to edit the videos. My aim was to compose an installation of two videos that faced each other and led the spectator between this dialogue. Each screen was split in three channels, playing multi-screen scenes. One same moment was shown, at the

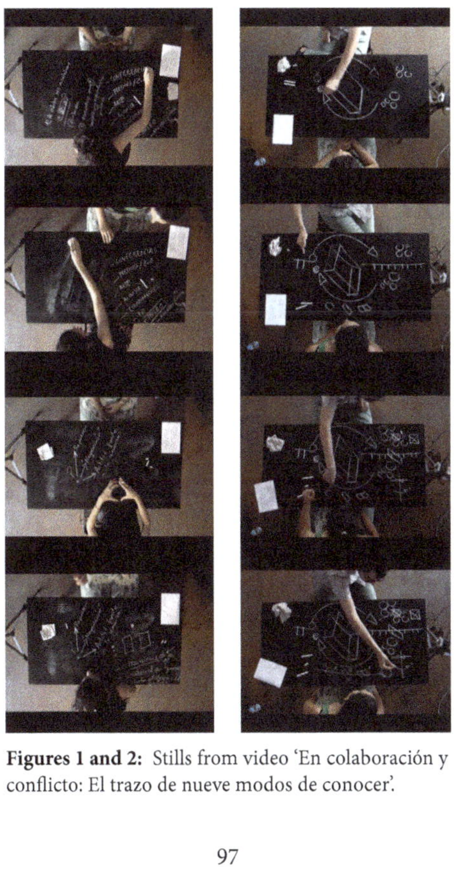

Figures 1 and 2: Stills from video 'En colaboración y conflicto: El trazo de nueve modos de conocer'.

same time, from three different perspectives and then, the experience was multiplied into a composition of different layers. The process of video editing was even more important than the final video work. It was in the decision-making process that I had to discriminate between what to keep and what could be dismissed. The task became a challenge to re-compose a new narrative not precisely of what had happened, but to give an account of how an artist and a curator produce knowledge in the process of artmaking.

I saw, regarded and listened to the video footage so many times. I had to build a script as clear as I could manage while editing such a complex composition. Reviewing Oriol and Núria's interviews, I identified nine ways in which they had generated knowledge in the artistic project. These nine ways of knowing became the parameters that influenced my decisions regarding the video footage. The narrative I was composing was developed according to these nine ways of knowing and was not limited to describing what actually happened in the interview.

In the process of finding the nine ways of knowing, I drew diagrams that helped me understand and organize my ideas.

During the analysis of my research, which entailed both editing the video and writing the dissertation, the diagrams were not used as mere illustrations of my ideas. Diagrams were spaces to think and allowed me to establish new orders, to imagine and create new epistemological possibilities.

It was through the process of diagramming that I grouped the nine ways into three spheres: social, spatial and political. These spheres reflected how Núria Güell and Oriol Fontdevila mentioned they produced knowledge and organized the nine key concepts: collaborators, feedback, mediation; layers, limits, hinges; interpellation, conflict, negotiation.

These key concepts of nine ways of knowing allowed me to trace bridges between art and other fields. These bridges were inexistent prior to the pedagogical relationship established during the project. And, therefore, based on the identified ways of knowing, I was able to question the notions of both the *artistic* and the *pedagogical* to unveil their transitive, ontological and disruptive being.

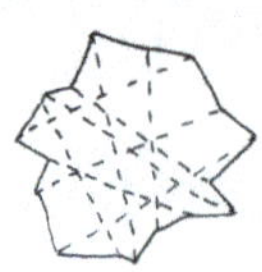

Figure 3: Social space of knowledge production.

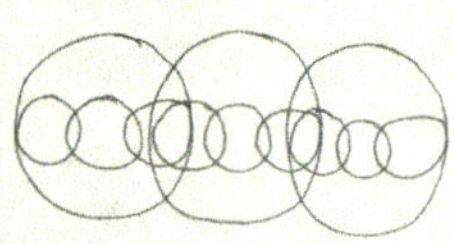

Figure 4: Nine ways of knowing.

These diagrams (Figures 3 and 4) were shown at BAK (Basis voor aktuele kust) in Utrecht as part of the exhibition, *A Call for Drawings* (24 April–12 July 2015).

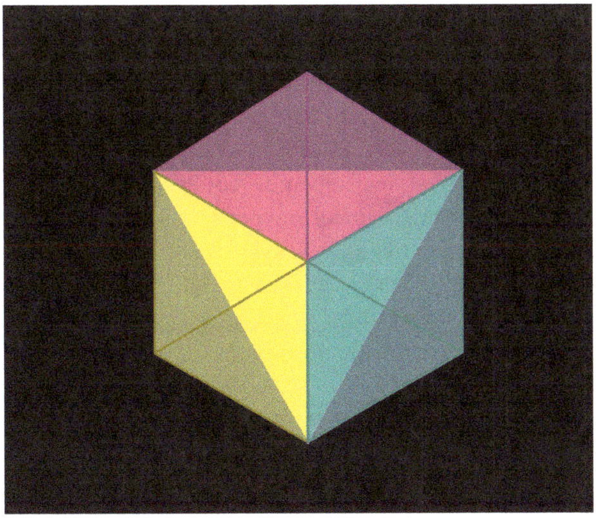

Figure 5: Prisma: a visualization of the nine ways of knowing resulting from my research. This figure summarizes the organization process in three major categories: the social, the political and the spatial.

At the end of my research, my dissertation drew conclusions that spoke to the impossibility of isolated or individual practices. Both the artistic and the pedagogical are an intervention on the significance wave, and therefore they are products of social, epistemological and pedagogical relations that conceive and assume knowledge and artistic productions as transitive and ontological processes.

> The consequences of refiguring pedagogy in this way are far reaching. They encourage us to ask what pedagogy *does* rather that what it means or how it means. Pedagogy as 'sensation construction' is not merely 'representational'. It's no longer a model that teachers use to set the terms in which already-known ideas, curriculums or knowledges are 'conditions of possible experience', pedagogy as sensation construction is a condition of possible experience of thinking. [...] Regarding pedagogy as experimentation in thought rather than representation of knowledge as a thing already made creates a profound shift in how we think of pedagogical intent of volition – the will to teach.
>
> (Ellsworth 2005: 27)

Following Ellsworth, I consciously worked with the artistic and the pedagogical as political notions. Not because of the theme they addressed, but because of their rapprochement to reality. I related to both concepts in order to build an active hinge that folded and unfolded through reflexivity to destabilize and question the given. Exceeding the educational, the pedagogical was able, thus, to provide a net of transitional and unstable subjects-yet-to-come.

Hence, artistic research weaves a web of localized and embodied knowledge that is engaged in epistemic reconstruction. It performs and shows art making and research as collective processes attempting to understand dialectics on the knowledge production of pedagogical and social (spatial and political) subjects.

At the end of my dissertation I introduced conclusions and also, mainly, a list of new interrogations. In the exercise of tearing and rebuilding knowledge, artistic research happened, as an event, or as a social, political and pedagogical relation; an active relationship that enabled me to relate different conceptual frameworks. This multiple-perspective research questions the statements that are taken for granted in education and opens up new spaces of epistemological possibilities. Disruptive artistic research not only produces representations, but generates a social space where the unknown can surprise our own understanding frameworks such that a new 'knowing us' is formed.

Therefore, artistic research could be assumed as a *revolutionary event* since, as Garcés (2013) would philosophically explain, it forms an 'us' that did not exist before. It is in the relationship, in the pedagogical relationship that a new 'us' changes what we were. We are re-formed in the in-between relation, to conclude that individual knowledge and individual artistic production are impossible. But artistic research is not only this revolutionary event, artistic research needs to maintain the different representation layers that value the importance of the process and its transitional conception, to give account of its own reflexivity. It is through this layered approach that artistic research becomes an encounter, an ongoing social space for reflection and learning that produces pedagogical subjects in relation. Finally, artistic research can be disruptive when it re-forms us as social, spatial and politically engaged artistic-researcher agents: when we become social and political (pedagogical) subjects in the epistemological weave of knowing and un-knowing.

References

Atkinson, D. (2011), *Art, Equality and Learning: Pedagogies Against the State*, Rotterdam: Sense.

Badiou, A. (1999), *El ser y el acontecimiento*, Buenos Aires: Manantial.

Bourriaud, N. (2004), *Postproducción: La cultura como escenario: modos en que el arte reprograma el mundo contemporáneo*, Buenos Aires: Adriana Hidalgo.

Caduff, C., Siegenthaler, F. and Wälchli, T. (eds) (2010), *Art and Artistic Research*, Zurich: Scheidegger & Spiess AG.

Calderón García, N. (2015), 'Irrumpir lo artístico, perturbar lo pedagógico: La Investigación Artística como espacio social de producción de conocimiento', PhD thesis, Barcelona: Universitat de Barcelona.

Ellsworth, E. (2005), *Places of Learning: Media, Architecture, Pedagogy*, New York and London: Routledge Falmer.

Garcés, M. (2013), *Un mundo común*, Barcelona: Ediciones Bellaterra.

Marrero Guillamón, I. (2008), 'La fábrica del conflicto: Terciarización, lucha social y patrimonio en Can Ricart, Barcelona', PhD thesis, Barcelona: Universitat de Barcelona.

Slager, H. (2012), *The Pleasure of Research*, Helsinki: Finnish Academy of Fine Arts.

Note

1 Along with Caduff et al. (2010), artistic research started in visual arts universities in 1990s in the English-speaking countries via Scandinavia and the Netherlands.

Chapter 9

Artmaking as Entanglement: Conceptualizing Agency through a Diffractive Methodology

Ramya Ravisankar

Telling the story

The challenge of attending to agency in artmaking is that to do so involves a bit of manoeuvring. For me, it involves telling the story of how one of my most robust, multi-year artmaking projects came to be. At first, I had no idea that I was even making artwork by tending to jasmine plants, collecting their flowers and drying these flowers on the kitchen counter. It started out as a utilitarian endeavour for me, the flowers fall off the plant if you do not pick them, and they smelled nice as they dried. It was not until I started to read about agency and materiality that I realized that my large collection of dried jasmine flowers was something more than a strange collection. It was natural for me to carry the insights from my research into my everyday and this is how I started to recognize the art in tending to my jasmine plants and drying their flowers. The narrative below describes how through my dissertation research, I discovered this project, relating my insights and memories with my examination of the agency of the jasmine plants.

For close to three years, I have engaged in a rather peculiar activity involving a few jasmine plants. At my home in Columbus, Ohio there are three jasmine plants with which I have a very close relationship. I prune, fertilize and fortify the soil; these acid loving plants are especially finicky during the winter months as the amount of sun and humidity shrinks. Keeping them alive in their dormant state becomes a challenge. On a few occasions I thought I killed these plants; the feeling I have when they begin to drop all of their leaves is a kind of deep grief. I think, 'how could I do this to them?' I have a deep sense of responsibility for them, and I have managed to bring them back from the brink each time they feel stressed. The elation I feel when the plants start to sprout new tendrils is as if I had the ability to bring them back to life. My care for these plants may seem one-sided, after all, I am doing a lot of work to keep my jasmine plants alive, but there is a beautiful and ephemeral benefit for me. During the summer months in Ohio, the jasmine plants thrive, probably because the weather resembles their tropical hot and humid native climate. It is in these months that the plants start to flower abundantly, and my joy is the act of going outside in the warm morning sun, just before it gets really hot, to pick jasmine flowers from my plants. The thing about jasmine plants is that you need to pick them to encourage new growth – so I pick the flowers that are about to bloom or have just bloomed. After I collect the flowers, I do a couple of things. Firstly, if there are only one or two flowers, I dry them on a plate or on the kitchen counter. The second option, with a collection of at least ten flowers, I string them together with thread so I can hang the stringed flowers in my kitchen and enjoy their sweet, intoxicating aroma for a few days. The fragrance transports me back to India and elicits memories of my visits and experiences in my ancestral homeland. My grandmother would show me how to string jasmine flowers together using a rather elaborate method of knotting resulting in a long chain of flowers strung together causing their fragrance to strengthen exponentially. Normally, you pick jasmine flowers in bud form rather than already bloomed because it is difficult to use traditional stringing techniques for already opened blooms. However, in my Ohioan jasmine growing scheme I never seem to get the timing right so I always have to use a needle and thread to string my jasmine flowers together – technically this is cheating, but it is the best I can do.

I try to augment the 'authenticity' of my endeavour by incorporating turmeric. I create a rudimentary dye using turmeric from my collection of spices and water. In India, we use turmeric as a healing salve to cool our bodies and add a golden undertone to our skin. Turmeric dyed thread is also used in many religious capacities in Hinduism, such as marriage ceremonies. Turmeric, like jasmine, is a smell that transports me back to my childhood, back to walking to the open-air market in Chennai to buy vegetables with my grandmother. This combination of material, turmeric and jasmine, is one that brings to mind so many vivid memories. It brings back the warmth and colour of my childhood. When I run my hands over the string dying it yellow, my hands too are stained. The gritty feeling of the powder is comforting. I then take the newly yellowed string, sit at my desk and create a garland of flowers. Sometimes I choose to include the older flowers that have become purple and died off on the plant. Sometimes I do not. On one occasion, the purple flower I tried to string fell out of my hand, so I decided that perhaps the older flowers would stay out of this particular string of flowers. Though I always reserve the right to change the rules on other flower strings, I tend to let the jasmine flowers decide where they want to go. I place the strings of flowers on my kitchen counter, so that I can smell them as I walk by. They stay there until they dry out completely, turning purple then brown. I take the dry brown flowers and put them in a kitchen drawer. At the end of the summer, I had dozens of flowers in the kitchen drawer and I did not know what to do with them. I did have many questions about this project. However, the central question I ask is: why do I carry on this ritual of tending, growing, stringing, smelling, drying and storing these jasmine flowers?

As I started reading the post-human/new materialist theory that undergirds my current research, I began to think about my jasmine flower ritual differently. I began to examine this ritual through a consideration of agential forces involved and I saw an opportunity to explore the agency of the jasmine plants. Did the plants enact a kind of agential force on me to make me tend them so carefully? Furthermore, I wondered how conceptions of this ritual would change by viewing it as a part of my artmaking practice. The best place to start was to take all of the dried jasmine flowers out of the kitchen drawer. I placed them on a table in my studio to take stock of the collection. There were dozens of individual dried flowers and four strings from the summer of 2015. I began placing the flowers on white paper and arranging them in various combinations which has become an important facet of my dissertation and exploration of materiality and agency in artmaking. This project has become a way for me to view artmaking as an entanglement of agential forces, rather than an activity that is directed from a sole human agent. Using Karen Barad's exploration of Donna Haraway's concept of 'diffraction' I read insights through one another – this is particularly useful in generating insights from reading my artmaking practice through concepts of new materialism. Barad introduces diffraction by evoking the visual metaphor of diffraction patterns as observed by dropping two pebbles into a pool of still water (Barad 2003, 2007). The radiating pattern caused by the two stones is multiplied when the waves produced by the individual pebbles meet. Waves going through one another results in more waves – this concept of reading concepts through one another to produce insights is what Barad describes as a diffractive methodology (Barad 2003, 2007).

This notion of diffraction is informed by Barad's knowledge of the physics of diffraction. She makes a distinction between the concepts of reflection and diffraction and she feels that going beyond reflection is a necessary step in a new materialist methodology. Diffraction is this attempt to transcend reflection. Barad states, '[t]o theorize is not to leave the material world behind and enter the domain of pure ideas where the lofty space of the mind makes objective reflection possible. Theorizing, like experimenting, is a material practice' (2007: 17). Here Barad describes how the notion of objectivity through reflection is perhaps misguided; we must recognize the real material and physical consequences that emerge through our discourses. To do this, we must attempt to set aside the urge to view the world without considering our presence in it and the influence of the world on us. By considering my jasmine ritual through artmaking and diffractively reading this ritual through the concepts of Barad's agential realism and new materialism, I look beyond reflections on artmaking and assess the real material engagements enacted through entanglements with the material of artmaking. Attending to materiality and its agency by reading these concepts through an ongoing artistic engagement, like my jasmine ritual, is a tactic that helps displace human-centred approaches to artmaking and brings forward insights that further the discussion of contemporary art practice. Expanding this discussion is a focus of my dissertation, which aims to develop a way to discuss materiality in contemporary artmaking as it continues to evolve with the ever-expanding practices enacted by artists.

It is important to delve into Barad's concept of agential realism as a method of attending to material/non-human agencies found in new materialism. Barad states:

> I propose 'agential realism' as an epistemological-ontological-ethical framework that provides an understanding of the role of human and nonhuman, material and discursive, and natural and cultural factors in scientific and other social-material practices, thereby moving such considerations beyond the well-worn debates that pit constructivism against realism, agency against structure, and idealism against materialism.
>
> (2007: 26)

Barad puts forward agential realism as a way to trouble the history of separation of epistemological, ontological and ethical concerns that undergird the way we view the agential roles. Agential realism, for Barad, becomes a way to move beyond whether we can attribute agency to human and non-human entities and she posits that the relationship between these entities is co-constitutive. Furthermore, she states that agency should not be viewed as an asset or an entity that is held by an agent. For Barad 'agency is not an attribute but the ongoing reconfigurings of the world' (2007: 103). Defining agency as a continually emergent phenomenon rather than a static, unchanging entity allows for the constant renegotiation of agential forces in artmaking. The co-constitutive entanglement of shifting agencies between artist and material in artmaking creates interesting and often unexpected paths. The artist manipulates the material, but the material may have other ideas. This notion is articulated by Sara Ahmed in her examination of her relationship with her table. Ahmed (as cited in Coole and Frost 2010) writes:

> As I type, I face the table, and it is what I am working on. I am touching the object as well as the keyboard and am aware of it as a sensuous given that is available for me. In repeating the work of typing, my body comes to feel a certain way. My neck gets sore, and I stretch to ease the discomfort. I pull my shoulders back every now and then as the posture I assume (a bad posture I am sure) is a huddle: I huddle over the table as I repeat the action (the banging of keys with the tips of my fingers); the action shapes me, and it leaves its impression through bodily sensations, prickly feelings on the skin surface, and the more intense experience of discomfort.
>
> (2010: 246–47)

In this passage, Ahmed recognizes and admits that her table exerts agency over her body and explores this notion through attending to her senses. The scene is familiar to most of us as we write more than we should at tables that contort our bodies and make our necks sore. The same soreness is present in most of my artmaking endeavours, the material of my artmaking shapes me, and so do the objects in my studio – my table, chair, computer, etc. The task of exploring the agencies of these materials for artmaking is a vital component of articulating contemporary artmaking practices. In my dissertation, I address how discussions of artmaking have mostly tended to focus on the material, the artwork and the artist. However, as illustrated by Ahmed, the creative process involves a deeper look at agency and materiality. In my dissertation I suggest that working through and with materiality, including one's workspace, allows an artist to develop a methodology that is diffractive and generative.

The insights brought to light by reading Ahmed's account through my own experiences with the jasmine flowers bring forward a major element of artmaking – the body of the artist. New materialist scholars contend that objects exert agencies over the body. This is where the notion of entanglement comes into play in a diffractive look at artmaking practices. Karen Barad sees entanglements as a way to recognize that things, particles, people and entities are created through their entangled states and as such are linked inextricably. Barad states:

> To be entangled is not simply to be intertwined with another, as in the joining of separate entities, but to lack an independent, self-contained existence. Existence is not an individual affair. Individuals do not preexist their interactions; rather, individuals emerge through and as part of their entangled intra-relating.
>
> (2007: ix)

Barad asserts that not only are agential forces at play in an entanglement, but the boundaries we construct between entities are not as finite as we may think. If we envision artmaking as an entanglement, then we must also consider what it means to consider ourselves linked to the entanglement to which we belong. Whether it is in the studio or in the world, we are shaped by both the human and non-human entities and both emerge as a result of entanglements. An artmaking entanglement can be conceptualized as a cloud in which the artist, their medium/material, concept and space have agency in the production of artwork. A discussion of artmaking that diffracts theories of new materialism should interrogate the agential roles of the elements of artmaking practice. Approaching artmaking as an entanglement allows for generative and diffractive discovery about the agencies of the artist, material and the elements of their entanglement.

As I continue engaging with these jasmine flowers through an artmaking practice guided by a diffractive methodology, I can attend to the agential pull of the flowers; this process of making is grown through the new materialist theories that guide my dissertation. This section from my dissertation offers a glimpse into how my research is rooted and developed through an engagement with jasmine. Reviews of pertinent literature, research insights and findings are developed more substantially in my dissertation. Reading my engagement with the jasmine flowers diffractively through my evolving understandings of artmaking and new materialism has allowed me to gain insights and develop new understandings of all of these areas, both separately and as they coalesce through this research process. In my ongoing reconfiguring with the jasmine plants, I never felt like I was in complete control of the situation. This begs the question: why is there such a solid boundary between maker and material in artmaking – and for that matter between subject/object and mind and body? This question is central to my dissertation and important to me as an artist who has never felt in complete control of her process. To me, these feel like arbitrary delineations because when observed, these concepts permeate, overlap and infuse with each other. By employing this diffractive methodology throughout my dissertation and reading insights from various artmaking practices, including my own, through post-human/new materialist theories, I hope to uncover ways to articulate the co-constitutive, entangled, ongoing negotiations of artmaking and materiality. To develop this concept further, it is necessary to continue to develop this diffractive method of inquiry to generate insights from entangled relationships with the material entities of artmaking. What I have provided here is merely a flower bud.

References

Ahmed, S. (2010), 'Orientations matter', in D. Coole and S. Frost (eds), *New Materialisms: Ontology, Agency, and Politics*, Durham: Duke University Press, pp. 234–57.

Barad, K. (1998), 'Getting real: Technoscientific practices and the materialization of reality', *Differences: A Journal of Feminist Cultural Studies*, 10:2, pp. 87–128.

——— (2003), 'Posthumanist performativity: Toward an understanding of how matter comes to matter', *Signs: Journal of Women in Culture and Society*, 28:3, pp. 801–31.

——— (2007), *Meeting the Universe Halfway: Quantum Physics and the Entanglement of Matter and Meaning*, Durham: Duke University Press.

Coole, D. and Frost, S. (eds) (2010), *New Materialisms: Ontology, Agency, and Politics*, Durham: Duke University Press.

Haraway, D. (1992), 'The promises of monsters: A regenerative politics for inappropriate/d others', in L. Grossberg, C. Nelson and P. A. Treichler (eds), *Cultural Studies*, New York: Routledge, pp. 295–337.

Chapter 10

A/R/Tographic Rhythm: Opening Conversations of Resistance and Accommodation as Scholarly Provocation

Anita Sinner, Verónica Sahagún Sánchez, Jennifer Wicks and Darlene St. Georges

We begin with a proposition: resistance within institutional contexts is enabled because of the necessary state of accommodation, and we are all, arguably, always between the relational dimensions of our desire to sustain individual autonomy for our research interests, and our need to operate within programme parameters. There exists a 'figurative equivalence' in this system of relations between resistance to protocol (dissimilarity) and accommodation of protocol (similarity), which brings into play what Rancière refers to as 'several kinds of intolerability' (2009: 94). Resistance-accommodation is part of the mechanism underscoring what Jackson (2013) describes as a mutual and reciprocal relation with the material realm. Simply, we are constructed within the differentials as a response to the institution in which our academic identities emerge.

Our resulting research is in part an expression of this sustained engagement, and we in turn influence the socio-spatial dynamics that we encounter in the institution (Martin and Kamberelis 2013). This facilitates opportunities and advances understandings of research issues through our voices, that is, we are not singular voices, but the production of theories, practices and experiences upon one another (be that researcher-participant, peer-peer, individual-institution and so on), along with the stories, network of associations and the many geographies produced in part by the materiality of our academic home (Mazzei 2013). Our a/r/tographic pulse attends to this delicate balance in an effort to foster productive and proactive academic change. The following exemplars chart a desire for unbelonging and belonging in the same instance, guided by notions of resistance-accommodation that serve to initiate conversations about our understandings in this case of what constitutes the parameters of doctoral research. By exploring this conceptual space, we seek to map paradigmatic shifts in institutional practices, and promote autonomy as scholars in ways that contribute to the advancement of cycles of knowledge within higher learning.

Veronica: Resistance as reverberations of the personal in the professional

My doctoral studies in art education were characterized by reverberations (or continuous shifts) in my understanding of what it entails to be an artist/teacher/researcher (Irwin and Springgay 2008). My initial goal was to successfully transition from a studio practice/instruction standpoint into the world of educational research without relegating my studio work to a secondary role in my professional practice. Achieving this transformation, however, required me to familiarize myself with the numerous trends of the arts in research emerging within the North American academy. Being originally from México, my review of these approaches soon led to reflections of how the parameters of what are acceptable knowledge production practices vary from one cultural landscape (Canada) to others (United States, México) and from one discipline (studio arts) to another (art education). My expectations of the kind of research that I would be doing as a doctoral student did not necessarily coincide with the qualitative research orientation that prevailed in the department upon my entry. And, most importantly, after having spent five years teaching studio arts in México, encountering unfamiliar educational environments and populations did not correspond to the professional aspirations that I had prior to my arrival to Canada.

In response to this scenario, I opted to work with a/r/tography, a methodology that had never been used in the programme before, but which, from my perspective, allowed me to fulfil the goal of turning my studio practice into the foundation of my research and my teaching. Due to a/r/tography being a form of situated inquiry 'informed by feminist, poststructuralist, hermeneutic and other postmodern theories that understand the production of knowledge as difference' (Irwin and Springgay 2008: xxi), I felt it was readily adaptable to my personal experiences as well as to my cultural background. I proposed to work with a/r/tography in order to develop a self-study with the purpose of consciously incorporating my origins, my past life in México and my professional strengths, to my educational research activities in Canada. Doing this a/r/tographic self-study was my way of accommodating the new educational environment without diverting myself from my initial professional aspirations. My expectation was that my acceptance of my state of 'un-belonging' would lead to a critical perspective (Rogoff 2000) of the world of educational research that I was encountering. This critical view, in turn, assisted me in the development of an educational research agenda in which my interest in Mexican vernacular textile traditions, art/craft practice and education merged.

In my a/r/tographic self-study, Mexican vernacular textile traditions became my point of departure for an autobiographical artmaking and writing inquiry. Working with my life history led me to engage with a practice of active resistance. This resistance involved avoiding language and imagery that provided a superficial reading of Mexican culture and the exoticization of my persona. As a non-native English speaker interested in fostering receptivity to peripheral views on art/craft practices within the western academy, this exercise was revealed as the ultimate translation (and political) challenge (Spivak 1993). Resistance also involved learning to tame my fear of being criticized for making my life history the main source of my research. Taking this risk, however, allowed me to clarify what kind of professional I wanted to be (or have become) after concluding my studies. This newly acquired professional identity is that of an educator who attends to the realities of minority groups who might be undergoing similar or even more challenging experiences of cultural dislocation.

Based on my experiences as an emerging scholar, I now view resistance-accommodation as a circular movement, rather than two opposing forces reacting to each other. Accommodation reflects an awareness of the circumstances in which the learner works to articulate his or her scholarly voice, whereas resistance stands for the learning process itself. Resistance is an ongoing process, or ever-shifting force, that has the power to transform consciousness. In my case, resistance also created reverberations of my life history within my scholarly practice. These reverberations expanded my view of what I could achieve as an art educator. Today, I embrace the momentum, letting it guide my way within a new learning cycle in my scholarly practice. With a deeper understanding of myself, I create openings for learners to share their individual experiences of resistance-accommodation within contemporary art/craft practice, and collaboratively, expand their view of what is knowledge, art and research.

Jennifer: Balancing on the back(s)lash – the liminal state of candidacy

Midway through the doctoral programme, I reflect on the space of PhD candidacy as an in-between state. A notion explored within the methodological praxis of a/r/tography, liminal balance refers to the navigation of differing spaces in an attempt to find equilibrium within contiguous identities – the artist, the researcher and the teacher. In my case, I seek to find balance on the backslash of 'r' in a/r/t through resistance and accommodation. While negotiating the suspended space that is candidacy, that is, not entirely student and not quite an academic, it is hard not to draw parallels between these proximate roles. I navigate multiple identities within the academy as a student, a research assistant, a graduate instructor, with each of these functions important to me in my trajectory as a future academic, and each requiring gestures of accommodation. With one foot on the shore and the other in the ocean, I am not quite there yet, and I work with a number of faculty members to gain access to a deeper understanding of how the academy functions, and how I may fit within it.

I have chosen a/r/tography to be the nucleus of my methodological practice in order to explore and integrate my three passions (making art, developing understandings and sharing what I have learned) into my research. A/r/tography is in its essence a creative practice. It complements my praxis as I seek holistic means by which to develop an understanding of community art education – my specific area of study. At the heart of my practice lies the notion of collaboration and my love for sharing, which reaches each of the trifecta identities in meaningful ways. Employing a collaborative a/r/tographical methodology began with a serendipitous encounter at a workshop in Oporto, Portugal, where I connected with Mariana, my doctoral research collaborator, also a PhD candidate in art education at the University of Porto. Together we are now exploring our transatlantic collaborative a/r/tography through our familial maritime histories and archives, weaving together our parallel stories through visual arts, sound, storytelling and new media installation.

The sharing of authorship and ownership of research findings and practice is a prime example of resistance and accommodation; outlined in my dissertation project of collaboration where we each own the data we have collected (Buford May and Pattillo-McCoy 2000: 83). This aligns with Giroux's (2001) definition of an act of resistance 'as an expression of a creative mode of cultural and social production outside the immediate force of domination' (108). When I think about power in the Foucaultian (1977) sense, in relation to the hierarchical structure of the academy, I believe that for students like me, resistance becomes something that will provoke questions of ethics and integrity, such as: is resistance possible in the academy today? Should I moderate my position to accommodate existing protocols, and if I do, is this then truly original research? What are the implications if I do not comply? Due to the foundational, hierarchical nature of traditional educational institutions, graduate students, in particular, are likely compelled to 'fall in line' with the political leanings of the institution to ensure a strong academic standing. Yet, to recognize research methodologies as the vehicles for power is 'to make an epistemic break with history' in ways that remap what the academy is becoming (Pascale 2011: 16).

At the same time, a/r/tography is also a hotly and openly debated methodology within our department and beyond in our field, despite wide acceptance across the academy and internationally. As echoed by my colleagues in this chapter, the validity of considering inquiry through multiple interwoven identities of creative practice is in question. Is it art or is it research? Or is it neither? Working with an alternate methodology that is rooted in such controversy can operate in two ways: I can align myself with like-minded scholars within the wider academy and in the field at large, and immerse myself in the fore of innovative thinking within this group; and/or simultaneously risk being marginalized within my home institution by employing a methodology that continues to be critiqued by those who hold more traditional approaches to research (a position that from an intellectual perspective is as valid as that of proposing something new). As I progress through the programme, I have come to an understanding that it is not in the binary of either/or, but in the necessity of both conversations that propels my work forward in ways akin to the essence of collaborative a/r/tography. Yet it is a precarious balance.

Through the development of communities of a/r/tographic practice both inside and outside of my institution, the use of collaborative methodologies and the sharing of knowledge and power, as well as co-authored knowledge production and dissemination, I believe we approach the 'radical notion of resistance [as] an expressed hope, an element of transcendence, for radical transformation' (Giroux 2001: 108), in ways that benefit us all in a wider sense as scholars, and move us closer to a dialogical approach to learning, research and knowledge production. By extension, within this space of candidacy, it is the /r/ of researcher that forms through the validity and receptivity of our work in progress, part of our rite of passage in the liminal spaces of the academy that leaves us vulnerable to the politics of space. It is through the process of resistance-accommodation that I try to navigate delicately, mindfully, with the knowledge that disrupting active equilibriums pushes both scholarship and positionality to a sustained and uncertain conditionality, an awareness that moves the form of my research study to the inter-contextual, where the self is always in relation to the institution, in a continuous, pensive state of becoming as a doctoral candidate.

Darlene: 'Wild Iris'

Her voice opens,
shifting realities
with her ancestral song;
dazzling butterflies,
igniting hummingbirds,
injecting the sun
into your veins.

As a doctoral student, I launch into my research interests conscious of the fact that in a broad sense I am operating within an institutional paradigm situated in historical understandings often derived from the Enlightenment, where a pragmatic disposition of logic and reason animated by empirical research methods has legitimized what is regarded as 'objective truth'. In this milieu, discourse generated through the methodological axiom of a/r/tography tends to destabilize such longstanding anthropocentric narratives, much as Bolt (2013) suggests of materiality and practice-based inquiry, which can provoke contentious debate around the parameters of what constitutes research. For instance, Pariser states that the legitimate use of the term 'research' is grounded in normative science and is founded on a positivistic epistemology (2009: 2), which supports his contention that arts-based inquiry is not 'research', and further, as articulated in my recent term paper, 'of all the arts-based practices, a/r/tography is probably responsible for more incoherent and "out there" "research" than almost any other research approach, other than that advocated by Dr. Timothy Leary' (Pariser 2015).

...residing in a garden of echoes,
where the dead return
to their hidden fountains,
She rises up and dances
in-between spaces;

While the use of generative methodologies that engage us in seeking deep understandings of what it means to be and become is new territory for research over the past decade, it can hardly be likened to the unethical and drug-induced approaches of Leary, at least in my view as a fledging graduate student. Nevertheless, I see critical issues surrounding arts-based methodologies as an essential part of the ebb and flow of the evolution of scholarship, and attending to such provocations as an opportunity to advance our understanding(s) about how innovative approaches can inform and broaden the scope of what constitutes research. As an emerging a/r/tographer, I see the work I do, in conjunction with the research unfolding in the wider a/r/tography community, as having the potential to transform and recontextualize the idea of theory and research by engaging us in questions about how we

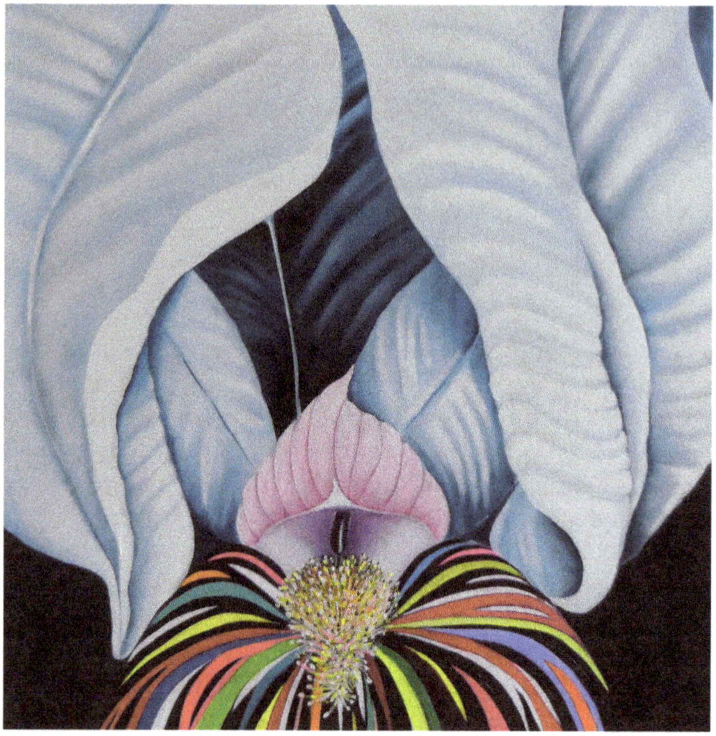

Figure 1: Darlene St. Georges, *Wild Iris*, 2016. Oil on canvas. © GAIA Studio.

can envision 'truth' (Boutet 2013). Should we not ask how my truth is different from your truth? How is truth situated in experience, in time and space, and how can truth be fluid and multifaceted (Boutet 2013)? Although it is outside the scope of this chapter to attend to these questions, in stating such, I consider how an amalgamation of diverse voices can benefit us on our journey of learning and teaching.

As a Métis woman, artist and poet, rooted in Indigenous ways of being, I struggle with internalized undercurrents of resistance of my own voice, reflective of a culture in which I grew up where subordination and womanhood were synonymous. In my artistic practice, I respond to this tractate positioning by enacting resistance through methods of interruption of dominant discourse to draw out my voice. My a/r/tographic creative work is situated within new materialism, a more fluid discourse between the realms of the body, mind and spirit in an unfolding hermeneutic (Barrett 2013) in which I harness visual imagery, text and sound elements to weave together my experiences of selfhood, identity, loss of identity, connection, disconnection, spirit, my relationship to the earth, my ancestors, Indigenous knowledge, dreams and memories. This is a methodological and ontological strategy that intends to disrupt established codes of language (Kristeva 1984) engaging me in an evolving inter-text through performative modes of knowledge production (Barrett 2013). My research animates the depth of reflexive processes of self-understanding and political agency in a cultural context of what it means, in effect, to be human. I emphasize emergent knowledge that can be unfinished, multiple and conflicting, which becomes an 'embodied [research] that is not a pre-determined or a stable interpretive scaffold, but part of a relational encounter' (Springgay et al. 2008: 159).

In choosing a/r/tography as my methodological approach I am engaging in a shifting paradigm that 'seeks to sypher; a wild imagining beyond deciphering' (Leggo 2015) — to conceive an educational and research orientation that moves beyond the structure of a hierarchical taxonomy on knowledge, towards a logic and discourse embedded in creative, metaphorical and dialogical practice(s). As an artist, researcher and teacher, I believe that as a society we rest on our ability to expand our perceptions and engage with our imaginative capacities to understand more deeply and broadly the extent of what truth can be. By expanding the parameters of what constitutes research, I seek to invite innovation and embrace the unfolding metamorphosis of scholarship in a provocative, creative, intellectual space that opens conversations rich with possibilities.

...she is the song of night bird,
currents in your heart,
distant silences,
magical glances;
Oxygen.

(St. Georges 2016)

Opening conversations: Engaging the spaces of resistance-accommodation

As part of our cycles of knowledge production, we profile three conditions of a/r/tographic accommodation through the horizontal and temporal dimensions in the doctoral journey: Veronica reflecting on the completed dissertation; Jennifer considering the state of candidacy; and Darlene initiating her doctoral programme of work. In turn, the vertical dimensions of movement to a post-qualitative paradigm emerged in our conversation, where negotiating resistance within our continually changing scholarly conditions is a fluid and uncertain venture. As scholars, our exchanges about a/r/tographic research as a form of resistance to the prevailing institutional climate, here and elsewhere, are equally informed by accommodating our work to meet academic requirements of the same institution. Veronica, Jennifer and Darlene are acutely aware of the discourse that is our shared (institutional) cultural production, and yet, collectively there is an effort to manifest a trans-discursive position to create openings for alternate forms of research to be considered. Such notions of resistance-accommodation are well aligned with Foucault's concept of discourse, and the production of knowledge that occurs at a given historical moment within an apparatus that enables forms of knowledge to exist, circulate and function, in this case in relation to our university, the programme and policies, the faculty and the graduate students themselves as part of the current regimes of truth (Foucault 1998). The challenge is then to move to a position of critical evaluation of the scope, depth and purpose of such a/r/tographic work where we are bound and unbound by resistance-accommodation as multiple selves with multiple subject positions, in tension with other conflicting positions we, and our colleagues, may also hold.

The cultivation of such generative tensionality, as Aoki suggests (Pinar and Irwin 2005), recognizes an elegance residing within the art of thinking that advances an academic culture of *writing against* through such dualisms, a forum that is particularly important in doctoral studies. We have come to welcome resistance-accommodation as worthy of embracing in the research equation, making scholarly provocations a mode of knowledge production where we are guided by understandings that the methodology, a/r/tography in this case, is a process of 'inventing again and again' (Taguchi 2013: 711). In this context, resistance-accommodation is positioned as creating spaces within the academy for deliberative conversations, mediating dialectics with the intent to resist not as disagreement, but to produce the kind of healthy discourse that diversifies possibilities of the idea, to be nurtured, refined and reconsidered, and accommodated in the course of becoming a scholar. Residing on the border of resistance and accommodation, we also inhabit the vigour of knowledge production, as Mazzei (2013) suggests. This situation is one we have often acknowledged in conversation, and by definition, as scholars we heed forces of cohesion balanced by forces acting in opposition, where the degree of our acts and actions correlate to the intensity of the collective intellectual effort to deliberate on the many dimensions of a/r/tography.

Acknowledgement

We would like to thank the Social Sciences and Humanities Research Council of Canada for funding our research.

References

Barrett, E. (2013), 'Materiality, affect, and the aesthetic image', in E. Barrett and B. Bolt (eds), *Carnal Knowledge: Towards a 'New Materialism' through the Arts*, New York: I. B. Tauris, pp. 63–72.

Bolt, B. (2013), 'Introduction: Towards a "new materialism" through the arts', in E. Barrett and B. Bolt (eds), *Carnal Knowledge: Towards a 'New Materialism' through the Arts*, New York: I.B. Tauris, pp. 1–14.

Boutet, D. (2013), 'Metaphors of the mind: Art forms as modes of thinking and ways of being', in E. Barrett and B. Bolt (eds), *Carnal Knowledge: Towards a 'New Materialism' through the Arts*, New York: I. B. Tauris, pp. 29–39.

Buford May, R. A. and Pattillo-McCoy, M. (2000), 'Do you see what I see? Examining a collaborative ethnography', *Qualitative Inquiry*, 6:1, pp. 65–87.
Foucault, M. (1977), *Discipline and Punish: The Birth of the Prison*, Toronto: Random House.
——— (1998), 'What is an author?', in J. Faubion (ed.), *Aesthetics, Method and Epistemology: Volume Two* (trans. R. Hurley and others), New York: The New Press, pp. 205–22.
Giroux, H. A. (2001), *Theory and Resistance in Education: Towards a Pedagogy for the Opposition*, rev. ed., Westport: Bergin & Garvey.
Irwin, R. L. and Springgay, S. (2008), 'A/r/tography as practice based research', in M. Cahnmann-Taylor and R. Siegesmund (eds), *Arts-Based Research in Education: Foundations for Art Practice*, New York: Routledge, pp. 103–24.
Jackson, A. Y. (2013), 'Posthumanist data analysis of mangling practices', *International Journal of Qualitative Studies in Education*, 26:6, pp. 741–48.
Kristeva, J. (1984), *Revolution in Poetic Language*, New York: Columbia University Press.
Leggo, C. (2015), 'Arts-based and contemplative practice', Play Building, http://www.joenorris-playbuilding.ca/?page_id=1329. Accessed 27 June 2016.
Martin, A. and Kamberelis, G. (2013), 'Mapping not tracing: Qualitative educational research with political teeth', *International Journal of Qualitative Studies in Education*, 26:6, pp. 668–79.
Mazzei, L. (2013), 'A voice without organs: Interviewing in posthumanist research', *International Journal of Qualitative Studies in Education*, 26:6, pp. 732–40.
Pariser, D. (2009), 'Arts-based research: Trojan horses and shibboleths', *Canadian Review of Art Education*, 36:1, pp. 1–18.
——— (2015), email to author, 22 September.
Pascale, C. (2011), *Cartographies of Knowledge: Exploring Qualitative Epistemologies*, Thousand Oaks: Sage.
Pinar, W. and Irwin, R. L. (eds) (2005), *Curriculum in a New Key: The Collected Works of Ted T. Aoki*, Mahwah: Lawrence Erlbaum.
Rancière, J. (2009), *The Emancipated Spectator* (trans. G. Elliott), London: Verso.
Rogoff, I. (2000), *Terra Infirma: Geography's Visual Culture*, London: Routledge.
Spivak, G. C. (1993), *Outside in the Teaching Machine*, New York: Routledge.
Springgay, S., Irwin, R. L., Leggo, C. and Gouzouasis, P. (eds) (2008), *Being with A/r/tography*, Rotterdam: Sense.
St. Georges, D. (2016), 'Wild Iris', unpublished poem.
Taguchi, H. (2013), 'Images of thinking in feminist materialism: Ontological divergences and the production of researcher subjectivities', *International Journal of Qualitative Studies in Education*, 26:6, pp. 706–16.

Chapter 11

To Reach the Unreached: Rhythms of Issues, Reflections, Writings and Art Practices

Jo Chiung Hua Chen

Graduate studies with a/r/tography

Since 2007, I have taught a graduate course called 'Art and Gender Studies' in the Fine Arts Department at National Taiwan Normal University. In this course, I introduced the methodology of a/r/tography and asked students to apply it for their final project. The content of the course focused on gender issues (Chen 2013). During the process, we explored gender stereotypes, inequality and social systems that generate power. Students were encouraged to reflect and discuss based on their personal experiences. In the final project, they were asked to make art that portrays their thoughts. These final projects amounted to a public exhibition and book collection. This course went well and we were able to secure grants from the Taiwan government to support this course, which continued for three years.

As one of the faculty members in the Fine Arts Department, I began to rethink the position of art education at this institute. Here, graduate studies, except art education, include several divisions such as art history and theories, Chinese studio and western studio. When students graduate from the studio division, a solo exhibition and a thesis are required. For the art education division, however, making works of art and exploring art practices as the central focus in graduate theses are not required and have not been done by graduate students before. Therefore, in my class, I encourage students to apply a/r/tography practice in their dissertations. Making works of art then serves as an approach to experience, understand, reflect and rethink art education pedagogy.

In 2010, Chi-Wen Chung took this 'Art and Gender Studies' course. Later on, she demonstrated a keen interest in a/r/tography and carried on exploring this practice as her master's thesis topic and based on her experience, we continued to have expansive conversations about how visual arts PhD theses would be formed as the basis for this chapter. In general, the thesis work towards visual art PhD dissertations would cover the nature of artistic practice, reflection and academic writings. The following example taken from Chi-Wen's master's dissertation focuses on 'gender'-based teaching and learning. In the near future, along with academic writing, the 'artistic practice' will deepen and enlarge to include a public show with a visualized curriculum development process and a concept map of teaching and learning.

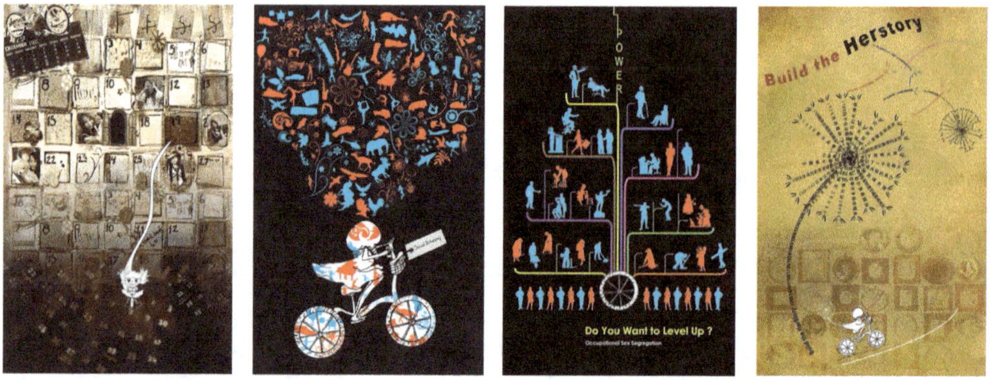

Figure 1: Chi-Wen's artworks for 'Art and Gender Studies' in 2010, NTNU (left to right: 1a, 1b, 1c and 1d).

A/r/tography rhythms: Translating issues, reflections, writings and art practice into teaching and learning

Graduate study in the Fine Arts Department is about self-empowerment and pre-service teacher training. From the a/r/tography class, we engaged in deep reflections about what we had encountered since childhood. It aimed to give a chance for students to renew themselves. At that time, Chi-Wen created four posters to express her thoughts on gender. One is entitled 'Memory' (Figure 1a). For Chi-Wen, memory helps her move towards her own self-expectation. She said:

> From the moment we were born, there are tears, joy, happiness, and sadness. All interact with each other to make different memories in the calendars of our hearts.
>
> (Chi-Wen 2010)

The second one is 'Dichotomy' (Figure 1b). In this artwork, a girl is riding a bicycle with cultural expectations in mind. She interrogated what she learned:

> Girls should obey, and be a good wife when married. Girls have to act like girls. Are you a girl?
>
> (Chi-Wen 2010)

At the same time, in the work of 'The Power of Men or Women' (Figure 1c), a wheel was loaded up with different power layers. She questioned the social system that creates inequality and power. On the other hand, she doubted the reality of art history and tried to 'Build the Herstory' (Figure 1d).

Transforming a/r/tography into art pedagogy

A/r/tography is a research methodology, a creative practice and a performative pedagogy (Irwin 2013). Using the experience of her graduate studies, Chi-Wen worked on her thesis proposal exam and gratefully got approval. In the beginning, she drew out a map to represent her research structure. This map creates a route from art practice into curriculum development.

Having gender concerns in mind, Chi-Wen followed the *National Gender Education Curriculum Guideline* (Ministry of Education 2008) and developed 'The Secrets of Arts & Gender' curriculum for junior high school. In this course content, she designed multiple learning activities to make students go through a self-reflective creation process. These learning activities cover appreciation and creation, and lasted for 8 weeks over 16 classes. A total of 29 junior high school students participated in this programme. Before the class started, she set up three topics in gender for the course: the first was 'gender stereotypes', the second was 'gender occupation' and the third was 'gender and power'. She continued to explore these topics and created artworks as teaching materials.

As well as 'Dichotomy' and 'The Power of Men or Women', she made three more pieces. One is called 'Gender Collage'. She juxtaposed images of real people in the background and added conventional values of gender on the figures' faces to invite people to rethink gender stereotypes. In the other, 'Schedule', she considered women's daily workload in contemporary life. Another one is 'Elite Standards'. This artwork expresses her criticism about the social measurements determining who is elite. The man and woman look like they are communicating or negotiating, but why is the man higher than the woman? Why does the man open his mouth and woman close her mouth? Why do textural differences exist between the two heads? Are there any special meanings here? She invites her students to look carefully at the form to imagine the implication of the images.

Besides her own artworks as appreciation objects, she also introduced artworks and films of internationally well-known female artists. She designed worksheets for students to investigate meanings, artistic ways to express ideas, gender consciousness and artistic and cultural differences. A total of seventeen classes were employed. One class was an introduction about how art expresses meaning, what influences from cultural contexts might be there and so on. Ten classes were for group investigation and discussion, while another six classes were for individuals to make art. Self-understanding, interpersonal relationships and self-exploration in gender are three main concerns when considering gender issues in lesson plans. Chi-Wen collected data from classroom observation, students' interviews, pre-test and post-test, students' feedback sheets and her reflective journals. She used qualitative methods to analyse these data for a better understanding of students' learning and teaching effects. Examples of student feedback included:

> I did not know any female artists before, now I know they are not only in Taiwan but also in other countries.
> Yes, I did believe girls can paint but why did no one mention this? Now I know it is because they are not recognized at the time.
> I believe art can been done by either man or woman. It is based on your ability.
> I will pay more attention to female artists' work.

In general, from the investigation of female artists' artwork, the project sharpened students' eyes and minds. They started to rethink the pictorial form and meanings; how do they interweave with each other? How do people get meanings from the form? After deep discussion, most of the students indicated that they understood how their teacher, Chi-Wen, created her works and what kind of thoughts on gender were implied. Students created paintings with different concerns, such as: 'Challenging the conventional way of dressing; boys could dress as girls', 'Start from the beginning, just like racing', 'Gender roles change when moving from a traditional society to a contemporary one', 'Girls can be bosses and boys can be secretaries', 'Boys can wear make-up and enjoy fashion just like girls', and 'Housekeeping is not only for girls' (the students' works can be found in the thesis Chung 2012: 174–79).

Later on, students were asked to create forms to express their thinking about gender roles in society. In their work, students explored gender roles, jobs and values through the pictorial world. For example, a student wrote:

> There are gender limits in our society, like boys should have short hair, wear pants. Girls could do beautiful stuff and boys are not allowed. So I would like to paint boys and girls but no one could figure out gender difference.

Another student took her personal experience from school that when running races, the teacher sometimes gave girls more time to finish. It was not equal, yet she felt girls' capabilities were no less than those of boys'. Therefore, she painted 'Equal in the running race'. In the next panel, the student said: 'in our tradition, dad works and mother takes over all the housekeeping. The work should be equally shared'. Then the next painting represents a man who acts as a secretary handing tea to his female boss. In the fifth the student argues that boys could work at a make-up counter of department store, and they could enjoy fashion like girls. The final rendering expresses the reverse in home life and gender roles. This is the scenery that the student usually sees at home. Here is the twist: Dad is cleaning the house and Mother has a cup of tea at the time.

Overall, these themes are explored around a personal journey that is punctuated by moments of inside problems. The issues draw out ideas using visuals by forming a system that makes sense. In this learning activity, Chi-Wen used art-based theory for students to form new insights through practices. As Sullivan (2014) asserts '[a]s researchers well-schooled in studio practices of many kinds, artists and art teachers understand that, as we grow, we learn things differently' (272). By designing proper and free learning environments, students were able to touch their living paths and tell their own meaningful stories in multiple ways. On the other hand, from the comparison of the results between pre-test and post-test, students demonstrated changes in their concepts of gender stereotypes. For example, after the lessons, fewer students believed that wearing skirts would make a girl more feminine. However, boys who were good at sports were much more qualified to take on a sport leadership job. Fewer students believed boys should be brave to be a man, and that being tender or dainty would be girlish.

Regarding occupational division, students also changed their minds on various statements. For example, they no longer believed that housekeeping and cooking are much more suitable for girls, or that a woman should quit her job once she's given birth. On the other hand, they still thought that boys were better at driving than girls, and careers were more important to men, meaning that they should be exempt from housework; Dad should work outside of the home, and Mother should be at home for the kids. As to gender power, student responses changed too. Fewer students agreed with the statement that Dad's salary should be more than Mother's; or that a man should achieve more than a woman; or that a man should get a higher position than a woman otherwise it is embarrassing; or that Dad should be the leader at home; or that boys are much better than girls at serving as a decision-maker. Therefore, this arts-based lesson based on a sociocultural investigation helped students develop deeper understandings about the meaning and importance of gender equality. Young people are the future. Their gender consciousness influences future society. The intrinsic and extrinsic values of art education are much more important than before. As a result, art plays a key role in Taiwan's new K–12 curriculum guideline, and art and aesthetic literacy is one of the common core literacies.

Theory and practice

As Walker (2014) argues, theory simply cannot do its work if it remains outside of practice. Theory and practice should be placed in the same spaces and territories. However, for reasons such as a lack of a common language, shared concerns, favourable circumstances and consequential exchange, they often remain separate (Walker 2014: 267). This study tried to overcome this dilemma. It focused on the 'Arts & Gender' curriculum development and evaluation. The course content included the features and knowledge of art, combined with gender issues, students' life experiences and art practices. The teacher plays the role of a self-conscious and reflective person, leading students to understand and criticize the construction of arts and gender from their self-experience, culture and social environment. The goal is to help students establish their gender consciousness and improve their future career development by initiating the creation of conscious ideas into practice to build up a traceable process. It echoes Sullivan's (1998) discussion of critical influences of visual arts research. According to Chi-Wen's pedagogy, this model is good not only for student learning but also for teachers who can use it for professional empowerment in artistic production.

The creation of the course on arts and gender combines self-experience, theoretical knowledge and self-reflection. By designing a curriculum and developing teaching concepts, the researcher can inspect his/her own gender consciousness during the creation process. Through the integration and switching between 'artist/researcher/teacher', which are the three roles based on a/r/tography, the processes and achievements of such creations can be used as teaching materials to impart arts and gender experience and consciousness onto students, leading them to think about arts and gender issues. The result of this study indicates students can understand the importance of the arts and gender, and exchange their affections and experiences with each other.

The curriculum of this study integrates the theory of art education, gender issues and students' life experiences. The rationale of the course matches our *National Gender Education Curriculum Guideline* in which student competence indicators are at the heart of course design (Ministry of Education 2008). The teaching strategies, which cover discussion and inquiry, help students to be autonomous learners. As to the students' learning, they were assessed by various resources collected through their portfolios. In all, based on the students' feedback and performance, we found this approach a successful example of curriculum design and instruction. It helps to develop art appreciation and cognitive competence, and it inspires students to inspect and criticize themselves, others, the environment and even our culture. Such reflection can be useful in their future career development. The results show the validity and feasibility of practising the 'Arts & Gender' curriculum.

For decades, art education research topics, methods and writing styles in Taiwan followed the general academic pattern that places an emphasis on educational concerns with less focus on art practice itself. Approaches to the development of art curriculum and pedagogy are popular topics for doctoral theses. In terms of methodologies, action research in classroom settings is often employed. But it is very rare to use 'making art' to develop teaching materials and to strengthen curriculum design ideology. If arts education is a subject for free exploration, a method for solving the challenges of life and a place for enjoying human experiences, then we should not limit our academic endeavours in narrow frameworks. We should embrace contemporary issues and employ design thinking to reflect, to write and then to take action during the process of art creation. This study demonstrates a possible way to create rhythms of issues, reflections, writings and art practices for research in art educational pedagogy in Taiwan. It also assumes to attract more art educators to engage in this field. The example discussed above tries to draw a picture of what a visual art research dissertation modelled on a/r/tography could be. We believe once we are willing to open up our traditional format, we will be free to access and realize our imaginations.

Acknowledgement

Chi-Wen was the author's advisee. The materials discussed and used from Chi-Wen Chung's thesis in this chapter are authorized and permitted by Chi-Wen Chung.

References

Chen, J. C. H. (2013), 'Deciphering gender concept ways to making meaningful works of art', in M. Lee and F. Long (eds), *Synthesis Interaction Innovation: Comparative Studies of Art Education between East and West: The 4th World Chinese Arts Education Symposium & Guangzhou Academy of Fine Arts*, Guangzhou: China, pp. 59–66.

Chung, C. W. (2012), 'The study of "Arts & Gender" curriculum development and evaluation: Process construction from the initiate of creating conscious, ideas, into practice', MA dissertation, Taipei: National Taiwan Normal University.
Irwin, R. L. (2013), 'Becoming a/r/tography', *Studies in Art Education*, 54:3, pp. 198–215.
Ministry of Education (2008), *National Gender Education Curriculum Guideline at Primary and Junior High School Levels*, Taipei.
Sullivan, G. (1998), *Critical Influence: A Visual Arts Research Project with Jayne Dyer and Nikki McCarthy: Exhibition Catalogue*, Australia: Ivan Dougherty Gallery of University of New South Wales.
——— (2014), 'The art of research', *Studies in Art Education*, 55:4, pp. 270–86.
Walker, S. (2014), 'A mutual reshaping: Theory and practice', *Studies in Art Education*, 55:4, pp. 267–69.

Chapter 12

Artistic Event as Pedagogy

Belidson Dias and Tatiana Fernández

Artistic events as pedagogy

This chapter travels through Tatiana Fernández's dissertation (2015) departing from the central idea that artistic events are also pedagogical in visual culture education. This premise lies in the convergence between the pictorial turn in education and the pedagogical turn in art. Drawing on cultural pedagogy, this research dissertation draws attention to what occurs in spaces of intersection between art and visual culture education and what might be the political and cultural implications of this intersection. Furthermore, it addresses how such occurrences are instituted in the spaces that promote educational events as aesthetic experiences.

Fernández's dissertation examines an interdisciplinary research project in art education, which combines theories and approaches from cultural studies, material culture, educational philosophy, visual culture, fine art and art education. It offers new understandings related to the political, methodological and existential meanings of artistic events produced in educational contexts. This thesis explores the potential of Poietic Learning Objects (PLO), developed for this research and born out of the appropriation of Learning Objects (LO) as concept. Poietic (from poiesis) is Greek and means pro-duction, referring to an act of transforming or 'unveiling the truth connected to neither practical consideration or willing intent' of the artist (jagodzinski and Wallin 2013: 85). This concept was explored through the critical undertaking of an arts-based oriented research case study analysis of poietic learning objects completed in a continuing education course. The subjects, who are called participants in Fernández's dissertation in accordance with participatory art principles, were art teachers from Brasília's private and public schools and teacher education programmes, and art, drama and pedagogy students. They created their own PLOs (or LOs) before applying them to their own teaching context and reflecting on their experience. The methods used to collect data were rooted in participatory art, conversations in online forums, focus groups, video sessions and the creation of their own object. The data was selected for relevance and structured into conversation charts and maps of the artefacts for later analysis.

Conceptualization

Fernández's research is about territories of coincidences, contaminations, hybridizations and intersections created by the convergence of the 'pictorial turn' (Mitchell 1995) and its influence over education and the 'pedagogical turn' in art (Bishop 2012). These turns are part of wider global cultural changes leading to art and education transformations. The former refers to the role of the visual in knowledge construction and power relations and how images manifest themselves in visual culture education trends. The latter refers to the recent trend within art wherein pedagogical projects are a medium within socially engaged art. Both turns point to the increasingly important role of the visual in knowledge construction and social transformation.

The research seeks to understand what happens when both turns converge in school classrooms and art teacher education contexts, which is the space/time of this artistic/pedagogical event. It also seeks to identify how and under what conditions the artistic event could be, at the same time, a pedagogical event in its own terms, and how spaces to promote educational events as aesthetic experiences could be established in school contexts.

The research departs from the idea of an event as a disruption in the order of things that are not yet discernible or comprehensible and therefore open to the unknown (Badiou 2005). An artistic event is an aesthetic experience of being in the world wherein there is a dynamic organization of forces that go from the construction of values to the accumulation of experiences. They are, at the same time, an anticipation for what is yet to come, as it includes the tensions and resistances that arise in the adaptations of the parts (Dewey 2005).

Artistic and pedagogical events are processes of change and learning between what we know and what we do not yet know, since what is already known, alone, does not lead to learning (Atkinson 2002). The problematic is thus constructed around the idea that both events are aesthetic and pedagogical at the same time when they are open to the unknown as a space of becoming. At this point they converge around the idea of poiesis, which, in its Greek origin, refers to a form of production that, different from today's relationship to industry, is a transformation from one state to another yet unknown (pro-duction). It is non-representational and it is differentiated from praxis as a willing action of the artist (jagodzinski and Wallin 2013).

The unfolding discussions of this research are related to educational philosophy, mainly cultural pedagogy (Giroux cited in Trend 1992), understood as cultural production, and cultural production as pedagogy. It is also related to visual culture studies and trends in contemporary art. In that context Fernández points to the conceptual foundations that allow her to identify intersecting spaces between contemporary art and education, as well as its political and cultural implications. The study included a brief discussion of modern artists that worked with pedagogical interfaces and contemporary artists involved directly with pedagogical projects.[1] It also discussed the importance of hybrid identities between artists, teachers and cultural agents in Latin America. However, as the research needed to establish a practice and actual ground for pedagogical experiences, the study was mainly focused on pedagogical and aesthetic experiences with PLO (or LO).

A/r/tographic perspective and learning objects

The intent of Fernández's dissertation is articulated as an arts-based research (ABR) methodology, framed within two perspectives.

Firstly, she used a/r/tography, an ABR and ABER methodology to deal with transitions between theory, practice and poietics as well as between artist, researcher and teacher subjectivities. These transitions are necessary to inquire into intersectional spaces defined as the spaces formed by art and education convergences and border epistemologies (Mignolo 2012) that are forms of knowledge construction in the tensions between dichotomies. Mignolo identifies these border epistemologies in the modern/colonial tensions. The fluid quality of the a/r/tographic methodology allowed her to address political issues through conceptual frames or renderings. Living inquiry was performed where questions arose from ontological orientations; given the particular situation she dwelled in as an art teacher working in a *decolonial* education policy process that surged with the social and political transformations in Bolivia since 2006.[2] The methodology favoured the contiguity of beings in plural worlds, as the artist/researcher/teacher, and helped to operate within openings in yet unknown hybrid spaces in educational contexts. It also permitted her to interweave creation, production, teaching and research and emphasize complementary relationships between image and text. From this perspective theory and practice are not viewed as a dichotomy, rather as dialectic. It allowed for an embodied research experience to unfold because it engaged in spaces where particular narratives relate art, education and research to life, to construct an inter-textual dialogue (Irwin and de Cosson 2004).

The second ABR perspective used in this research is Sullivan's study on transcognitive practice (2002, 2010), which considers the multiple ways in which artists do research. In this dissertation it was important to understand the ways in which artists work and artworks operate in cultural contexts. In that regard it was an important methodological frame of reference to study the intersections, contaminations and convergences of theory/practice/poetics that occur in the convergence between the pedagogical turn in art and the pictorial turn in education.

Sullivan (2010) structures different frameworks in which visual knowing is constructed in art. These frameworks were useful to analyse the data collected in the continuing education courses in order to observe what the learning artefacts (LO or PLO) produced (ideas, forms and situations); how they were conceived (thinking in language, medium or context); and in what contexts they worked (communities, systems or cultures).

Within these methodological frameworks, the dissertation is both a theoretical and philosophical study of these turns and their implications in art and visual culture education. Praxis is interwoven with theorization and achieved through pedagogical practices in diverse educational contexts within the continuing education courses. The research subjects studied the same authors reviewed in Fernández's theoretical research. Poiesis was set in motion through the appropriation and transformation of the LO educational concept, which is attached to standardized educational policies (conceived in the spectre of the learning economy from a market point of view), to turn it into PLO proposals that focused on situated knowledge. Moreover, the poietic was also interwoven with theory and praxis by introducing, for example, fiction into the process of learning theory.

Originally, the LO concept emerged from the new information and communication technologies being applied to education, training and distance educational systems (Hodgins 2000). They are conceived as modular, interactive, reusable, self-explained learning virtual objects designed for autonomous learning with instant feedback. They range from simulation environments, videogames or role-playing games to simple webquests or content presentations. It draws its concepts, protocols, methods and languages from computer sciences and is characterized by metadata to be stored and retrieved on the Internet, and by standardized procedures and product assessment (IEEE 2000).

The PLO concept, on the other hand, privileges unexpected outcomes over assessment standards, imagination over mimesis, creative and relational processes over repetitive fixations, participative construction over transmitting-absorbing principles and existential settings over prefabricated fit-for-the-market ones. In essence, they prioritize a pedagogy of dissent where there are possibilities to construct spaces of subjectivity, agency and participation.

Fernández introduced the students to the concepts, political contexts, advantages, possibilities and tools for LO when applied to visual culture education and then presented the PLO concept. They also explored the objects as 'participants'. Within that experience they invented, created and produced their own PLO (or LO) for their own students/participants in formal, non-formal and informal education contexts.[3] The challenge of the PLO concept was neither to disclose knowledge for the learner as a 'correct-incorrect' dichotomy, nor to expect hegemonic outcomes from learning activities. For a pedagogical artefact (LO) to be poietic it should create ruptures, cracks, holes, be open to a plurality of responses, allow for subjectivity, differences and dissidences, imagination and aesthetic experience (corporeal).

In that sense PLO operated as a concept for pedagogical artefacts that was meant to provoke aesthetic events in which everyone took risks to perform in spaces of power that dared to visualize the tensions between knowing and not knowing. This also valued difference, expressed through singular ways of seeing, and dissent, that is demonstrated through the plural ways of seeing.

In the same manner, knowing and not knowing function as parts of the same movement of existence that does not separate singularity from plurality, real from virtual, past from future, subject from object or self from otherness. Learning is viewed as an existential process (Dewey 2005; Atkinson 2002) in which the singularity of the self and the plurality of the many can operate as a form of social reconstruction, and these processes are aesthetic and political because they are spaces of angst, fear, anxiety and tension. In other words, the differences between LO and PLO are political because the students are participatory subjects in a manner similar to the contemporary emancipated spectator (Rancière 2011), or a spectator that has an active role in a cultural process.[4]

Fernández created five PLOs specifically produced for the subjects of the continuing education course as a way of learning about cultural pedagogies. One of them was a co-authored comic book between her and the 'participant'.[5] The narrative featured a fictional conversation, based on videos of different conferences, between four educators and artists (Henry Giroux, William Pinar, Gayatri Spivak and Anton Vidokle[6]) that focused on border-crossing discourses of art and education with the intention of introducing their ideas. The 'participant' was invited to be part of the comic book by establishing a dialogue with the intellectuals using text and image interventions.[7] The results were different comic books with the fictional dialogues established with the subjects.

Thinking anew

The focus of the course and the research was the subjects' learning objects (PLO or LO) and experiences. In that regard, three key guiding questions were used to analyse the subject's artefacts, processes and conversations:

1. What can poietic learning objects do? This question focused on implications on the political level. From the twenty regular subjects, seven concluded, applied and reflected upon the results of their LO or PLO, and presented them in the final meeting of the class. In order to analyse them they were classified by the intensity and degree of openness, by the deviation of openness and by the relevance of the project. The analyses showed that through PLO, students are active participants in the construction of knowledge that goes beyond what art means towards what art can do or provoke, while through LO, on the other hand, students and teachers remain in traditional hierarchical systems.
2. What was produced with poietic learning objects and how was it produced? This question focused on the strategies, methods and methodologies used by all of the twenty subjects that went through the creation and application in educational contexts. The analyses showed that PLO (and even LO) emphasizes the visual role in the construction of knowledge wherein ideas are formed through thinking in a language, a medium and a context. Yet, we also found that for most of the subjects the PLO was a challenge. Subjects from educational backgrounds had difficulty thinking in poietic ways and subjects from artistic backgrounds had difficulty thinking in terms of pedagogical processes.
3. What kinds of effects do poietic learning objects form and what are they formed by? The question focused on implications on the existential level. The analyses showed that in the process of constructing their own artistic/pedagogical event zones, the participants of the continuing education courses changed the way they saw themselves and their practice. The majority were on a quest to learn ways to recreate themselves, unsatisfied with the current state of education, but willing to find ways to be creators. The PLO artefacts were formed by the desire to cross borders in visual art education, and the resulting artefacts have the potency to form fluid identities.

One of the most effective artefacts was the PLO *Queresquanto*,[8] which is a paper fortune teller game for her fourth-grade students to assess learning processes in a popular culture class. The subject collected a series of poietic proposals or challenges to create a game, as if she was thinking in popular circle dance, writing a poem, or inventing a new *capoeira* fight-dance step. The outcomes were the creation of poems, dance movements, performances, narratives and images.

In follow-up discussions, the subject described her difficulty thinking in pedagogical and poietic terms because it required opening up to the uncontrolled or unplanned in a very controlled and planned context. But once she grasped a solution within the tensions between what is planned, what she wants and what she could not imagine might be learned, she found a space where both events could happen concurrently.

Not all the artefacts created in the continuing education courses had openness or managed to get out of the 'correct-incorrect' dichotomy, although they all sought to have some sort of aesthetic experience. There were card games with art history images; a virtual museum where the students/participants curated their own art room; webquests; a set of texture objects in boxes and bags to work with or to produce from; propositions to create aesthetic maps; performances; board games; video games and structures to construct forms.

In addition, many students realized that the LO and PLO were precariously structured, not arriving at a satisfactory solution for the subject or the educational context while the subjects were experimenting. However, some were resourcefully completed. Nevertheless, these artefacts were not the artistic event that many would expect from a PLO. What can be considered an artistic event is what occurred in between, even if the process was not completed. For many of the subjects it was the leading ideas that were constructed in singular manners for different contexts, discussed collectively and presented to their peers in many stages of the process that provoked a turn, a rupture with the order of things in art teaching.

Spaces of convergence

The analyses of the conversations and the production of PLO (and LO) for visual culture education revealed that in the space formed by the convergence of the turns, it is possible for a class to operate as an artistic event; however, it requires courage to cross borders of prescriptive practices because it has political and cultural implications. One implication is that the participant becomes the emancipated spectator. The student is a 'participant' in the process of knowledge construction and this allows for a disruption of hegemonic structures of cultural production. Another implication is the democratic distribution of the sensible (Rancière 2010, 2011), or the ways in which social roles are distributed, where there is space for singularity, difference and dissidence, pointed towards conflict zones that disrupt processes of invisibility, visual control and centre-periphery dichotomy.

The use of arts-based methodologies and a/r/tographic approaches points towards the ethico-aesthetic paradigm (Deleuze and Guattari 2002), which considers the political role of the aesthetic in the creation of subjectivities to articulate a new ethic of understanding alterity and collective identities. This process allows for the disruption of traditional art education principles subordinated to science models and art institutions subordinated to power relations. Instead it proposes that art is a metadiscipline, and a complex form of knowledge construction.

References

Atkinson, D. (2002), *Art in Education: Identity and Practice*, Dordrecht: Kluwer.

Badiou, A. (2005), *Being and Event*, New York: Continuum.

Bishop, C. (2012), *Artificial Hells: Participatory Art and the Politics of Spectatorship*, London: Verso.

Deleuze, G. and Guattari, F. (2002), *Mil Mesetas: Capitalismo y Esquizofrenia* (*A Thousand Plateaus: Capitalism and Schizophrenia*), Valencia: Pre-Textos.

Dewey, J. (2005), *Art as Experience*, New York: Penguin Group.

Fernández, T. (2015), 'Evento artístico como pedagogia' ('Artistic event as pedagogy'), PhD thesis, Distrito Federal: Universidade de Brasilia.

Hodgins, W. (2000), 'The future of learning objects', in D. Wiley (ed.), *The Instructional Use of Learning Objects*, http://reusability.org/read/. Accessed 29 March 2017.

Institute of Electrical and Electronics Engineers (IEEE) (2000), 'Learning Technology Standards Committee (LTSC)', *Draft Standard for Learning Object Metadata*, http://ltsc.ieee.org/. Accessed 29 March 2017.

Irwin, R. L. and de Cosson, A. (2004), *A/r/tography: Rendering Self through Arts Based Living Inquiry*, Vancouver: Pacific Educational Press.

jagodzinski, j. and Wallin, J. (2013), *Arts-Based Research: A Critique and a Proposal*, Rotterdam: Sense.

Mignolo, W. (2012), *Local Histories/Global Designs: Coloniality, Subaltern Knowledges and Border Thinking*, Princeton: Princeton University Press.

Mitchell, W. J. T. (1995), *Picture Theory*, London: University of Chicago Press.

Rancière, J. (2010), *Dissensus: On Politics and Aesthetics*, London: Continuum.

——— (2011), *The Emancipated Spectator*, London: Verso.

Sullivan, G. (2002), 'Artistic thinking as transcognitive practice: A reconciliation of the process-product dichotomy', *Visual Arts Research*, 22:1, pp. 2–17.

——— (2010), *Art Practice as Research: Inquiry in Visual Arts*, Thousand Oaks: Sage.

Trend, D. (1992), *Cultural Pedagogy: Art, Education, Politics*, New York: Bergin & Garvey.

Notes

1 Artists discussed include Tania Bruguera, Pablo Helguera, Anton Vidokle, Jan Verwoert, Pawel Althamer, among others.

2 In 2006 Evo Morales won the elections and became the first Indigenous president of the Republic of Bolivia.
3 Formal education has an official national or regional curriculum. Non-formal education is where there is a planned curriculum, but it is not part of an official curriculum. Informal education is where there is no curriculum.
4 The emancipated spectator is not a transformation from ignorant into a scholar, but the idea of an intellectual emancipation that is the ground of equality of knowledge.
5 Comic Book Damage Control, continuing education course, UnB/IdA/VIS: http://estagio-deartista.pro.br/artedu/OAP_oficina/giroux/front_controle_danos.htm. Accessed 29 March 2017.
6 Giroux is a critical pedagogy educator and researcher, Pinar is a curriculum researcher, Spivak is a postcolonial researcher and philosopher and Vidokle is an artist engaged in pedagogical projects.
7 'Exposição curso de extensão OAP' ('PLO continuing education course exhibit') in MyDocu-menta platform: http://www.mydocumenta.com/f/index.php?proyecto_token=35C419BC8E11ED0673054D1071AD1669. Accessed 29 March 2017.
8 The artefact can be seen in a video made of the continuing education courses between 06:39 and 10:00 at http://estagiodeartista.pro.br/artedu/OAP_oficina/2/video.htm. Accessed 29 March 2017.

Chapter 13

Parsing Creative Influence through Comparative Visual Research Methods

Justin B. Makemson

For the purposes of this chapter, I refer to comparative visual research methods that encourage participants to propose and support connections between two objects within a series of researcher-generated prompts as structured symbolic object comparisons. For example, the structured symbolic object comparisons in my own dissertation research prompted participants to seek out, propose and support connections to objects somehow representative of their current artistic identities, projected future artistic identities and the creative influence of 'significant artistic others' or more socially recognized artists. The discussion that follows expands on the research potential of structured symbolic object comparisons and outlines the practical application of comparative visual methodologies in the context of the author's dissertation research into creative influence and student artistic identities (Makemson 2014).

Comparative research involving structured symbolic object comparisons is similar in practical application to other creative or arts-based methodologies in that the researcher is called upon to interpret both visual and verbal elements, i.e. what some researchers refer to as 'representational forms' and 'artful discourse' (Cahnmann-Taylor and Siegesmund 2008; Finley 2003). The participants in my dissertation project submitted personal artwork for review and selected images from a digital collection, although they also openly critiqued the images that they created or found online as a mode of demonstrating social and personal-level value systems. Tallack (2004) provides a four-tier taxonomy helpful in defining the value systems connected to creative and interpretative action: personal, situated, transitive and intercultural artistic values (I came up with the latter three designations for Tallack's different tiers). I repurposed Tallack's taxonomy as a qualitative measure of participant demonstrations of value systems in the data collected through creative self-histories, portfolio presentations and think-aloud comparative search protocols.

To expand briefly on the theoretical foundations of comparative visual research – in semiotic or symbolic exchanges, created objects function as visual texts. Considering that the created object's symbolic significance can be situated both in personal and social experience, objects are demonstrative of the value systems of their creator, interpreter and the socio-historical circumstances of their creation and/or interpretation (Appadurai 1986; Benjamin 2006; Dewey 1934; Gauntlett 2007; Hegel 1998; Kopytoff 1986; Schlereth 1985). Singular interpretative frames contribute context, complexity and nuance to the object's interpretation; therefore, the deconstruction of the object's symbolic significance becomes considerably more comprehensive with the addition of interpretative frames (Albers

2007; Eisner 1998; Oberhardt 2001; Vallance 2004). Comparative visual methods defined in semiotic terms concentrate on the 'critical aspects' (Kress and van Leeuwen 1996) of two objects being compared and then parse which critical aspects form the basis of the participant's proposed comparison. While the prospect of using one object to deconstruct the properties of a second object and by extension reveal something about the value system of the object's creator is relatively unexceptional in the domains of visual interpretation and aesthetics (Arnheim 1969, 1971; Efland 2002; Langer 1942, 1957; Reid 1968; Zeki 2011), the practical application of comparative treatments remains relatively underrepresented in visual research initiatives. I found limited methodological precedent or no record of ongoing comparative visual studies when I began preparation for my dissertation project. Comparative visual research initiatives historically concentrate on the physiological and psychological mechanisms involved in reviewing two objects at the same time, rather than the implementation of comparative methods to better understand other more socially grounded phenomenon (Bauhoff et al. 2010, 2011; Galpin et al. 2008; Pomplun et al. 2001). I did find records of researchers employing comparative methods to study values systems in teacher training and social work education (Gould and Harris 1996), to study self-other relationships in the workplace (Gauntlett 2007) and to study the perceived social significance of distinctive architecture within a local environment (Arefi 2013). While informative, these prior initiatives did neither explicitly relate to the study of artistic identities or creative influence, nor procedurally did they comparatively consider the visual properties or symbolic interrelationship of two created objects, something I treated as prerequisite to my research concentration.

Research defines social self-identification, creative, artistic or otherwise, as a succession of negotiations and/or exchanges between intrinsic and sociocultural agents, wherein the individual's reflexive reconciliation of self-other and self-environment boundaries helps to define, refine and then re-define social identities (Bakhtin 1993; Loevinger and Blasi 1976; Cooley 1902; Deci and Ryan 1991; Frith 2007; Fuchs 2003; Maturana and Varela 1975; Piirto 2009; Reid 1981; Ryan 1991; Schwartz 2002; Walsh 2002; Waterman 1984). Furthermore, the reconciliation of social identities requires multiple points of reference, most notably reference related to perception of self, relationship to others and integration into a social community (Halverson 2005). I concluded, following significant literature review that a comparative research treatment best suited the study of a social construct that was defined through reflexive comparison – and also that existing comparative methodologies insufficiently addressed the specific needs of the dissertation project. I therefore refocused my dissertation research to better address creative influence and designed a three-stage research protocol that appropriated conceptual and procedural elements from the qualitative practices of portraiture (Lawrence-Lightfoot and Davis 1997; Lightfoot 1983), narrative analysis (Chase 2005; Labov 1972, 1997; Labov and Waletsky [1967] 1997), think-aloud protocol analysis (Ericsson and Simon 1980, 1984, 1998; Newell and Simon 1972) and search-based protocol analysis (Case 2002; Guinee et al. 2003; Kari and Savolainen 2007; Rolston 1987; Sloane 2003; Xie 2000).

In overview, I prompted participants in the first stage of data collection to develop and present short narrative self-histories of symbolically significant artistic experiences. In recounting their creative experiences, participants self-identified as artists, defined the social role of the artist, described and categorized their own artwork and creative practices and discussed creative associations and interests, in most cases with minimal direction or input from the researcher. Participants reported on topics including early interest in the arts, cultural and familial background, educational experience, formal training, career goals, as well as creative development, partnerships, breakthroughs and setbacks. As I previously referenced, the reflexive narrative stage of data collection was designed and administered as constructive discourse between participant and researcher; I left discussion intentionally open-ended and flexible in structuration and sequence.

In the second stage of data collection, I prompted participants to share and discuss examples of personal artwork representative of their larger student portfolio. To facilitate these portfolio presentations, I contacted each participant in advance and instructed them to bring digital copies of three selected works to our scheduled session; the only stipulation I placed on participant selections was that the artwork had to be somehow representative of the student's present means of artistic self-identification. I then uploaded the copies into a digital database at the beginning of the session. Several participants opted to bring original artwork instead of the requested digital copies; in these situations I photographed the work and uploaded the digital copies to the database for later reference. Per the first stage of data collection, I treated portfolio presentations as a constructive discussion between participant and researcher and left the process of discussion intentionally flexible and open-ended. To close discussion of each selected artwork, I prompted participants to define the exact properties of the work that made it more or less representative of their present artistic identities and/or preferred mode of working. I reviewed data from the first two stages of collection and identified inferences suggestive of narrative 'turning point' events (Denzin 1989; Feldman 1982; Labov 1997; McAdams et al. 2001), thematic structures (Gauntlett 2007), and visual and verbal expressions of artistic value systems (Reid 1968; Tallack 2004). Because the first two stages of data collection and interpretation primarily set up the initial points of comparison, I am waiting to further elaborate on comparative methodological treatments until the third stage of the dissertation project.

In the third and most overtly visual and comparative stage of data collection, I prompted participants to complete a series of think-aloud search protocols using an online collection of digital images (www.artstor.org). The individual prompts in my research protocol included directions for participants to search for an image or object somehow representative of their 'current artist identities' (Figure 1), to search for an image or object somehow representative of their 'projected future artist identities' (Figure 2), and to search for an image or object somehow representative of artwork participants 'appreciated or enjoyed viewing' – I framed this final prompt less formally as a search for the participant's 'significant artistic other' (Figure 3).

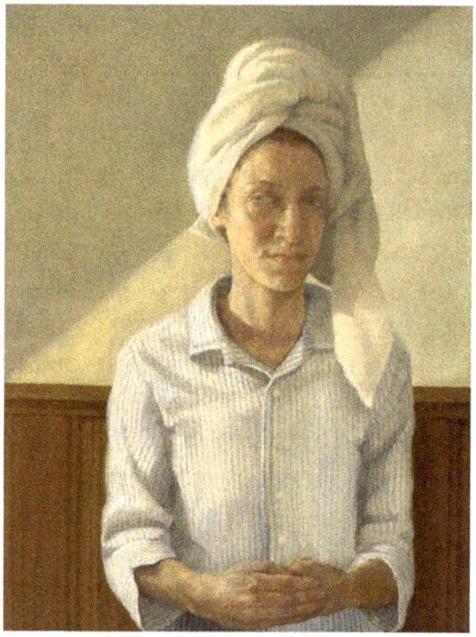

Figure 1: Student artwork, titled *Self Portrait with Towel*. The research participant proposed and supported connections to Rogier van der Weyden's *Saint George and the Dragon*, 1432–35. Reprinted with permission of the artist.

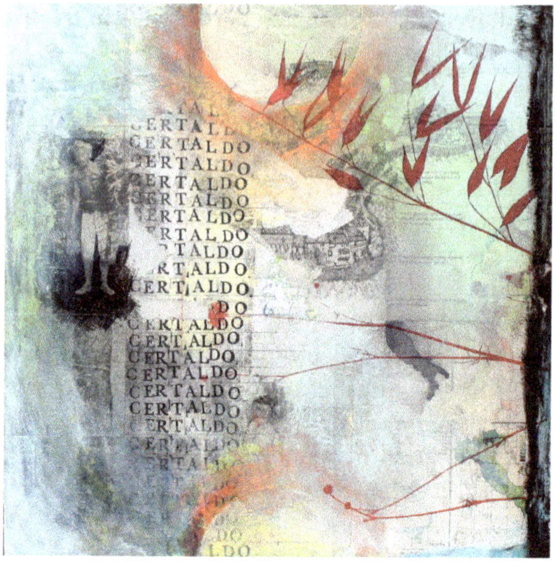

Figure 2: Student artwork, titled *Certaldo Alto*. The research participant proposed and supported connections to John Baldessari's *The Overlap Series: Trees*, 2001. Reprinted with permission of the artist.

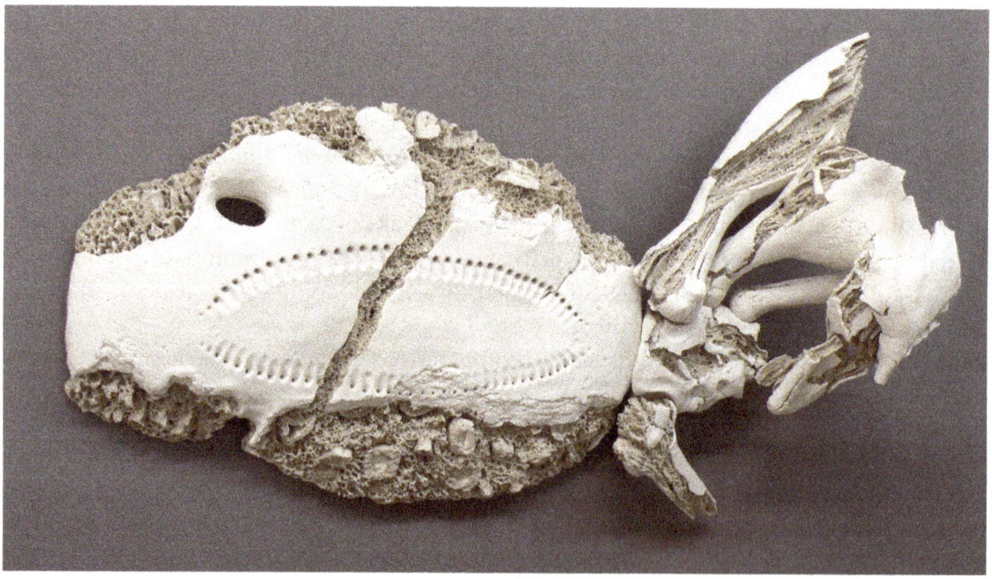

Figure 3: Student artwork, titled *Homologization #3*. The research participant proposed and supported connections to Italo Scanga's *Potato Famine*, 1979. Reprinted with permission of the artist.

During the search process, I created a record of the participants' self-reports and an audit trail of the structure and sequence of participants' search forms, i.e. the combinations of words or phrases participants typed into the search engine to formulate a search (Guinee et al. 2003). Participant search forms ranged from 'Chauvet+cave' and 'Rogier+van+der+Weyden' to 'dark+surreal+moody' and 'contemporary+sculpture+natural' and I recorded the participants' use of key word searches, advanced searches, faceted searches and orientations towards browsing or more direct forms of searching. While the Artstor collection of fine art and visual culture artefacts is extensive (during the period of this research Artstor contained over 1.5 million digitally archived images and objects), several participants reported having a specific image or object in mind for a given prompt, only to discover that it was not part of the collection. Interestingly, I found that the collection's limitations compelled participants to consider only the properties most central to their proposed comparisons and in most situations served to clarify or strengthen the symbolic connection between objects. In select cases wherein participants pushed back against search parameters, I encouraged them to share images and objects found elsewhere on the Internet, but only after they had selected a surrogate selection from the Artstor collection.

In addition to in-protocol self-report, participants reflexively examined the search and selection process and discussed their selected symbolic objects at the conclusion of each search protocol. For example, participants in the first protocol examined and discussed the objects representative of their current artist identities in relationship to their own portfolio of artwork and creative practices: here participants were prompted to consider similarities and differences between the search selection and their own artwork; participants projected how they could see themselves taking on a similar creative endeavour; and participants explained the nature and strength of association with the search selection. The reflexive self-examinations of the other two protocols also followed this template.

Following prompted search sessions, I examined search protocol data and digital copies of student artwork for evidence of compositional, conceptual, formal-material, affective and biographical similitude, i.e. interpretative measures derived from more traditional frameworks of visual interpretation (Fiore and Nelson 2003; Garber 1996; Greenberg 1961; jagodzinski 1991; Lakoff and Johnson 1980; McFee 1998). Although unknown at the time of my dissertation project, the interpretative measures I established for the third stage of my research roughly correspond to Walker's (2001) different classifications of creative problem solving: aesthetic, conceptual, technical, expressive and stylistic.

To better define the project's five interpretive measures, compositional similitude signified commonalities in formal design elements and principles; this point of analysis examined colour palette, implementation of line, distribution of form and space, rendering of objects, surface treatment and visual representation. Conceptual similitude signified commonalities in creative intent or in the artists' attempt to address similar creative problems; this point of analysis examined creative content, ideation, intent, themes, messages, symbol use and purpose. Formal-material similitude signified commonalities in materials and methods; this point of analysis examined the processes and resources invested in the creative act, as well as the artists' valuation of creative processes and resources. Affective similitude signified commonalities in emotive or tonal visual elements; this point of analysis examined the image's emotional impact on the viewer and the means employed by the artist to achieve the desired affect (I also addressed considerations of emotional sensitivity/authenticity and effectiveness of artistic treatment within this measure). Biographical similitude signified commonalities in shared events and circumstances within the artists' respective life histories; this point of analysis examined biographical elements such as educational experience, formal training, family life, precocity and disability, socioeconomic status, peer relationships and geographic origins. To help facilitate the coding of the object comparisons, I developed a simple five-point scoring system, with a score of five indicating a strong positive correlation between the objects in the given interpretative measure and a score of one indicating a strong negative correlation between the objects in the given interpretative measure. I recorded these five scores in conjunction with other data to develop an understanding of the relationship between participants' portfolio of artwork and think-aloud search protocol selections. I concluded the third stage of my research by cross-referencing the scores from the interpretative measures with participants' in-protocol and post-protocol self-reports.

Based on these summative comparative visual interpretations, I integrated findings from all three data threads to construct individual portraits with corresponding portrait synopses for each of the participant's social artistic identities. In my dissertation project I referred to the condensed narrative representations as 'seven portraits of artistic self'. Resulting portraits synthesized the perspectives of the participants and researcher, so the portraiture method of presentation provided readers with multiple vantage points for the consideration of emerging patterns in the research. Moreover, the seven portraits and related portrait synopses presented an opportunity for me to share my findings in a manner that was informative, relatable, accessible and applicable to researchers as well as classroom art teachers. Due to the methodological focus of this book, I do not plan to address the findings of my research other than to say that I found comparative visual research incredibly effective in dealing with questions of creative influence within a small population of student artists. What I discovered using comparative visual methods broadly reinforced findings from the earlier literature review: (1) self-identification is primarily a socially situated phenomenon; (2) student artists rely heavily on the work of other artists to define their own creative practice; and (3) symbolic evidence of self-other and self-environment reconciliations is readily available in student-created objects and related artful discourse.

In closing, the discussion portion of my dissertation document examined numerous pedagogical implications for a reflexive and socially negotiated definition of artistic self-identification; however, one of the things I neglected to consider is the possibility of teacher-designed symbolic comparative exercises as a component of regular classroom instruction. In terms of pedagogical relevance, research suggests that student artists develop social awareness and by extension become self-critical of creative practices between the ages of 10 and 13 years old – Lowenfeld (1945) refers to this social acuity in creative action as the 'dawning realism' or 'gang stage' of artistic development, while Hurwitz and Day (2012) refer to this time period as the 'preadolescent stage' of artistic development. Both parties frame preadolescence as a critical developmental stage wherein students decide whether or not to continue involvement in creative activities. In other situations, socially invested creative action can precede the preadolescent stage of artistic development by several years, e.g. when early elementary age artists employ conversational strategies to negotiate creative dilemmas and readily imitate representational forms found in visual culture, teacher exemplars and the artwork of neighbouring students (Sless 1978; Duncum 1999). Citing the sizable creative and social influence of significant others within an educational environment, I propose that teacher-designed symbolic comparisons have the potential to clarify student positions regarding the value of their own artwork and the work of other artists. Since the completion of the dissertation project, I have incorporated structured symbolic comparisons into several of my own teaching assignments. In one project students propose and support connections linking visual and popular culture objects to objects found in galleries and museums; in another project, students interpret, restage, photograph and digitally manipulate a culturally significant work of art and later critique the intertextual relationship between original and reinterpreted images. I have regularly used information from these and other similar projects to help guide curriculum development and to better understand the specific instructional needs and interests of my students.

References

Albers, P. (2007), *Finding the Artist Within: Creating and Reading Visual Texts in the English Language Arts Classroom*, Newark: International Reading Association.

Appadurai, A. (1986), 'Introduction: Commodities and the politics of value', in A. Appadurai (ed.), *The Social Life of Things: Commodities in Cultural Perspective*, Cambridge: Cambridge University Press, pp. 3–63.

Arefi, M. (2013), 'The structure of visual difference: A comparative case study of Mariemont and Lebanon, Ohio', *Urban Design International*, 18:4, pp. 296–312.

Arnheim, R. (1969), *Visual Thinking*, Los Angeles: University of California Press.

——— (1971), *Entropy and Art: An Essay on Disorder and Order*, Berkeley: University of California Press.

Bakhtin, M. (1993), *Towards a Philosophy of the Act*, Austin: University of Texas Press.

Bauhoff, V., Huff, M. and Schwan, S. (2010), 'The influence of expertise on comparative visual search performance', *Journal of Vision*, 10:7, pp. 1309–09.

——— (2011), 'The effect of temporal distance on comparative visual search', *Journal of Vision*, 11:11, p. 1325.

Benjamin, W. (2006), 'The storyteller', in D. Hale (ed.), *The Novel: An Anthology of Criticism and Theory 1900–2000*, Malden: Blackwell, pp. 361–78.

Cahnmann-Taylor, M. and Siegesmund, R. (2008), *Arts-Based Research in Education: Foundations for Practice*, New York: Routledge.

Case, D. (2002), *Looking for Information: A Survey of Research on Information Seeking, Needs, and Behavior*, San Diego: Academic Press.
Chase, S. (2005), 'Narrative inquiry: Multiple lenses, approaches, voices', in N. K. Denzin and Y. S. Lincoln (eds), *The Sage Handbook of Qualitative Research,* 3rd ed., Thousand Oaks: Sage, pp. 651–79.
Cooley, C. (1902), *Human Nature and the Social Order*, New York: Charles Scribner's Sons.
Deci, E. and Ryan, R. (1991), 'A motivational approach to self: Integration in personality', in R. A. Dienstbier (ed.), *Nebraska Symposium on Motivation, 1990*, vol. 38, Lincoln: University of Nebraska Press, pp. 237–88.
Denzin, N. (1989), *Interpretive Biography*, Newbury Park: Sage.
Dewey, J. (1934), *Art as Experience*, New York: Perigree Books.
Duncum, P. (1999), 'What elementary generalist teachers need to know to teach art well', *Art Education*, 52:6, pp. 33–37.
Efland, A. (2002), *Art and Cognition: Integrating the Visual Arts in the Curriculum*, New York: Teachers College Press.
Eisner, E. (1998), *The Enlightened Eye: Qualitative Inquiry and the Enhancement of Educational Practice*, Englewood Cliffs: Prentice Hall.
Ericsson, A. and Simon, H. (1980), 'Verbal reports as data', *Psychological Review*, 87:3, pp. 215–51.
——— (1984), *Protocol Analysis: Verbal Reports as Data*, Cambridge: Harvard University Press.
——— (1998), 'How to study thinking in everyday life: Contrasting think-aloud protocols with descriptions and explanations of thinking', *Mind, Culture, and Activity*, 5:3, pp. 178–86.
Feldman, D. (1982), 'A developmental framework for research with gifted children', in D. Feldman (ed.), *New Directions for Child Development: Developmental Approaches to Giftedness and Creativity*, San Francisco: Jossey-Bass, pp. 31–46.
Finley, S. (2003), 'Arts-based inquiry in QI: Seven years from crisis to guerrilla warfare', *Qualitative Inquiry*, 9:2, pp. 281–95.
Fiore, R. and Nelson, H. (2003), *Recognition, Responsibility, and Rights: Feminist Ethics and Social Theory*, New York: Rowman and Littlefield.
Frith, C. (2007), *Making up the Mind: How the Brain Creates Our Mental World*, Malden: Blackwell.
Fuchs, C. (2003), 'Structuration theory and self-organization', *Systemic Practice and Action Research,* 16:2, pp. 133–67.
Galpin, A., Underwood, G. and Chapman, P. (2008), 'Sensing without seeing in comparative visual search', *Consciousness and Cognition*, 17:3, pp. 672–87.
Garber, E. (1996), 'Art criticism from a feminist point of view: An approach for teachers', in G. Collins and R. Sandell (eds), *Gender Issues in Art Education: Content, Contexts, And Strategies*, Reston: National Art Education Association, pp. 21–29.
Gauntlett, D. (2007), *Creative Explorations: New Approaches to Identities and Audiences,* New York: Routledge.
Gould, N. and Harris, A. (1996), 'Student imagery of practice in social work and teacher education: A comparative research approach', *British Journal of Social Work*, 26:2, pp. 223–37.
Greenberg, C. (1961), *Art and Culture: Critical Essays*, Boston: Beacon Press.

Guinee, K., Eagleton, M. and Hall, T. (2003), 'Adolescents' internet search strategies: Drawing upon familiar cognitive paradigms when accessing electronic information sources', *Journal of Educational Computing Research*, 29:3, pp. 363–74.

Halverson, E. (2005), 'InsideOut: Facilitating gay youth identity development through performance-based youth organization', *Identity: An International Journal of Theory and Research*, 5:1, pp. 67–90.

Hegel, G. (1998), *Hegel's Aesthetics: Lectures on Fine Art*, vol. 1, Oxford: Oxford University Press.

Hurwitz, A. and Day, M. (2012), *Children and Their Art: Methods for the Elementary School*, 9th ed., Belmont: Wadsworth.

jagodzinski, j. (1991), 'A para-critical/sitical/sightical reading of Ralph Smith's *Excellence in Art Education*', *Journal of Social Theory in Art Education*, 11, pp. 119–59.

Kari, J. and Savolainen, R. (2007), 'Relationships between information seeking and context: A qualitative study of internet searching and the goals of personal development', *Library and Information Science Research*, 29:1, pp. 47–69.

Kopytoff, I. (1986), 'The cultural biography of things: Commoditization as process', in A. Appadurai, *The Social Life of Things: Commodities in Cultural Perspective*, Cambridge: Cambridge University Press, pp. 64–91.

Kress, G. and van Leeuwen, T. (1996), *Reading Images: The Grammar of Visual Design*, New York: Routledge.

Labov, W. (1972), *Language in the Inner Cities: Studies in the Black English Vernacular*, Philadelphia: University of Pennsylvania Press.

——— (1997), 'Some further steps in narrative analysis', *Journal of Narrative and Life History*, 7:1–4, pp. 395–415.

Labov, W. and Waletsky, J. ([1967] 1997), 'Narrative analysis: Oral versions of personal experience', *Journal of Narrative and Life History*, 7:1–4, pp. 3–38.

Lakoff, G. and Johnson, M. (1980), *Metaphors We Live By*, Chicago: University of Chicago Press.

Langer, S. (1942), *Philosophy in a New Key: A Study in the Symbolism of Reason, Rite, and Art*, Cambridge: Harvard University Press.

——— (1957), *Problems of Art: Ten Philosophical Lectures, Volume 35*, New York: Charles Scribner's Sons.

Lawrence-Lightfoot, S. and Davis, J. (1997), *The Art and Science of Portraiture*, San Francisco: Jossey-Bass.

Loevinger, J. and Blasi, A. (1976), *Ego Development: Conceptions and Theories*, San Francisco: Jossey-Bass.

Lightfoot, S. (1983), *Good High School: Portraits of Character and Culture*, New York: Basic Books.

Lowenfeld, V. (1945), 'Tests for visual and haptical aptitudes', *The American Journal of Psychology*, 58:1, pp. 100–11.

Makemson, J. B. (2014), 'Seven portraits of artistic self: A qualitative examination of self in the reflexive narratives and artwork portfolios of postsecondary art students', PhD thesis, Bloomington: Indiana University.

Maturana, H. and Varela, F. (1975), *Autopoietic Systems*, BCL Report 9.4, Urbana: University of Illinois.

McAdams, D., Josselson, R. and Lieblich, A. (2001), *Turns in the Road: Narrative Studies of Lives in Transition,* Washington DC: American Psychological Association.
McFee, J. (1998), *Cultural Diversity and the Structure and Practice of Art Education*, Reston: National Art Education Association.
Newell, A. and Simon, H. (1972), *Human Problem Solving*, Englewood Cliffs: Prentice Hall.
Oberhardt, S. (2001), 'The pedagogy of the art museum: Re-viewing the four frames', *Counterpoints*, 167, pp. 119–58.
Piirto, J. (2009), 'Eminence and creativity in selected visual artists', in B. MacFarlene and T. Stambaugh (eds), *Leading Change in Gifted Education*, Waco: Prufrock Press, pp. 13–26.
Pomplun, M., Sichelschmidt, L., Wagner, K., Clermont, T., Rickheit, G. and Ritter, H. (2001), 'Comparative visual search: A difference that makes a difference', *Cognitive Science*, 25:1, pp. 3–36.
Reid, L. (1968), 'Knowledge, morals, and aesthetic education', *Journal of Aesthetic Education*, 2:3, pp. 41–54.
——— (1981), 'Intuition and art', *Journal of Aesthetic Education*, 15:3, pp. 27–38.
Rolston, H. (1987), *Science and Religion: A Critical Survey,* Philadelphia: Temple University Press.
Ryan, R. (1991), 'The narrative of the self in autonomy and relatedness', in J. Strauss and G. R. Goethals (eds), *The Self: Interdisciplinary Approaches,* New York: Springer, pp. 208–38.
Schlereth, T. (1985), 'Material culture and cultural research', in T. Schlereth (ed.), *Material Culture: A Research Guide*, Lawrence: University of Kansas, pp. 1–34.
Schwartz, S. (2002), 'In search of mechanisms of change in identity development: Integrating the constructivist and discovery perspectives on identity', *Identity: An International Journal of Theory and Research*, 2:4, pp. 317–39.
Sless, D. (1978), *Visual Thinking,* Adelaide: Radio University 5UV.
Sloane, D. (2003), 'Internet search approaches: The influence of age, search goals, and experience', *Library and Information Science Research*, 25, pp. 403–18.
Tallack, M. (2004), 'Critical studies: Values at the heart of art education', in R. Hickman (ed.), *Art Education 11–18: Meaning, Purpose, and Direction*, London: Continuum, pp. 105–23.
Vallance, E. (2004), 'Framing the art experience: Beyond museums', *Visual Arts Research*, 30:2, pp. 126–30.
Walker, S. (2001), *Teaching Meaning in Artmaking,* Worcester: Davis.
Walsh, D. (2002), 'Constructing an artistic self: A cultural perspective', in L. Bresler and C. M. Thompson (eds), *The Arts in Children's Lives*, Dordrecht: Kluwer, pp. 101–11.
Waterman, A. (1984), *Psychology of Individualism*, New York: Praeger.
Xie, I. (2000), 'Shifts of interactive intentions and information-seeking strategies in interactive information', *Journal of the American Society for Informational Science,* 51, pp. 841–57.
Zeki, S. (2011), *Splendors and Miseries of the Brain: Love, Creativity, and the Quest for Human Happiness*, West Sussex: John Wiley and Sons.

Chapter 14

Artworks in Residence: Semiosis, Transmediation and ZPD

Julie Wren, Susan Wright and Marnee Watkins

Background

Young children's engagement with artworks has long been recognized as a significant feature of visual arts curricula. An example is the Australian curriculum, which highlights children's exploration and interpretation of artworks as a means to developing effective communication (Australian Curriculum Assessment and Reporting Authority 2016). Two key approaches have underpinned visual arts pedagogy: cognitive and sociocultural.

The cognitive approach refers to how children *perceive* artworks. It emphasizes developmental theories with a focus on children's arts-based language, particularly as related to adult-style responses and critiques (Leeds 1989). In contrast, the sociocultural approach considers personal meaning as being mediated through an individual's interaction with artworks and people (Savva 2003).

The challenge with these approaches has been in capturing children's deep engagement. Langer (1953) describes deep engagement as intrinsically driven exploration with genuine interest and enthusiasm that leads to new learning. She adds that experiences with artworks require an ongoing process of interpretation, continual refinement and clarification over time. Vygotsky emphasizes that deeply engaging experiences are only possible when one encounters 'the rhythmic patterns of the creative product', where the viewer interacts with the *actual* artistic object (Connery 2010: 23) rather than reproductions.

Providing young children with actual artworks and opportunities for deep engagement in social contexts has been problematic for researchers and teachers (Savva 2003; Tickle 1996). The doctoral dissertation project described in this chapter incorporated a unique semiotic methodology, where professionally produced artworks (paintings and sculptural works) were displayed in the kindergarten classroom over prolonged periods of time. The 'residing' artworks as semiotic and cultural tools provided opportunities for the children's extended and sustained engagement (sometimes over many days). They provoked children's semiosis (i.e. semiotic meaning-making) through a gradual and unfolding process of engagement, where the mind, body and emotions worked together, symbiotically, and where children's play-based encounters were mediated by social-cultural norms, rules and conventions.

Aims of the doctoral study

The aim of the study was to ascertain how deep engagement with artworks enables young children to explore, construct, appropriate and convey meaning about themselves and their world. Specifically, the focus was on how regular interactions with artworks allow children's semiosis to be transmediated through the multiple modes of embodied action, talk and the creation of their own artworks.

The unique feature of this visual arts dissertation is its methodology that involved the teachers and parents as co-researchers. Collaboratively, the co-researchers collected evidence of the 4-year-old children's semiotic transmediation at school and home. The unfolding nature of the children's semiosis became the focal feature determining subsequent residencies (e.g. the next artworks to be installed, the types of teacher interventions to be used). Additionally, the extensive use of participant video ethnographic techniques captured and made visible moments of semiotic action, some of which may have otherwise been unnoticed.

Methods

Participants, residing artworks and the co-construction of meaning

The participating children were 4-year-old kindergarteners, in a metropolitan school in Perth, Western Australia. All eighteen children in the class participated; however, data were collected on only six case-study children (three boys and three girls), selected by their teachers for their differences in interests, learning style preferences (e.g. visual, oral, embodied) and experiences with art.

In total, 33 artworks, on loan from nine professional artists, were displayed in the classroom in two-weekly residencies, over twenty weeks. Each residency had from two to five artworks on display, which focused on one theme (e.g. maps, family relationships, tea-parties). The artworks comprised of paintings and sculptural works (static, moving and sound-making), ranging in size from fitting into a child's hand, to occupying the space equivalent to a desk. They were displayed in prominent positions, with natural light and a large floor-space directly in front. The artworks were specifically selected to reflect the children's interest to help them make connections with the themes, content and elements in the artworks.

The school's pedagogic principles were inspired by the Reggio Emilia social-constructivist approaches to education. Hence, the artworks were seen as provocations and the children were encouraged to engage with them at their own volition throughout each day. Children were also provided with follow-on access to materials/resources (e.g. blocks, dolls, drawing tools) and spaces that stimulated their indoor and outdoor play within and across multiple modes (e.g. talk, drawing, construction and creative movement).

The focus was on how children expressed what they thought, felt and imagined through signs. A sign could be 'anything – a word, a gesture, an object, etc. – that stands for something or someone' (Danesi 1993: 2). Signs are a 'central fact of human existence' (Vygotsky cited in Ma 2014: 379).

Semiosis (i.e. semiotic meaning-making) refers to the innate capacity of people to create, appropriate, understand and express signs of all kinds. This process includes the acquisition of signs through sensory systems, after which they are perceived and interpreted to make meaning. Signs are then expressed through activity that may include a range of verbal and non-verbal modes, such as speech, drawing, movement, dance and storytelling. This dynamic activity leads to the creation of schemas of symbolic processes and objects that ultimately enables the development of new perspectives and meanings. This creative process involves flexible, holistic approaches, rooted in feelings, imagination and cognition. It is dependent on the individual's idiosyncratic capabilities and dispositions that make their meaning-making unique (Danesi 1993).

'Transmediation', as coined by Suhor (1984: 25), describes a process whereby the content and expression of one sign system is recast into another (that consists of different affordances), leading to the reconstruction of knowledge itself. Transmediation is a fundamental process for young children in particular, because they utilize multi-modal symbolic systems long before they are served by written text. Knowledge creation through transmediation is a continual process of transformations.

Opportunities for repeated viewing and continuous interpretation provided the children with time for the effect of the artwork and their actions to emerge (Vygotsky [1925] 1971). These were extensively expressed through various forms of play (e.g. imaginative, role play, dramatic). Play featured as the children's expression of signs. Games and dramatic enactments were frequently re-played, allowing the children to cross-modally express their ideas and feelings associated with the artworks.

The co-researching team: Data collection and analysis

The task of capturing semiotic transmediation in action became a shared labour between two classroom teachers, the pedagogista (art teacher) and the (doctoral) researcher during school time, in the classroom and playground. Parents of the case study children collaborated by also collecting information at home.

As a co-researching team, each member documented their naturalistic observations of the children's narratives, embodiment and artistic creations that related to the artworks. Members used hand- and/or computer-written notes (EDUCA, www.geteduca.com). They photographed the children's artefacts, such as drawings, sculptures and paintings, during production and on completion.

The researcher also used extensive video documentation in the classroom, which provided a comprehensive record of child-child and adult-child interactions. It captured the complexity and nuances of moment-by-moment encounters. Four small cameras were used – three fixed around the classroom and one hand-held. The video captured ephemeral artefacts, like dances, creative movement and role plays. The researcher was supported by the

Collaborative Research Network (CRN) through a funded fellowship programme (between Edith Cowan University Research Institute in Perth, and the University of Melbourne) with the aim of further developing video-based research.

At the end of each residency, the researcher met with the teachers in semi-structured meetings where they reviewed data from the preceding residency. They presented multiple perspectives and drew inferences that informed the researcher's ongoing analysis. It also informed subsequent residencies. For instance, the teachers arranged schedules, sought alternative resources and planned special activities. In total, there were seven meetings with the teachers.

Two semi-structured interviews were held with the parents. Additionally, there were numerous informal spur-of-the-moment meetings before and after school. The parents also contributed via email. Extensive data were generated during each residency. Analysis and interpretations from each residency were presented to the teachers and parents by the researcher for their verification and scrutiny. Data were stored, collated and analysed using NVivo 10 qualitative data-analysis software. The multiple perspectives of the co-researchers were used to validate the different phenomena and verify four broad NVivo nodes (oral, artistic, embodied and social). This rigorous open coding of all data generated 95 codes (oral – 34; artistic – 14; embodied – 15 and social – 32). Narrative inquiry was used to present the children's lived experiences across temporal (chronological), personal, social and spatial dimensions.

The researcher liaised between the co-researching team in Perth and the two doctoral supervisors at the University of Melbourne (co-authors of this chapter). The supervisors became critical peer reviewers to the co-researching team in Perth. They probed excerpts of data to identify any blind spots, checked for internal validity (e.g. consistency between data, potential bias, evidence-based findings and interpretations) and assessed each code's reliability in relation to the semiosis that was transmediated in the school and home settings. Their unique contribution to this external auditing process aided in the enhancement of the case study trustworthiness, credibility and dependability.

The processes and products that emerged from this study

The co-researching team became increasingly invested in the study as data from each residency yielded informative insights and contributed to increasing understandings about young children. As the team worked together, a sense of comfort, familiarity and routine developed. By the latter stages of the second residency, the teachers and the researcher adopted unique roles, such as becoming the children's play-mates or 'interlocutors', entering the children's zone of proximal development (ZPD) by participating in imaginative play and suspending disbelief, listening and seeking clarification (Wright 2010: 28). This gave the co-researchers an opportunity to deeply access the children's realities from two orientations: the children's inner (intentions and expressions) and their outer (self-interpretations and expressive activity) realities (Vygotsky [1925] 1971) and understand how the children mediated co-constructed meaning within a range of contexts (John-Steiner et al. 2010).

The teachers also implemented pedagogic approaches such as Visual Thinking Strategies (VTS) (Housen 2007), which supported children's theories and philosophies about each of the artworks. The VTS was adapted to a 15- to 20-minute, semi-structured, child-focused but teacher-facilitated activity, implemented two to three times a week for each of the five residencies. It made visible how the children shared their perceptions, feelings and thoughts with others in the group, and how they grappled with complex problems as they co-constructed knowledge.

The teachers also supported the development of a class-wide ZPD. This was a dynamic, multi-directional process that unified thoughts and emotions. It encouraged the unfolding of joint activities that incorporated interaction and scaffolded experiences. It supported conditions for meaning-making and processes of cross-modal transmediations – oral, artistic, embodied – within social contexts (John-Steiner et al. 2010).

Parents reported becoming increasingly mindful and involved with their child's responses to artworks at home. They also supported their child's ZPD by providing novel and extended activities (e.g. visiting galleries), sourcing art and craft materials and talking with their child about artworks. The parents recounted ZPD events through photographs, video clips and narratives. For example, as children appropriated the three-dimensional qualities of the residing sculptural artworks, they began creating their own sculptures at home. One parent relayed how she relinquished several kitchen utensils for her child's sculptural work. The collecting and sharing of data among the co-researchers became an insightful process. Eventually, a ZPD evolved among the co-researchers as greater understandings about young children's multi-modal semiotic transmediations emerged.

Documentation over time and across contexts: An excerpt of Victoria's semiosis and the co-researchers' collective knowledge creation

Longitudinal tracking of children's engagement occurred in two ways: when two co-researchers (e.g. a teacher and the researcher) simultaneously became involved in discussion or imaginative play with a child/or a group of children, or when a child expressed an idea to one co-researcher, which was then subsequently followed up by another researcher, later in the day, or the next. Similarly, ideas expressed during VTS discussions at school were tracked and documented by parents at home. An example is when in the second residency, Noam discussed with a teacher his theories about how the artist's sculpted teapots were made. His mother reported that, at home that evening, she had provided him with clay-like materials on his request so he could test his earlier theories.

An example of the co-researchers longitudinal tracking and documenting is evident with Victoria (aged 4 years, 8 months). On the first day of the first residency, Victoria expressed an interest about a particular icon in an artwork that represented fireworks. The artist, Sara

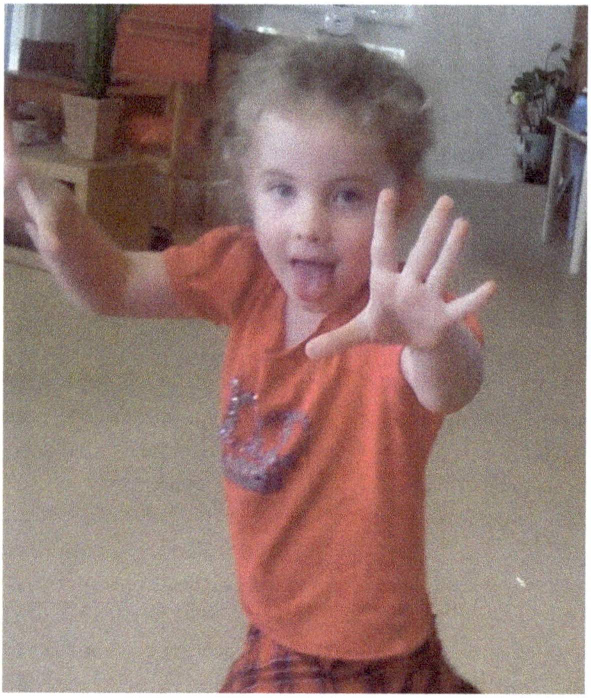

Figure 1: Victoria dancing the fireworks.

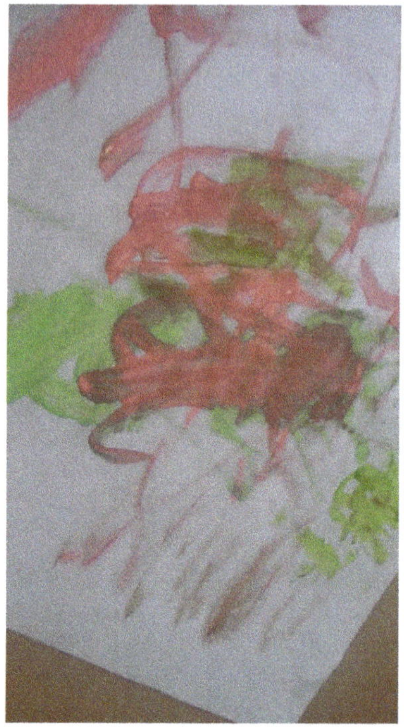

Figure 2: Victoria's painting of her dance moves.

Drake (www.saradrake.com), used shiny beads, threaded on wire, affixed to a canvas and protruding outwards, to depict fireworks during Australia Day celebrations. The following afternoon, after a VTS session, Victoria said to the researcher 'Julie, watch me sing the fireworks'. This cross-modal, metaphoric invitation to watch her dance was expressed with both hands in an opening-closing gestural action (depicting the twinkling light of fireworks). Gestures often preceded her whole body actions. Her dance was inspired by the form and her imagined content of the fireworks icon. It involved twirls of her body, repeated spreading of both arms upwards then slowly downward in a soft-floaty movement, facial expressions of concentration (tongue poking out), eye movements that followed her arms then feet, and her previously rehearsed hand actions (see Figure 1) as she 'became' the fireworks. Immediately afterwards she painted a picture of her dance moves (see Figure 2). Her mother reported that this painting was brought out that evening and showcased during a family performance of her dance. Victoria asked her mother to hold up her painting, so she would know her dance moves.

Victoria had a predisposition to dance. It proved to be her preferred mode across subsequent residencies. However, she also used several other modes – talking, painting and later, the creation of an accompanying song to enhance the meaning of her dance. Converting the meaning from one sign-system into another extended her thinking and feeling and therefore strengthened her expressions. The process of transmediation across these modes was gradual, as if she was trying each for their potential to accommodate her immediate needs, but always returning to her signature mode of dancing (using her whole body, or parts, such as her arms or hands).

Transmediation of children's semiosis: Transformations of teachers'/researcher praxis

The co-researching team agreed that capturing semiosis in action was an authentic process that offered a deeper awareness into how children expressed knowledge. As such, it provided unique and comprehensive insights. An example was when a child demonstrated his understanding of a complex concept of 'perspective' (that the class had previously grappled with) by instructing the teacher where to stand to take photos. Below is an excerpt from a teacher's transcript during the first semi-structured interview.

TEACHER-1: So today Mike [child] had made something with the clay and he said, can you take photos for my portfolio, and I said sure ok … so he bent down low so he could be in the photo, and he said you have to take three photos from different 'perspectives', and I said sure. Where will I take the next photo from? He went around the table and pointed there and from there [Teacher-1 pointed to high above the desk and then at desk level but from a distance away].

Another example is in the fifth residency where the children transmediated in response to Helen Seiver's nest sculptures (www.helenseiver.com). Although the emptiness of the nests was an intended message by the artist, emptiness created cognitive dissonance for the children (who thought that empty nests would be unhappy) so they filled the void by drawing pictures of birds and 'flying' them into the nests. This act was a semiotic critique by the children who commented that the artist would be thankful they had completed the sculpture for her.

Over the course of the five residencies, the co-researchers became highly astute in identifying and capturing moments of children's semiotic action. For the teachers, this provided an opportunity to become aware of children's cognitive and affective transformations as they occurred in the moment. Documentation of learning had already featured strongly in these teachers' practice; however, they reported that they had become even more proficient in noticing, tracking, articulating and documenting the process of semiotic transmediation as it unfolded to the benefit of their pedagogical practices.

Conclusions

This chapter has described how a research project investigated young children's meaning-making when the children were deeply engaged with artworks. The challenge of capturing semiosis in action was approached through a unique methodology where the teachers, parents and the (doctoral) researcher became a team of co-researchers collaboratively capturing, documenting and sharing extensive longitudinal data at school and home, over five, two-weekly residencies.

Also unique to this study were the methods the co-researchers used to enter the children's zone of proximal development as play-mates or interlocutors, from which emic perspectives were possible. A ZPD also evolved for the co-researchers themselves as the process of understanding children's semiosis gradually became evident and the significance of their learning was shared among the group.

An extension to the co-researching team was established when the doctoral supervisors (located on the other side of the continent) became critical peer reviewers and auditors. They probed and checked the data and inferences for the co-researching team in Perth, and in so doing, added a measure of scrutiny, trustworthiness and dependability to the study.

While the methods described in this study might be appropriate for other studies, clearly each study of this nature will have its unique journey and outcomes. It is hoped that other researchers will adopt aspects of this unique methodology to authentically and comprehensively investigate young children's semiotic transmediation.

References

Australian Curriculum Assessment and Reporting Authority (2016), *The Arts,* Education Services Australia, http://www.australiancurriculum.edu.au/the-arts. Accessed 14 February 2017.

Connery, M. C. (2010), 'The historical significance of Vygotsky's psychology of art', in M. C. Connery, V. P. John-Steiner and A. Marjanovic-Shane (eds), *Vygotsky and Creativity: A Cultural-historical Approach to Play, Meaning Making and the Arts,* New York: Peter Lang, pp. 17–26.

Danesi, M. (1993), *Messages and Meanings: An Introduction to Semiotics,* Toronto: Canadian Scholars' Press.

Drake, S. (2016), 'Illustrated 3D maps and globes', http://www.saradrake.com/. Accessed 14 February 2017.

EDUCA (2017), 'Online communications and documentation in one simple platform', http://www.geteduca.com/. Accessed 14 February 2017.

Housen, A. (2007), 'Art viewing and aesthetic development: Designing for the viewer', *VTS: Visual Thinking Strategies,* http://www.vtshome.org/. Accessed 7 May 2015.

John-Steiner, V., Connery, M. C. and Marjanovic-Shane, A. (2010), 'Dancing with the muses: A cultural-historical approach to play, meaning making and creativity', in M. C. Connery, V. P. John-Steiner and A. Marjanovic-Shane (eds), *Vygotsky and Creativity: A Cultural-historical Approach to Play, Meaning Making and the Arts,* New York: Peter Lang, pp. 3–16.

Langer, S. (1953), *Feeling and Form: A Theory of Art,* London: Routledge and Kegan Paul.

Leeds, J. (1989), 'The history of attitudes toward children's art', *Studies in Art Education,* 30:2, pp. 93–103.

Ma, J. (2014), 'The synergy of Peirce and Vygotsky as an analytical approach to the multimodality of semiotic mediation', *Mind, Culture and Activity,* 21:4, pp. 374–89.

Savva, A. (2003), 'Young pupils' responses to adult works of art', *Contemporary Issues in Early Childhood,* 4:3, pp. 300–13.

Seiver, H. (2014), 'Birdland', http://www.helenseiver.com/view/archive/birdland-goldilocks-region. Accessed 14 February 2017.

Suhor, C. (1984), 'Toward a semiotics-based curriculum', *Journal of Curriculum Studies,* 16:3, pp. 247–57.

Tickle, L. (1996), *Understanding Visual Art in Primary Schools,* London: Routledge.

Vygotsky, L. ([1925] 1971), *The Psychology of Art,* Cambridge: MIT Press.

Wright, S. (2010), *Understanding Creativity in Early Childhood: Meaning-Making and Children's Drawings,* Thousand Oaks: Sage.

Chapter 15

Connections, Disruptions and Reconfigurations: The Implications of Aesthetic Experience for Doctoral Research in the Visual Arts

Boyd White and April Mandrona

Finding common interests

We, the authors, have a common interest in aesthetic education, more specifically, the contributions of aesthetic experience to learning. However, in my (Boyd's) case, the teaching takes place in an arguably privileged setting, the university classroom and museum/gallery spaces. I was interested to see how aesthetic experience might play a role outside the confines of a university setting. April's recent doctoral research provided such a setting – a rural community in South Africa, a community beset by issues of poverty, post-apartheid racism, anti-child bias and epidemic illness, particularly HIV and AIDS. Although, at the time of this writing, we worked in the same faculty and department[1] and we knew we had common interests, we had not had much opportunity for conversations about our respective projects. We thought this paper would provide a good opportunity to begin that conversation. Dialogue, to us, suggests something invitational, exploratory. Further, community-based art education, and the research connected with it, depends on a sharing mindset. It is not top-down. For these reasons, dialogue seemed a reasonable format to adopt for this chapter. Preliminary discussions centred on Suzi Gablik's (1991, 1992) notion of connective aesthetics.

APRIL: Boyd, can you give me a brief overview of Gablik's concept of connective aesthetics?

BOYD: Gablik first introduced the phrase in her book *The Re-enchantment of Art* (1991) and elaborated upon the idea a year later in an article titled 'Connective aesthetics'. As the term 'connective' suggests, Gablik was trying to move beyond Baumgarten's ([1750] 1961) notion of aesthetics. Baumgarten was persuaded that 'the senses have an underlying principle, or logic' (White 2009: 25) and that principle, for Baumgarten, was beauty. But judgements of beauty ultimately result in reliance upon a standard. And standardization, in turn, implies repetition, imitation. Kant, in his *Critique of Judgement* (1790), maintained this emphasis on 'conformity to standards' (Crowther 1985: 63) and insisted that such conformity could only be arrived at through a process of disinterested attention. Contemporary thinkers, Gablik among them, reject the notions of disinterest and standardization in favour of engagement (see also Berleant 1991). However, Gablik rejects the notion of separation between art and daily life. She does not reject the notion of beauty. 'I think beauty is intrinsic to life on earth' (Gablik and Merriott 2007: 336). But certainly there is no standard in Gablik's concept of beauty, as her examples of artistic practice illustrate. What is more important to Gablik is the principle that art should take an ethical stance: '[w]e are all being called, in our understanding of what art is, to move beyond the mode of contemplation to something that is more participatory and engaged [...]' (Gablik 1998). By 'engaged' Gablik means to confront the world as it is, to wrestle with its problems. Gablik says, 'I think we need to have some compassion for the human plight' (Gablik and Marriott 2007: 338). In short, Gablik rejects the notion of art as an individualistic capitalist enterprise in favour of one that attempts to address the ills of the world through passionate community-minded interaction with the world.

APRIL: I find the concept of participatory community engagement particularly interesting, as it suggests that everyday activities can operate as a space of potential from which new values and sentiments may arise. Can you say more about how Gablik's aesthetic theory takes up the aesthetic/affective aspects of vernacular creative practice?

BOYD: To expand a little on what I mentioned before, Gablik's theory of art combines social, aesthetic and moral dimensions. The intertwining of those three foci implies a transdisciplinary[2] emphasis – people working jointly to move beyond the restrictions of their own areas of specialization. Art requires a sharing of perspectives and methods. Likewise, her concept of aesthetics requires a dedicated sharing, hence her use of the term *connective*. Out of that sharing, new perspectives may arise, and with them, altered values. Is it possible that your project in South Africa might be said to exemplify some of Gablik's ideas?

APRIL: My introduction to South Africa occurred through my involvement with the Rural Teacher Education Project, which offers practicum opportunities for pre-service teachers from the University of KwaZulu-Natal. I was invited to participate as an onsite coordinator by Dr. Claudia Mitchell, one of the project co-founders from McGill University. My participation was a springboard for connecting with specific rural communities.

The central question of my dissertation asked, 'what can we make with this?' The artmaking, which utilized local and found resources (knowledge and materials), was intended not only to build artistic skills but also to provide opportunities for creative expression.

BOYD: Attention to formal artistic skills appears to be of minor interest to Gablik. My sense is that Gablik associates artistic skills with the commercial, competitive artworld. The nurturing of creativity, on the other hand, is certainly a key concern of hers. She says: 'I believe there is a new evolving relationship between personal creativity and social responsibility [...]' (Gablik 1991: 6).

APRIL: To pick up on her phrase 'personal creativity and social responsibility', the purpose of my research was to work collaboratively with rural, resource-constrained communities, with particular focus on young people, in order to develop and implement art activities that responded to context.

In the research context, the role of artmaking as pedagogy, creative expression, social responsibility and products used for exchange was not easily teased apart. The end purpose of an artwork was often unpredictable and the intentions for it often shifted, depending on the need and wants of the participants and those around them.

The interactions between the participants and myself were built around collaborative artmaking and a form of reflexive ethnography. I viewed the artmaking and the ethnography as operating in tandem to develop my research into a more ethical, dialogic and empowering practice, and also to explore what meaning these concepts had in the particular context. The reflexive aspect of constructing an ethnography served as an ongoing evaluative mechanism for how I interacted with the community.

For example, our explorations of substances like clay and wood brought up questions about what it might mean to be connected to the land as a young black person. Under apartheid in South Africa, black people were confined to rural areas and were prohibited from travelling unless they had official documents indicating that they could enter urban areas for purposes such as work. Historically, urban centres have been cast as comparatively civilized with populations that are wealthier, more educated and healthier. The role of rural areas in sustaining collective survival, however, is occluded. The relationship between the contemporary young people with whom I worked and 'the land' is understandably complex.

BOYD: Do you mean a kind of love/hate relationship?

APRIL: Perhaps what these young people were articulating was the layered and nuanced ways in which rural and urban locales and the associated value systems interact in contemporary South Africa. They often expressed to me a desire to leave the rural areas, as they felt their location had few opportunities to offer. Some of them had never left the countryside and they wanted to travel to the coastal city of Durban to see the ocean and investigate the attractions of the urban centre, such as shopping malls. On another occasion, a group of girls announced emphatically that they hated speaking their mother tongue, isiZulu. One member added that just because they were black, outsiders assume they have strong ties to all aspects of their 'culture' but in fact they actively chose to reject various identifiers. On the other hand, they also recognized the value of their participation in certain activities. For example, when I proposed the idea of making things out of clay as an activity, one of the girls said, 'I know where to get clay'. When we arrived at the spot, it was possible to tell that people had been digging in specific areas, perhaps for months or years. The river was a place where many things seemed to happen. Cattle drank from it, people washed clothes, clay was dug and there were sometimes offerings related to spiritual belief systems. The river is definitely connected to community life in both concrete and more abstract ways. That is, this clay digging activity connected them to larger systems of cultural and community practices.

BOYD: It seems as though your participants actively considered social ties and/or constraints. And one might argue that their concern with the variables in their materials, such as clay, showed aesthetic, even formal interests. What about Gablik's third focus, the moral component? Gablik regrets the secularization of our contemporary western culture. So, for her, the moral is intimately connected with spirituality. Did you get any sense of that influence in your participants?

APRIL: Gablik contends that due to the relationship between capitalism and art institutions, artists are often disconnected from the social, spiritual and environmental life of communities. But the influence of the capitalist marketplace is far reaching, especially in poor areas and with young people that crave financial independence. I think the art of these young people highlights the fundamental difficulties of working against capitalism. These young people have been consistently marginalized by that very system, but their survival and that of their community is also dependent upon it.

BOYD: If I can return to the topic of ethnography for a moment, could you say more about the artmaking and ethnography operating in tandem? That is, I understand how ethnography provided you with a lens through which to study the community's involvement in artmaking. I wonder if your ethnographic inclinations also influenced the directions that the art projects took and ultimately, your views on art education.

APRIL: My ethnographic lens influenced how I thought about and contributed to the artistic activities of the young people in terms of what materials or topics I introduced and discussed. I was prompted to think deeply about materials and what meanings they had in the context. Found and repurposed items became central to our artmaking. Often it was only after the materials had been deemed unneeded or useless by adults that they were accessible to the young people.

BOYD: You mention local specificity – materials and traditions. Can you elaborate on that, and perhaps explain how children's artmaking responded to certain community issues? Was there any art education in the community prior to your arrival? I am curious to know how you persuaded the people that artmaking would be a positive contribution to the community.

APRIL: South Africa has a rich heritage and contemporary expressions of various art forms that are present throughout the country – ceramics, basketry, beadwork, photography and other hybrid and street-based practices like graffiti and performance. Aesthetic devices find a presence everywhere in the country, but formal school-based art instruction tends to be located in private, well-resourced or government schools. There continues to be a disconnect between official policies on art education in schools, what is happening on the ground, and in art institutions. There are persistent barriers to accessible art education opportunities in rural communities, as well as for lower income areas more generally. Rural locales are still recovering from a history of strategic underfunding and racist schooling policies.

Formal art education exists in the schools I worked with under the arts and cultures curriculum, but this is a broad subject area and visual arts education was dependent on the resources available to the teachers, which were minimal. Informally, many of the students made art independently or engaged in intergenerational art practices such as beading.

BOYD: So, in a sense, your work with the community's youth was a natural extension of certain social practices already in place. South Africa's rich heritage of material culture – the beading, ceramics and so forth – point to strong connections to the land, the people and their histories. And yet, as you point out, that cultural richness is acquired informally. Formal education largely ignores this connection. Projects like yours would appear to be a necessary extension of informal education, to acknowledge and celebrate connectedness, between oneself and one's material culture, and between oneself and others. Can you talk a little about your research project in terms of how it was manifested in daily interactions with the community's youth?

APRIL: My research in art education explored notions of bricolage, or working with what is at hand. Through this approach I sought to further support what was, as you suggest, already happening in the communities. I invited interested young people to participate and they brought with them existing skills, knowledge and aspirations. We focused on assemblage, sewing, beading, woodworking and ceramics. These activities were an opportunity for us to develop alternative creative spaces. The relationship with systemic issues emerged organically as we made things together. The participants attempted to create social forms that challenged their sense of alienation engendered by disease, violence and poverty. Let me clarify this point, as I am referring to both the artworks and the social processes involved in production. The artworks may not have directly taken up social issues in terms of symbolic meaning. For example, none of the students made work that was about 'AIDS', 'exclusion' or 'poverty' explicitly. Rather, the making of art with their peers could be described as acts of solidarity or creative resistance that helped to strengthen existing social bonds or create entirely new ones. It was the act of coming together as a working group in the creative moment that was particularly important to them. In turn, for some, the art sessions served as the impetus to a source of income and the formation of additional peer or family art groups.

BOYD: You emphasize the participants' use of 'what is at hand'. Often the materials available to the young people were what the adults deemed worthless. This suggests that in this context it is not only about raw materials but also community values. Could you elaborate?

APRIL: There appeared to be several things at play. In some cases, the original socially assigned value of materials such as scrap wood seemed to be maintained after the young people had transformed them into art objects. In one instance a participant was offered money by one of the teachers for a wooden bench he had built, but it was considerably less than what they were being sold for by local adults. This situation may have reflected general attitudes towards the work of young people as 'not real work'. Conversely, another participant described how, after seeing what she had made from clay, her grandmother insisted she continue to pursue the activity to decorate their home. Whether or not adults saw the young peoples' art as meaningful contributions to local visual culture was dependent on relational specifics.

BOYD: So your initiative spurred an awareness of common interests and a desire for communal action. Certainly such desires conform to Gablik's definition of art as a shared endeavour, although I am not sure her related notion of transdisciplinarity would apply here. Would it be fair to say that the artmaking enabled a degree of self and community expression that was previously unarticulated?

APRIL: While the participant groups could be described as homogenous in terms of demographic indicators such as age, race, ethnicity and education level, they each brought unique approaches to the artworks. By my working with them as someone with different life experiences and expertise, perhaps we were engaging in a communal transdisciplinary effort, albeit on a very small-scale. Although the young people are by no means professionals operating within particular intellectual domains, the example of creating with clay implies connections between geography, ecology, art and chemistry.

I find Glynis Cousin's work on researcher positionality, and reflexivity helpful. Her approach acknowledges difference and the effects of unequal social structures, but also explores ways of possible connection, in this case between researchers and participants. Cousin (2010) suggests that reflexivity includes proposing to participants 'possible horizons of meaning: (Holstein and Gubrium 1997: 125), and perhaps the skill of the researcher [...] may be more important than their personal biography and status as an insider or outsider' (15). Collaboratively negotiating an alternate vocabulary or mode of representation for experiences, emotions and larger issues can become a vehicle for the articulation of realities that may otherwise be nameless or formless. Through both teaching and artistic expression, the possibilities of an 'enabling vocabulary' (Cousin 2010: 15) expand in multiple directions.[3]

Concluding comments

In this chapter we have introduced Gablik's concept of aesthetics to show how it could be applied to April's research in a rural South African context.

The connections to which we initially alluded are apparent in participants' use of local materials, in their shared efforts at artmaking and in their perspectives on their world. The disruptions are exemplified in participants' desire for something more for themselves – for a move beyond traditional community constraints and towards a more democratic sharing of power and resources; for an end to enduring poverty, disease and violence; and for a move beyond stereotypes, both western and homegrown.

Reconfigurations are represented in the re-use of otherwise abandoned or ignored materials, an emerging and enlarged sense of self-identity among the participants, and a perception of art education that takes place outside the classroom and is unconstrained by separation of craft from western notions of art. The artwork produced as a result of April's project is decidedly instrumental in purpose.

The participants in this project were not introduced to Gablik's theory. Indeed, concerns centred on pragmatic day-to-day challenges. Nonetheless, we hope that we have illustrated how Gablik's aesthetic theory provides a research framework for understanding and addressing those challenges.

References

Baumgarten, A. G. ([1750] 1961), *Aesthetica*, Hildesheim: G. Olms.

Berleant, A. (1991), *Art and Engagement*, Philadelphia: Temple University Press.

Cousin, G. (2010), 'Positioning positionality: The reflexive turn', in M. Savin-Baden and C. H. Major (eds), *New Approaches to Qualitative Research: Wisdom and Uncertainty*, New York: Routledge, pp. 9–18.

Crowther, P. (1985), 'Fundamental ontology and transcendent beauty: An approach to Kant's aesthetics', *Kant-Studien*, 76:1–4, pp. 55–71.

Gablik, S. (1991), *The Re-enchantment of Art*, New York: Thames & Hudson.

——— (1992), 'Connective aesthetics', *American Art*, 6:2, pp. 2–7.

——— (1998), 'The nature of beauty in contemporary art', http://moncon.greenmuseum.org/papers/gablik.pdf. Accessed 12 February 2017. Originally published in *New Renaissance*, 8:1.

Gablik, S. and Marriott, J. (2007), 'Of tipping points and sinking ships: A conversation between James Marriott and Suzi Gablik', *Studies in Art Education*, 48:4, pp. 336–40.

Holstein, J. and Gubrium, J. (1997), 'Active interviewing', in D. Silverman (ed.), *Qualitative Research: Theory, Method and Practice*, London: Sage, pp. 113–29.

Kant, I. ([1790] 1957), *Critique of Judgement* (trans. J. C. Meredith), Oxford: Clarendon Press.

Mandrona, A. (2014), 'What can we make with this? Creating relevant art education practices in rural KwaZulu-Natal, South Africa', PhD thesis, Montreal: Concordia University, http://spectrum.library.concordia.ca/979094/1/Mandrona_PhD_F2014.pdf. Accessed 26 October 2018.

White, B. (2009), *Aesthetics Primer*, New York: Peter Lang.

Notes

1 April has since accepted a position at Nova Scotia College of Art & Design.
2 Transdisciplinarity is a rather different notion from multidisciplinarity. The latter maintains methodological specialization but attempts to adapt it to fields outside its normal purview.
3 Sections of the above text have appeared previously in 'What can we make with this? Creating relevant art education practices in rural KwaZulu-Natal, South Africa' (Mandrona 2014).

Part 3

Provoking Doctoral Programmes

Chapter 16

Navigating Ethics Protocols for Artistic Research: Strategies for Graduate Student Researchers

Lorrie Blair

Practice-led research (see, for example, Vaughan 2005), practice as research (Sullivan 2010), research-creation (Chapman and Sawchuk 2012; Manning 2015) and studio-based inquiry (Barrett and Bolt 2010) are some of the many labels given to the activities involved with the creative process and the production of artworks in academic settings. While the names differ, there is consensus among these authors that artmaking is a way of knowing and of generating new knowledge. Chapman and Sawchuk note that '[k]nowledge is produced as creative work, and not simply through its analysis and interpretation' (2012: 14). Sullivan supports this notion, stating that artistic research has the capacity 'to create knowledge that can help us understand in a profound way the world we live in and how we learn to make sense of it' (2010: xi).

Who and what govern the ethics policies for research?

Ethical protocols and regulations differ among countries and research sites. Some are more casual in their approach, while others are quite stringent (Koski 2012). However, all research must comply with the host country's laws protecting human and animal research. For example, in the United States, the Department of Health and Human Service's (2009) *Code of Federal Regulations, Human Subjects Research* is charged with the protection of human subjects. The Canadian Institute of Health Research, Natural Science and Engineering Research Council, and the Social Science and Humanities Research Council's (2014) *Tri-Council Policy Statement of Conduct for Research Involving Humans* determines the guidelines and principles for research in Canada. Both documents set out clearly defined rules for a peer-review process. In the United States, the review committee is called an institutional review board (IRB) and in Canada, a research ethics board (REB). Research sites such as schools or hospitals often have their own ethics procedures and review boards and approval from one's university may not be reciprocated. Indigenous and community cultural practices may need separate consideration and consent. When publishing their findings, researchers may be required to demonstrate that their research adheres to the ethical standards of their home country or, in some cases, from the country in which the journal is published (McGrath et al. 2010).

While templates for ethics approval vary among research sites, most deal with four principles: potential for harm, confidentiality, informed participation and freedom to discontinue. Briefly, the researcher must clearly articulate the benefits of the research both to the participants and to society as a whole. Participants must know the level of privacy they will be afforded by the researcher. They must know they are the subjects of research, and how and when the researcher is collecting data. Usually, they must be given adequate information to permit them to know what the researcher is studying. Participants who provide information must be informed of how and where their information will be published or presented. Lastly, participation must be voluntary and participants have the right to withdraw from the research. Artistic research complicates many of these principles, including notions of who is a participant. For example, if an artist makes a painting about her youth, in which her parents can be identified, are her parents research participants? Are those who view the painting regarded as participants? These questions will be taken up in greater detail later in the chapter.

Animal research is governed by policy and all proposed academic research involving animals is peer reviewed. Again, laws and policies differ greatly from country to country. And like research with humans, researchers must conduct research in compliance with both the host country and their home country, if different. For example, the *Canadian Council on Animal Care in Science* (1989) guides animal research in Canada and the National Research Council (2011) oversees ethical treatment in the United States. The policies establish the three 'r's: replace, reduce and refine. Replacement refers to finding ways to replace animals with other systems, such as computers or by replacing certain species with others thought to have lower potential for pain. Reduction means designing studies to use the minimum number of animals possible and refinement means enhancing animal welfare to minimize pain and stress. According to these policies, animals may be used in research only if there are no possible alternatives and researchers must demonstrate best efforts to find an alternative to using animals for research have failed. If animals are to be used, the research must demonstrate that the species chosen for the study is best suited to answer the research question (American Psychological Association 2012).

History is replete with examples of ethically questionable artistic practices involving animals, including Guillermo Vargas's exhibition of a starving dog chained to a wall and Marco Evaristti's *Helena* (2000), featuring ten blenders, each filled with water and holding a single gold fish (Cashell 2009). Audience members were aware of the consequences of pushing the blender's buttons and two did just that. In many cases, the artists and their defenders argue their art benefits society because it was intended to provoke, shame or disgust viewers (Cashell 2009). Vargas claimed to raise awareness of the plight of animals, though only after an Internet backlash (Gigliotti 2010). It may be said these artists are responding to animal cruelty and suffering by inflicting the same. In response to such artwork, the College Art Associate adopted the three 'r's and further state, '[n]o work of art should, in the course of its creation, cause physical or psychological pain, suffering, or distress to an animal' (2011). However, guidelines differ from standards, in that standards require mandatory compliance, whereas guidelines allow review boards to make decisions based on judgement. The fact that animals cannot give their consent to being experimented on is a major point of contention for any use of animals in research (Kerr 2016).

Some researchers are exploring the notion of animals as co-creators. For example, a recent interspecies art collaboration between some tent caterpillars and two graduate students, Alison Reiko Loader and Christopher Plenzich, featured video installations, handmade textiles, drawings made by the caterpillars and custom viewing boxes housing research insects raised on site (Loader 2015a). The researchers followed ethical protocol, which included a consideration of how the invasive and destructive caterpillars would be ethically killed at the end of the exhibition (Loader 2015b). Loader and Plenzich inhabited the space for much of the exhibition to care for caterpillars and monitor them for any signs of stress (Loader 2015a). At the end of the exhibition, Loader and Plenzich were required to kill the caterpillars in the way they would die naturally in the cold climate. For this, they slowly reduced the temperature, mimicking winter. They could not release them into nature because these caterpillars are an invasive species. There was no backlash in this case, for potentially a number of reasons, including public perception.

Addressing the potential for harm in artistic research

Researchers are required to identify the risk for harm and indicate how they will minimize its effects on participants. Risk levels range from minimum to high, and include physical, psychological, financial and social risks. Research is deemed to have minimal risk when harm or discomfort is not more than that which one would encounter in everyday life and when participants are healthy adults over the age of 18. Boydell et al. (2011) note that artistic modes of representation create heightened experiences that increase the likelihood of making an impact, be it positive or negative. For example, some photo elicitation methods may include 'evocative imagery' that 'holds the danger that participants might suffer emotional harm from reliving upsetting events' (Boydell et al. 2011:11). In this regard, Cox et al. (2014) posit that the use of arts in research can cause harm not normally considered by ethics committees. This is especially the case when participants are individuals marginalized by society or when research deals with emotionally charged subjects (Holtby et al. 2015). Cox et al. remind researchers who invite others to co-create that, 'it may be difficult for participants to fully understand the effects of producing images' (2014: 12). This is amplified when participants are unfamiliar with academic modes of presenting and exhibiting art. At times, art is created in a supportive environment, which can give the participants a false sense of security. Guta et al. warn that, 'they may not fully be prepared for a diverse spectrum of reactions from the general public (which can sometimes be quite negative)' (2014: 8). They recommend researchers help participants understand the consequences of sharing work and consider if some works should not be shared. They also note that researchers should make participants aware that 'once a piece is shared (especially online) it is nearly impossible to be removed from the public domain' (Guta et al. 2014: 6).

The potential of harm usually applies to participants but some artists cause deliberate harm to themselves. For example, Marina Abramovic and Chris Burden, both active in the 1970s, used their bodies as their medium. Burden, for *Shooting Piece* (1971), asked a friend to shoot him with a handgun. He claims the shot was intended to graze his left arm, but the friend missed and 'instead blew away a large piece of flesh' (Goldberg 2001: 159). Abramovic's *Rhythm 0* (1974) involved the artist standing in a gallery for six hours, surrounded by objects, including knives, scissors, a needle and a loaded gun. Abramovic permitted spectators to use the objects in any way they wanted. According to Goldberg, '[b]y the third hour, her clothes had been cut from her body with razor blades, her skin slashed; a loaded gun held to her head finally caused a fight between her tormentors, bringing the proceeding to an unnerving halt' (2001: 165). Eliza Bennett's work, *A Woman's Work Is Never Done* (2012), provides a more recent example of self-harm. Bennett sews designs directly into her hands, a 'gruesomely precise handiwork [that] serves to remind the viewer of the strife of women laborers, many of whom are paid far less than their male counterparts' (Pitt 2014: 1).

Self-harm in Canada is not illegal, but depending on provincial legislation, it can result in assessment and/or detention in a medical facility; in the United States the right to intentionally injure one's own body without suicidal intent is protected by the 14th amendment of the United States constitution (Rezek 2009). However, the right to harm one's self does not extend to allowing others to harm the artist. Burden's friend and anyone who might have pulled the trigger of the gun in Abramovic's performance are subject to laws prohibiting such behaviour. Additionally, their performances place audiences at risk. Exhibits and performances can have unintended consequences for audiences, and Boydell et al. warn that audience members who view artistic research may be placed on 'dangerous emotional terrain' (2011: 10). They posit, '[i]mages or experiences have emotional overtones that stay with us, even if hidden for a time in the recesses of our consciousness, only to return and provoke at a later time' (2011: 10). They recommend audience members be given information about the research in advance of an exhibition or performance, and that researchers have a plan to debrief audiences and offer support to audience members who are negatively impacted by the work. For example, when Yehudit Silverman (2010) screens her documentary film, *The Hidden Faces of Suicide*, which features her research with those who lost love ones to suicide; she allows time for audience members to discuss the film and she makes available contact information about local groups such as Family Survivors of Suicide and Suicide Action crisis lines.

Informed participation and confidentiality

Artist-researchers must provide participants with the opportunity to give informed consent before the research begins and allow them to determine their preferred level of confidentiality in presentations, publications and exhibitions. Generally, an exhibition or performance is equated to a scholarly presentation, which does not require audience members to sign consent forms (Cox et al. 2014). Members of the audience are regarded as participants when the artist generates information through audience participation and iterative design.

Members of the audience became participants when they used the blenders in Evaristti's exhibition or interacted with Abramovic. Blackstone et al. suggest that: 'In areas such as performance, installations, and interactive new media, prior advertisement or introductory descriptions of the creative work [...] constitute the necessary information for the participant to buy a ticket, attend a gallery, or initiate a computer session' (2008: 9). They suggest researchers post warnings about candid photography or highly violent content, but regard attendance as voluntary as long as members of the audience are free to leave at any time.

Levels of confidentiality range from fully identified to fully disclosed. Boydell et al. (2011) note that some review boards insist all participants be completely anonymous. This poses serious problems for photographers, videographers and film-makers. In some instances, anonymity is impossible to achieve. Researchers who plan to use identifiable visual data should plan for lengthy review times. Being known and 'being seen is not an uncomplicated desire for many marginalized individuals' (Holtby et al. 2015: 1), and people who appear in artworks, such as videos, can be vulnerable. Citing ethical concerns for those who work with communities affected by HIV, Guta et al. (2014) suggest using drama to recreate events on video or to stage photographs to provide greater anonymity.

Tracy Emin and Sophie Calle, both celebrated artists, create artworks that involve others without their consent. For her work, *The Address Book*, Calle purportedly found an address book on a Paris street and copied its pages before returning it anonymously to the owner. She then contacted individuals listed in the book to gather information about the owner. Without the owner's knowledge or permission, Calle published her findings in the newspaper, *Libération* (Calle 1988). Tracey Emin's tent, *Everyone I Ever Slept With* (1997), was appliquéd with the names of everyone with whom the artist shared a bed (Kalb 2013). If contextualized as artistic research, it is unlikely that Emin's and Calle's works would be granted ethics approval. In most cases, researchers must obtain ethics approval for research that identifies individuals in any written texts, visual images or oral presentations. These individuals are entitled to the same rights as participants in any other research. The subject of Calle's work neither consented to be part of the work nor was he given the freedom to discontinue.

Admittedly, the need to protect a participant's rights can conflict with the researcher's artistic vision. Such was the case for graduate student Ciciola-Izza (2014) who used family photographs as personal visual memories to explore self-identity and social roles in the context of her marriage, motherhood and daughterhood. The resulting artworks included collages and paintings of these memories. Because her elderly mother was unable to give consent to appear in the artwork, Ciciola-Izza elected to make the work as an artist but not present it in her thesis. She instead included written reflections taken from her journal about making the artwork. The compromise allowed Ciciola-Izza to make personally meaningful work while ensuring the ethical integrity of her research. It should be noted that this case provides one example of ways in which students can work with review committees. Another ethics review committee might have rejected this compromise, or have suggested an alternative. There are no definitive answers to the many ethical questions that artist-researchers may face and it is advisable for graduate students to ask questions and dialogue with their supervisors about any potential ethical dilemmas.

Working with review boards

Government guidelines require that review committees be comprised of faculty members from various disciplines to ensure that the proposals are viewed from multiple perspectives. Each review committee is unique. It is possible that some committees will have no artist representation. Some committee members may be unfamiliar with the artistic milieu and some may be unsympathetic to artistic research. The onus is on the artist-researcher to justify the benefits of the proposed inquiry as research, not argue its value as art. Freedom of expression does not apply in this way to other disciplines.

Research ethics boards have the authority to approve, require modifications or deny requests. There are no definitive answers to ethical questions and one ethics committee might approve a request, while another denies it. Universities usually have procedures to appeal the decision, but arguing with an ethics review board will delay the research process. These delays can have an adverse impact on graduate students with strict timelines for completion. Those planning to conduct international research should consider partnering or collaborating with local researchers who are likely to be aware of the rules, laws and customs that guide animal or human research in their county.

It is time to leave behind metaphors of the ethics approval process as a border crossing or as a hurdle to jump over in order to get on with research. Ethical practice is an integral part of research. Instead, the ethics review process can help graduate students to become critically aware of the rights of those who participate or co-create knowledge, and of the rights of audience members to whom they present their findings. By working collaboratively with ethics review committees, graduate students can pave the way for future researchers by providing valuable feedback that will improve how committees assess requests for art research. They can provoke a greater understanding of the ethical challenges of artistic research and encourage committees to make changes to existing protocols to better reflect the nature of artistic research.

References

American Psychological Association (APA) (2012), 'Guidelines for ethical conduct in the care and use of nonhuman animals in animal research', http://www.apa.org/science/leadership/care/guidelines.aspx. Accessed 1 June 2015.

Barrett, E. and Bolt, B. (2010), *Practice as Research: Approaches to Creative Arts Enquiry*, London: I. B. Tauris.

Blackstone, M., Given, L., Lévy, J., McGinn, M., O'Neill, P., Palys, T. and van den Hoonaard, W. (2008), *Research Involving Creative Practices: A Chapter for the Inclusion in the TCPS*, http://www.pre.ethics.gc.ca/eng/archives/policy-politique/reports-rapports/ricp-ripc/. Accessed 1 June 2015.

Boydell, K., Volpe, T., Cox, S., Katz, A., Dow, R., Brunger, F., Parsons, J., Belliveau, G., Gladstone, B., Zlotnik-Shaul, R., Cook, S., Kamensek, O., Lafrenière, D. and Wong, L. (2011), 'Ethical challenges in arts-based health research', *The International Journal of Creative Arts in Interdisciplinary Practice*, 11, pp. 1–17, www.ijcaip.com/archives/IJCAIP-11-paper1.pdf. Accessed 30 June 2015.

Calle, S. (1988), *Suite Vénitienne*, Seattle: Bay Press.

Canadian Council on Animal Care in Science (1989), 'Guidelines', http://www.ccac.ca/en_/standards. Accessed 25 June 2015.

Canadian Institute of Health Research, Natural Science and Engineering Research Council of Canada, and Social Sciences and Humanities Research Council of Canada (2014), 'Tri-council policy statement: Ethical conduct for research involving humans', http://www.pre.ethics.gc.ca/eng/policy-politique/initiatives/tcps2-eptc2/Default/. Accessed 1 June 2015.

Cashell, K. (2009), *Aftershock: The Ethics of Contemporary Transgressive Art*, London and New York: I. B. Tauris.

Chapman, O. and Sawchuk, K. (2012), 'Research-creation: Intervention, analysis and "family resemblances"', *Canadian Journal of Communications,* 37:1, http://www.cjc-online.ca/index.php/journal/issue/view/138/showToc. Accessed 31 May 2014.

Ciciola-Izza, R. (2014), 'Mother/Art: A journey into selfhood, motherhood and art education through personal works', MA dissertation, Montreal: Concordia University.

College Art Association (CAA) (2011), 'The use of animal subjects in art: Statement of principles and suggested considerations', http://www.collegeart.org/guidelines/useofanimals. Accessed 1 July 2015.

Cox, S., Drew, S., Guilleman, M., Howell, C., Warr, D. and Waycott, J. (2014), *Guidelines for Ethical Visual Research Methods,* Melbourne: The University of Melbourne, https://artshealthnetwork.ca/ahnc/ethical_visual_research_methods-web.pdf. Accessed 12 August 2015.

Gigliotti, C. (2010), 'Heartburn: Indigestion, contention and animals in contemporary art', *Antennae: The Journal of Nature in Visual Culture*, 14:Fall, pp. 25–34, http://www.antennae.org.uk/back-issues-2010/4583475279. Accessed 3 June 2015.

Goldberg, R. (2001), *Performance Art: From Futurism to the Present*, New York: Thames & Hudson.

Guta, A., Flicker, S., Travers, R., Greene, S., Munro, L., Strike, C. and Switzer, S. (2014), 'HIV CBR Ethics fact sheet #4: Ethical issues in visual image-based research', Improving the Accessibility of Research Ethics Boards for HIV Community-Based Research in Canada, http://www.hivethicscbr.com/. Accessed 15 August 2015.

Holtby, L., Klein, K., Cook, K. and Travers, R. (2015), 'To be seen or not to be seen: Photovoice, queer and trans youth, and the dilemma of representation', *Action Research,* 13:4, pp. 317–35.

Kalb, P. (2013), *Art Since 1980: Charting the Contemporary*, London: Laurence King.

Kerr, D. (2016), 'Why won't artists leave animals alone? On the questionable ethics, and rising popularity, of critter art', *Artspace Magazine*, http://www.artspace.com/magazine/interviews_features/the_big_idea/animal-art-ethics-53858. Accessed 30 September 2016.

Koski, K. (2012), 'Ethics and data collection in arts-based inquiry: Artist-researcher embedded in medical education', *International Journal of the Creative Arts in Interdisciplinary Practice*, 11, www.ijcaip.com/archives/IJCAIP-11-paper4.pdf. Accessed 30 June 2015.

Loader, A. R. (2015a), 'En masse', http://alisonloader.com/en-masse/. Accessed 1 November 2016.

——— (2015b), personal correspondence, 27 May.

Manning, E. (2015), 'Against method', in P. Vannini (ed.), *Non-Representational Methodologies: Re-Envisioning Research*, New York: Routledge.

McGrath, J. C., Drummond, G. B., McLachlan, E. M., Kilkenny, C. and Wainwright, C. L. (2010), 'Guidelines for reporting experiments involving animals: The ARRIVE guidelines', *BJP: British Journal of Pharmacology*, 160:7, pp. 1573–76.

National Research Council (2011), *Guide for the Care and Use of Laboratory Animals*, Washington, DC: National Academies Press.

Pitt, B. (2014), 'Woman artist embroiders her own hand; Internet erupts in debate', http://bust.com/arts/11785-woman-artist-embroiders-her-own-hand-internet-erupts-in-debate.html. Accessed 15 August 2016.

Rezek, N. (2009), 'Is self-harm a constitutionally protected right?', *Quinnipiac Health Law*, 12, pp. 303–31, www.quinnipiac.edu/.../14_12QuinnipiacHealthLJ303(2008-2009).pdf. Accessed 12 November 2016.

Silverman, Y. (2010), *The Hidden Faces of Suicide*, Canada.

Sullivan, G. (2010), *Art Practice as Research*, Thousand Oaks: Sage.

United States Department of Health and Human Services (2009), 'Human subjects research: Code of Federal Regulations', https://www.hhs.gov/ohrp/regulations-and-policy/regulations/45-cfr-46/index.html. Accessed 12 June 2014.

Vaughan, K. (2005), 'Pieced together: Collage as an artist's method for interdisciplinary research', *International Journal of Qualitative Methods*, 4:1, pp. 1–21, https://www.ualberta.ca/~iiqm/backissues/4_1/html/vaughan.html. Accessed 2 April 2014.

Chapter 17

Examining the Case for Artful Participatory Inquiry in the Visual Art Education Doctorate

Kathryn Grushka and Allyson Holbrook

Arts-informed approaches

The transforming potential of arts-informed approaches has emerged as a new and substantive theme in visual art education not least in visual art education doctorates (Haseman 2015; Knowles and Cole 2011). A visual art education doctorate is driven by the discipline of education and the latter embraces a spectrum of epistemological positions from empirical work through philosophy to cutting-edge qualitative arts-informed inquiry methods. Arts-informed inquiry methods employ a focus on the 'artistic, disciplined and imaginative qualities of the arts' in the qualitative paradigm (Knowles and Cole 2008: 3) and respond to the increasing connectivity between knowledge domains, literacy forms and interpretations. The methods cross boundaries and create bridges from one discipline to another (jagodzinski and Wallin 2013; Rees 2010), an approach that is particularly pertinent in modern, cross-disciplinary, problem-solving contexts.

When framing a study, the doctoral student in visual arts education must identify and articulate the educational purpose and potential contribution of their study. They also need to become aware of how the dominant educational terrain is shifting and is challenged by arts-informed research perspectives that carry post-qualitative ideas (Lather and St. Pierre 2013). These ideas provoke questions and tensions around issues of discipline, contribution, quality and the forms of the visual art education doctorate.

This chapter focuses on the problematics of artful participatory inquiry practices in visual art education research for the mainstream education community. The potential of this method to reflect and represent the complexities of learning in new communication environments, such as the learning encounters between teachers/students and their relational pedagogies (Cole 2011), will be discussed. The initial section will explore how artful inquiry, within arts-informed research, embraces post-qualitative theory in seeking to represent knowledge as an assemblage able to capture knowledge as non-linear, non-hierarchical, unstable, shifting, mobile and multiple (Deleuze 1990; Masny 2016).

Those who adopt artful inquiry in art education research transform their inquiry approaches in efforts to best capture, analyse and render the agency of the learner or the pedagogical event. Academics in education and the social sciences question the limits of transferability, validity and the contribution of these methods and their representational approaches for personal and social transformation. The chapter raises issues arising from this research orientation and provides an example of a research learning space that crosses digital and material practices. Artful participatory inquiry is presented as an inquiry perspective in the new digital, e-learning visual studio environment as best situated to digitally capture the interactive reflexivity between student and teacher, and render research insights in the form of relational entanglements (Lather 2016) accessible for the wider academy.

Artful inquiry in visual education research

Artful inquiry within doctoral research has emerged in response to the ongoing quest of researchers to legitimize the arts as ways of knowing in qualitative research (Barone and Eisner 2012; Fleming et al. 2015). This has materialized in part by co-opting established methods (jagodzinski and Wallin 2013) from disciplinary fields such as ethnography, auto-ethnography, phenomenology, narrative and critical theory, among others, to extend the reach of artistic academic thinking within educational research.

Artful inquiry carries visual symbolic forms that include, but are not limited to, arts-based methods (Finley 2005), auto-ethnographic narrative methods (Denzin 2006), collage methods (Butler-Kisber and Poldma 2010), poetics of inquiry (Prendergast et al. 2009) and arts-based self-study methods (Mitchell et al. 2005).

Among a growing number of approaches, artful inquiry in visual education research aims to describe the aesthetic learner experience, whether teacher or student (Springgay 2011), in curriculum and pedagogical research (Sameshima and Irwin 2008), and as embodied and performatively generated for personal agency (Semetsky 2003). Artful inquiry acknowledges that the teachers' or learners' subjectivity, or 'becoming' or 'being', are manifest in contradictory, schizoid forms. As subjectivity assemblages they are malleable and shifting, often unable to be contained or defined. Artful inquiry also acknowledges that the dialogues between the learners (teacher/student) reveal *possibilities* (Deleuze and Guattari 1987) and should be seen as spaces open to multiple interpretive positions.

In turn, a/r/tography (Irwin et al. 2006; Springgay et al. 2005) has emerged as a genre/sub-field for the visual educator community. It is described as a re-territorization of the visual art doctorate, 'mobilised in the image of the artist's creative impulse' (jagodzinski and Wallin 2013: 87). The approach begins with a commitment to a process of thinking that draws on the imagination continually moving beyond what is, to what could be through the capture of transformative learning spaces. With an auto-ethnographic framing, it resides in the practices of artists, researchers and educators (Irwin and de Cosson 2004). A/r/tography also seeks a poetic communicative position over traditional educational descriptive methods (Rees 2010). Image and text are not separate or illustrative to each other but interconnected and interwoven to enhance learning (Springgay et al. 2005).

A/r/tography has transnational traction in arts and education research (Burke et al. 2014; Dixon and Senior 2011; Gouzouasis et al. 2013), along with teacher self-study as arts-informed research (Grushka and Young 2014; Mitchell et al. 2005). It also continues to draw interest from researchers across transdisciplinary contexts (Biggs and Büchler 2007; Haseman 2015).

Issues and controversies in the translation to new knowledge

There is concern expressed in the literature about the homogenization of methods and knowledge (Gidley 2013) in connection with qualitative research in the past decade. The post-qualitative researcher, in rejecting the 'brute' qualities of qualitative ways of knowing, has become an emancipating and invigorating space for artists. Yet even those who lead in the post-qualitative educational realm tell of the struggle to maintain dialogue with others in the discipline (St. Pierre 2014). Researchers who work with artful inquiry resist the educational rhetoric of complexity reduction that moves towards uniformity (Gough 2011). Instead it is focused on relational pedagogies, complexity and the expressive and constructed emergence of knowledge. By foregrounding uncertainty (Sameshima and Irwin 2008), artful inquiry is positioned in the post-qualitative turn, wherein knowing is not privileged over being (Lather and St. Pierre 2013) and insights take a plastic form. Evolving from the ideas of bricolage, this approach seeks to reveal different interpretive complexities to the assemblage (Masny 2016) and brings to bear different artistic forms in order to reveal ontological moments as learning. Rosiek identifies this as a methodology located in an ontology that 'co-constitutes' a relationship 'between inquiry practice' and 'future possibilities' (2013: 692). In addition, artful inquirers are skilful semiotic practitioners who generate material representations that carry boundary qualities. Boundary qualities in artful forms hold possibilities and the mapped effects of differences (Davies 2018). Artful forms enact indeterminacy, can be read from different epistemic positions and thus disrupt traditional academic boundaries (Barad 2014). With mainstream education research still firmly committed to the representation of epistemic matters and pedagogical theories linguistically, the capacity of artful inquiry to communicate within mainstream educational research looms as an issue.

The problem with post-qualitative knowledge production

Visual educator researchers are opting for the concept of productive assemblage or a mixing of artistic forms within non-hierarchical materialist ontologies located in Deleuzian thought (Sameshima and Irwin 2008). They are responding to a post-qualitative position that considers productive assemblages as spaces that give rise to the possibilities of events and intensities. For Deleuze and Guattari (1987) these spaces are smooth, dynamic, borderless and nomadic. Deleuze (1993) in his work on the fold further extends this space to one that is continually folding and offers up unlimited diversity of combinations. For Barad (2014) this space is also a differencing space of intra entanglements as well as offering up new patterns of engagement when producing knowledge. This position argues that educational research must break the ties with methods-phenomenology, logical positivism and linear and representational logic (St. Pierre 2014), along with the logic of investigating current teaching practice through an examination of past student learning and past pedagogical acts. Such acts have been represented often from a bricolage of artist, teacher, researcher interpretive perspectives, which then take on an intentional form. Rosiek (2013: 696) calls the post-qualitative shift a 'temporal inversion in pragmatic inquiry' to move beyond interpretive representations to the creative generation of new concepts (Masny 2016). This productive force is affectively driven, drawing on the inner complexities of the mind to bring forth new forms or ways of rendering the imagination of the learner. Arts-based methods of representation in visual art education research have gained levels of legitimacy, such as visual narratives or montaged methods of interpretive insights (Grushka 2010), yet they too are problematized within the post-qualitative knowledge space. How can the visual art educator represent their research in order to reveal the entanglement between processes and co-constructed productive meanings located in relational ontological spaces of learners' and teachers' voices (Stetsenko 2008)? How does the researcher capture the problematics of representing such voices (which in the visual arts may lie within the yet-to-be resolved-ideas of an artwork), while at the same time recognizing and accepting the gap between different desires, experiences, intensities, material encounters, actions, flows or speculative understandings (Mazzei 2013)? How can the burgeoning knowledge that is manifest within a learning moment or event be communicated and made accessible to the wider educational academy?

The problem of interpretation and audience

MacLure describes representations in qualitative research as a 'back-formation', 'sedentary, categorical and judgmental' (2013: 659), presenting a barrier to change and the emergence of new knowledge. To counter this limitation, artful methods straddle modes of 'practice/reflection' associated with 'artmaking' and 'the poetics of material experimentation and personalization', and the practices of 'text making' (Cabeleira 2015: 379). The need for a coherent narrative voice is abandoned (Mazzei 2013), as artful inquiry instead opts for revealing sense within reflexive artistic forms as imaginative possibilities (Hayes et al. 2014). Yet the art forms selected to communicate becoming as an event and the possibilities of burgeoning interpretations, remain shaped by the collective experiences of audiences and prompt legitimate questions for doctoral researchers about whom they seek to reach.

Critics of arts-informed inquiry say it is neither art nor research (Pariser 2009; Rees 2010). Others claim it has special ontological status and a research discourse that cannot be transferred within or across the disciplines of the academy (Kjorup 2010). The frustration with artful inquiry is that traditional academics do not think of the arts, or artful methodologies, as giving rise to worthwhile new knowledge, despite inroads over the last decade (Johnson 2010).

The problem with mapping and self-rendering

For a doctoral student to make a contribution to knowledge, they have to have encountered and understood the antecedents to that knowledge, its history and its theories, even if they are being rejected. Post-qualitative research and artful inquiry did not develop in a vacuum and post-qualitative thinking requires post-formal thinking and an appropriate pedagogy (St. Pierre 2014; Gidley 2013). This is the challenge for visual arts educators, as ultimately researchers have to communicate effectively what and how they know if workable transdisciplinary research is to occur.

The positivist stance in research places the self at the centre of the inquiry (object), and understandings emerge from a logo-centric interrogation of the past in order to deal with the present. Post-qualitative research shifts from a fixed external objective reality towards a decentred self or a practice-in-action (Haseman 2015: 334). Contradictions exist when artful inquiry has a preoccupation with self-exploration and self-rendering (jagodzinski and Wallin 2013: 85), attracting similar criticism about subjectivity claims as does auto-ethnographic research and action narrative research (Heikkinen et al. 2007; McCarthy 2014). The problem for the visual art education research community, who argue that the universal 'emerges from the particular' (jagodzinski and Wallin 2013: 57) is that knowledge resides, evolves and shifts with the centred researcher self, with attendant issues ever present in arts research higher degrees (Simmons and Holbrook 2013).

Cartographic methods such as visual mapping or topographical analysis have also been co-opted by arts researchers to reveal process or action (Smith 2015) shifting beyond traditional qualitative analyses of coding (Lather and Pierre 2013). Mapping as diagrammatic reasoning is not the sole domain of artists, many researchers map, plot or draw connections and relationships between data to represent models or fixed schemas. Indeed any artistic symbolic, metaphoric or abstract construct of research data also renders a fixed form. In short, academic protocol requires artists to lock down their understandings. Cartographies of becoming (Masny 2013) are presented as able to map the shifting lines of unpredictable rhizomic directions, and contemporary art maps demonstrate this very process in a variety of aesthetic forms (Obrist 2014). Mapping, nonetheless, can render spatial complexity in many aesthetic forms as a decentred activity where voices, imaginings and ideas intersect.

Artful participatory inquiry in the photographic e-learning environment

Artful participatory inquiry was conceived as a methodology suitable for researching the photographic e-learning environment (Grushka et al. 2014; Grushka and Bellette 2016) and teacher/learner pedagogies for transformational knowledge. Its application to visual art education research may offer ways to work productively with criticisms of current arts-inquiry approaches applied in educational settings. Participatory inquiry is active learning, a knowledge generation practice between teacher and student, emerging from the intersection of the critical/reflective teacher self and participatory research in education (Kemmis 2011). When combined with arts inquiry the focus is on the relational attention we give to how phenomena exist as qualities, artistic renderings and dialogical spaces, between participants (teachers and students) and their learning entanglements as they emerge through their own and other interactions such as audiences, including learning peers.

Implicit in artful participatory research is the idea that contemporary studio learning in schools and universities is now influenced by an interconnected global ecology and visual arts education researchers can access the mapping and productive power of social media and the computer 'machine'. The computer, with its multisemiotic digital communication structures (Bailey and van Harken 2014) and socially curated lenses, drives mobile participatory capacities (Cochrane and Antonczak 2013). Human and non-human interactional materialities combine to render *collaborative learning as* 'embedded, situated, distributed and co-constructed' (Stetsenko 2008: 477).

Virtual and e-feed platforms are able to actualize the decentred self; software tools are able to manage multimodal and text-based data, and have the computational capacities to gather and analyse multiple forms of generated data as flows or cartographies of meaning. Artful inquiry in the e-learning environment as a space where ideas and images are deposited, manipulated and distributed may be an option that has the potential to (re)position visual elements as actualizing forces within new media 'process-power' (Parikka 2012: 98). It also has the contemporary semiotic force to straddle epistemological fields while still allowing the artistic forms of research to be represented. For instance, Grushka and Bellette (2016) provide examples of how the student voice in e-learning journals can be co-present with the teacher reflective voice in ways that represent the spaces and flows as complex juxtaposed voices when using e-feed and e-portfolio spaces.

The addition of artful participatory inquiry could be described as plugging into the voices of participants within collectively performed assemblages (Livesey 2010). The assemblages can be virtual and/or material interactions that connect and produce knowledge as creative participation (Gaztambide-Fernández 2015). They do not emanate from a single subject or conversation but are 'body-less' enactments (Mazzei 2013: 733), ontological spaces that track and reveal conceptual insights to be analysed and reflected upon by the educational researcher, teachers and learners.

Research spaces in the e-learning context of artful participatory inquiry are argued as able to replace linear narratives with new digital spatial forms (van Alphen 2014). Artful inquiry in the e-learning participatory research carries this non-linear spatial construct (Grushka et al. 2014). While a screenshot may look like a series of emergent ideas pasted and grouped by both teacher and student without resolution, they represent the entangled thinking of this co-constructed learning in virtual and digital process. Also present are:

- The artefacts, the embodied and performative representations of artistic learning.
- Computer software: artefact and text(s) capture, recording devices as time based data. The data they generate can be used for analysis, image manipulation, production, storage,

documentary and archival access and retrospective analysis. While captured and coded in real time, its retrieval can mirror the iterative thinking of learning teacher/student and carry multifaceted voices and concepts.
- The e-feed journal: journaling is integral to artful inquiry (Butler-Kisber and Poldma 2010). The e-feed journal for instance takes the form of a blog. It re-conceptualizes the journal as evidence of a relational ontology emergent between human and non-human materialities, between multifaceted studio production and social media activities. It can capture critical dialogues between self and others, theoretical, historical or aesthetic choice and artisitic intent through concepts or artefacts, or by collapsing time-coded cognitive work as iterations or imaginings.

Discussion

Can artful participatory inquiry with a focus on the decentred self as practice-in-action offer a new pedagogic position? One that additionally harnesses the computation power of digital voice(s), captures the co-constructed and (possibly digitally) re-presented nature of learning. Its complex assemblages can be named, tracked and verified from either existing educational concepts and/or rendered through new artful forms. Such methods provide continuous access points to multiple digital data sets including artefacts, digital software files and e-journals. Traditional qualitative inquiry methods of 'observation' and 'interview' can be added to further strengthen the interpretive legitimacy of the voices occupying this emerging virtual research space. For example, the overlaying of digital data sets supports verification and checking of information to enhance validation. Reasoning through relational materialities can be digitally mapped and multimodal renderings (such as video bites, audio and blog reflections) can be easily collapsed to generate new intersections and reveal meaning.

The problems associated with mapping and self-rendering as fixed knowledge forms (jagodzinski and Wallin 2013) can be addressed by revealing shifting or unstable stories or events mapped as affective learning moments. For example, a series of screenshots can reveal this complexity. The multiple layering of digital files can simultaneously reveal and render emergent ideas as processes, imaginings and multiple interpretations. When artistic virtual renderings of multiple learning events are layered to reveal complexity, they acknowledge the collaborative transformations of audiences and learners. The researcher aims not to present a coherent narrative but reveal the complexity and relationality of the phenomena of study.

Artful renderings do not reject subjectivity claims. They aim to pry open ontological spaces and their relationships and re-represent them as digital encounters in order for the audience to imagine and make sense of the cognitive moments presented. Intensities can be revealed through screenshots that show the cutting together-apart and bleeding ideas of Barad (2014). Artful participatory inquiry can imagine futures now currently limited by fixed and stable forms (Mazzei 2013). Scepticism of the academy that the visual art researcher can shift beyond an ontology of self, firmly present in the productive spaces of personal artistic renderings remains a challenge for visual art educator researchers. Art education researchers who are seeking research that resonates more broadly in qualitative educational research must address such concerns. Artful participatory inquiry opens a space where the visual art educator can acknowledge their affective self, learner voices and their co-constructive presence in the generation of knowledge. It can also reveal how the relationality of learning folds or overlays and can be visualized as cartographic flows within an evidence-driven digital trail. Visual learning as empirical evidence can then lever our understanding of the ontological productive space with a capacity to demonstrate the imaginative and indeterminate nature of embodied learning in visual arts education.

Challenges for artful inquiry

As mainstream education research remains firmly committed to the representation of epistemic matters and pedagogical theories, the challenge for artful inquiry is how to render its relational ontological insights about cognition, embodiment, material and digital ontologies in learning in ways that resonate with the wider educational academy. Doctoral students in visual arts education are challenged by artful inquiry methods carrying post-qualitative ideas, as all representations, in any art form, require the fixing of ideas from past events. Criticisms about the limitations of artful inquiry methods need to be addressed. They must investigate how an ontology of self is caught up in the messiness of virtual relational materialities and that while digital evidence abounds, it also struggles to map and render knowledge within and across these boundaries as they re-represent visual art education research.

Artful participatory inquiry employs a research space constructed in real-time and spatially tagged. It is interactive, non-linear and participatory. Its methods provide points of connection between the image as object, the student and their relational aesthetic choices, and the praxis of the teacher. Decentring the teacher/learner/self by drawing on social media learning tools, the e-journal and the process-power of digital media platforms together with the cartographic power of the computer opens additional ways to evidence events and texts. This e-learning research site may well have legitimacy and reveal the next space of teacher and learning research.

References

van Alphen, E. (2014), *Staging the Archive: Art and Photography in the Age of New Media*, London: Reaktion Books.

Bailey, N. and van Harken, E. M. (2014), 'Visual images as tools of teacher inquiry', *Journal of Teacher Education*, 65:3, pp. 241–60.

Barad, K. (2014), 'Diffracting diffraction: Cutting together-apart', *Parallax*, 20, pp. 168–87.
Barone, T. and Eisner, E. (eds) (2012), *Arts Based Research*, Thousand Oaks: Sage.
Biggs, M. and Büchler, D. (2007), 'Rigor and practice-based research', *Design Issues*, 23:3, pp. 62–69.
Burke, G., Peterken, C., Hall, C. and Bennett, R. (2014), 'Belonging, being and becoming in the arts through a/r/tography: (Re)imagining early childhood education', *Australian Art Education*, 36:2, pp. 22–39.
Butler-Kisber, L. and Poldma, T. (2010), 'The power of visual approaches in qualitative inquiry: The use of collage making and concept mapping in experiential research', *Journal of Research Practice*, 6:2, pp. 1–16.
Cabeleira, H. (2015), 'The politics and the poetics of knowledge in higher arts education', *International Journal of Education Through Art*, 11:3, pp. 375–89.
Cochrane, T. and Antonczak, L. (2013), 'Mobile social media as a catalyst for creative pedagogy', *EC-TEL 2013 Eighth European Conference on Technology Enhanced Learning: Scaling Up Learning for Sustained Impact*, Paphos, Cyprus, 18 September.
Cole, D. R. (2011), *Educational Life-Forms: Deleuzian Teaching and Learning Practice*, Rotterdam: Sense.
Davies, B. (2018), 'Ethics and the new materialism: A brief genealogy of the 'post' philosophies in the social sciences', *Discourse: Studies in the Cultural Politics of Education*, 39:1, pp. 113–27.
Deleuze, G. (1990), *Negotiations*, New York: Columbia University Press.
——— (1993), *The Fold: Leibniz and the Baroque* (trans. Tom Conley), Minneapolis: University of Minnesota Press.
Deleuze, G. and Guattari, F. (1987), *A Thousand Plateaus: Capitalism and Schizophrenia*, London: Athlone Press.
Denzin, N. (2006), 'Analytic autoethnography, or déjà vu all over again', *Journal of Contemporary Ethnography*, 35:4, pp. 419–28.
Dixon, M. and Senior, K. (2011), 'Appearing pedagogy: From embodied learning and teaching to embodied pedagogy', *Pedagogy, Culture & Society*, 19:3, pp. 473–84.
Finley, S. (2005), 'Arts-based inquiry, performing revolutionary pedagogy', in N. Denzin and Y. Lincoln (eds), *The Sage Handbook of Qualitative Research*, 3rd ed., London: Sage, pp. 681–94.
Fleming, M., Bresler, L. and O'Toole, J. (2015), *The Routledge International Handbook of the Arts and Education*, New York: Routledge.
Gaztambide-Fernández, R. (2015), 'Thinking beyond the human', *Curriculum Inquiry*, 4:3, pp. 245–48.
Gidley, J. (2013), 'Global knowledge futures: Articulating the emergence of a new meta-level field', *Integral Review*, 9:2, pp. 145–73.
Gough, N. (2011), 'Foreword', in D. R. Cole (ed.), *Educational Life-Forms: Deleuzian Teaching and Learning Practice*, Rotterdam: Sense.
Gouzouasis, P., Irwin, R. L., Miles, E. and Gordon, A. (2013), 'Commitments to a community of artistic inquiry: Becoming pedagogical through a/r/tography in teacher education', *International Journal of Education and the Arts*, 14:1, pp. 1–23, http://www.ijea.org/v14n1/. Accessed 4 March 2016.
Grushka, K. (2010), 'Montage as visual art research', *Australian Art Education*, 33:1, pp. 72–91.

Grushka, K. and Bellette, A. (2016), 'Artful inquiry in the e-learning journal', *Learning Landscapes: Artful Inquiry: Transforming Understanding through Creative Engagement*, 9:2, pp. 261–79.

Grushka, K. and Young, B. (2014), 'Using arts-based methods in pre-service teacher education: Perzine pedagogies', *Studying Teacher Education: A Journal of Self-Study of Teacher Education Practices*, 10:3, pp. 275–89.

Grushka, K., Bellette, A. and Holbrook, A. (2014), 'Researching photographic participatory inquiry in an e-learning environment', *McGill Journal of Education*, 49:3, pp. 621–40.

Haseman, B. (2015), 'The radical in arts education research', in M. B. Fleming and J. O'Toole (eds), *The Routledge International Handbook of the Arts and Education*, New York: Routledge, pp. 334–44.

Hayes, M., Sameshima, P. and Watson, F. (2014), 'Imagination as method', *International Journal of Qualitative Methods*, 14:1, pp. 36–55.

Heikkinen, H., Huttunen, R. and Syrjala, L. (2007), 'Action research as narrative: Five principles for validation', *Educational Action Research*, 15:1, pp. 5–19.

Irwin, R. L. and de Cosson, A. (2004), *A/r/tography: Rendering Self through Arts-Based Living Inquiry*, Vancouver: Pacific Educational Press.

Irwin, R. L., Beer, K., Springgay, S., Grauer, K., Xiong, G. and Bickel, B. (2006), 'The rhizomatic relations of a/r/tography', *Studies in Art Education*, 48:1, pp. 70–88.

jagodzinski, j. and Wallin, J. (2013), *Arts-Based Research: A Critique and Proposal*, Rotterdam, Boston and Taipei: Sense.

Johnson, M. (2010), 'Embodied knowing through art', in M. Biggs and H. Karlsson (eds), *The Routledge Companion to Research in the Arts*, New York: Routledge, pp. 141–51.

Kemmis, S. (2011), 'A self-reflective practitioner and a new definition of critical participatory action research', in N. S. Mockler (ed.), *Rethinking Educational Practice through Reflexive Inquiry: Essays in Honour of Susan Groundwater-Smith*, New York: Springer, pp. 11–29.

Kjorup, S. (2010), 'Pleading for plurality: Artistic and other kinds of research', in M. K. Biggs and H. Karlsson (eds), *The Routledge Companion to Research in the Arts*, London and New York: Routledge, pp. 24–43.

Knowles, J. G. and Cole, A. (2008), *Handbook of the Arts in Qualitative Research*, Thousand Oaks: Sage.

—— (2011), 'Drawing on the arts, transforming research: Possibilities of arts-informed perspectives', in L. Markauskaite, L. Freebody and J. Irwin (eds), *Methodological Choice and Design: Scholarship, Policy and Practice in Social and Educational Research*, 9th ed., Dordrecht, Heidelberg, London and New York: Springer, pp. 119–31.

Lather, P. (2016), 'Top ten+ list: (Re)thinking ontology in (post) qualitative research', *Cultural Studies, Critical Methods*, 16:2, pp. 125–31.

Lather, P. and St Pierre, E. (2013), 'Post-qualitative research', *International Journal of Qualitative Studies in Education*, 26:6, pp. 629–33.

Livesey, G. (2010), 'Assemblage', in A. Parr (ed.), *The Deleuze Dictionary*, Edinburgh: Edinburgh University Press, pp. 18–19.

MacLure, M. (2013), 'Researching without representation? Language and materiality in a post-qualitative methodology', *International Journal of Qualitative Studies in Education*, 26:6, pp. 658–67.

Masny, D. (2013), *Cartographies of Becoming in Education: A Deleuze-Guattari Perspective*, Rotterdam: Sense.

——— (2016), 'Problematizing qualitative research: Reading a data assemblage with rhizoanalysis', *Qualitative Inquiry*, pp. 1–10.

Mazzei, L. (2013), 'A voice without organs: Interviewing in posthumanist research', *International Journal of Qualitative Studies in Education*, 26:6, pp. 732–40.

McCarthy, T. (2014), 'Introduction', in H. U. Obrist (ed.), *Mapping It Out*, London: Thames & Hudson.

Mitchell, C., O'Reilly-Scanlon, K. and Weber, S. (eds) (2005), *Just Who Do You Think We Are? Methodologies for Autobiography and Self-Study in Education*, London and New York: Routledge.

Obrist, H. U. (2014), *Mapping It Out*, London: Thames & Hudson.

Parikka, J. (2012), 'New materialism as media theory: Media natures and dirty matter', *Communication and Critical/Cultural Studies*, 9:1, pp. 95–100.

Pariser, D. (2009), 'Arts-based research: Trojan Horses and Shibboleths. The liabilities of a hybrid research approach. What hath Eisner wrought?', *Canadian Review of Art Education*, 36, pp. 1–8.

Prendergast, M., Leggo, C. and Sameshima, P. (2009), 'Poetic inquiry', *Educational Insights*, 13:3, pp. 743–44.

Rees, J. (2010), 'Art education in Canada: Reflections from scholars impacting the field', *International Journal of Education Through Art*, 6:1, pp. 25–40.

Rosiek, J. (2013), 'Pragmatism and post-qualitative futures', *International Journal of Qualitative Studies in Education*, 26:6, pp. 692–705.

Sameshima, P. and Irwin, R. L. (2008), 'Rendering dimensions of a liminal currere', *Transnational Curriculum Inquiry*, 5:2, pp. 1–15.

Semetsky, I. (2003), 'The problematics of human subjectivity: Gilles Deleuze and the Deweyan Legacy', *Studies in Philosophy and Education*, 22:3&4, pp. 211–25.

Simmons, B. and Holbrook A. (2013), 'From rupture to resonance: Uncertainty and scholarship in fine art research degrees', *Arts and Humanities in Higher Education*, 12:2&3, pp. 204–21.

Springgay, S. (2011), 'The ethico-aesthetics of affect and a sensational pedagogy', *The Journal of the Canadian Association for Curriculum Studies*, 9:1, pp. 66–82.

Springgay, S., Irwin, R. L. and Kind, S. (2005), 'A/r/tography as living inquiry through art and text', *Qualitative Inquiry*, 11:6, pp. 897–912.

St. Pierre, E. A. (2014), 'A brief and personal history of post qualitative research toward post inquiry', *Journal of Curriculum Theorizing*, 30:2, pp. 2–19.

——— (2016), 'Rethinking the empirical in the posthuman', in C. A. Taylor and C. Hughs (eds), *Posthuman Research Practices in Education*, London: Palgrave Macmillan, pp. 1–14.

Stetsenko, A. (2008), 'From relational ontology to transformative activist stance on development and learning: Expanding Vygotsky's (CHAT) project', *Cultural Studies of Science Education*, 3:2, pp. 471–91.

Chapter 18

Some Iberian Perspectives about Arts-Based and Artistic Research in Arts Education

Teresa Torres de Eça and Ângela Saldanha

Juan Carlos Araño, a well-known researcher in art education in Spain, pointed out art as experience and experience as knowledge as a starting point to discuss research in art education (Araño 2015). Art education needs more scholars studying problems or questions that are timely and that contribute to current policy debates or dilemmas of practice across a great variety of research methods. Quantitative, qualitative, artistic or arts-based methods are all necessary to enrich knowledge in our field. According to Araño, to understand where we are now in the field of research in art education we should look to the work of John Dewey (1934) and the three essential axes pointed out by him: a pragmatic view to construct the aesthetic world; reflections about knowledge through art and science from an experiential strand; and a vision of the living creature. Araño also refers to cognitive studies and especially to Jerome Bruner (1960) and Elliot Eisner (1991) who challenged the positivists who shaped research for many decades. Jerome Bruner helped us to search for research tools more adapted to art and education. For many years, art education researchers did not question recognized ways of doing research. Instead we used methods from other fields and adapted them to our needs. Similar to Araño, Spanish researcher Fernando Hernández acknowledges Elliot Eisner's influence (Eisner and Peshkin 1990) and the narrative inquiry turning point, particularly with Denzin and Lincoln (2000) who were among the most influential authors of research methods for researchers in Portugal and Spain in the last decades. We welcomed the rise of narrative inquiry with Michael Connelly and Jean Clandinin (Clandinin 2007; Clandinin and Connelly 2000). Postmodern views affected our ways of understanding education, as well as art and design and history, moving us away from the so-called 'scientific methods' and positivist epistemology (Hernández and Rifà 2011), and we are now moving to activist forms of collaborative research (Pardiñas and Trigo 2012).

Sometimes art education researchers need other ways for collecting and analysing data and reporting results that are more related to the subject of our studies. For example, images such as video, photography and drawings have been widely used in many fields of research (Margolis and Pauwel 2011; van Leeuwen and Jewitt 2002) as data, not as research methods. Artistic processes of thinking, analysing, synthesizing and exposing theory and practice only very recently entered the field of research, mainly designated as arts-based research methods or ABR – an inclusive term that describes methods that use art and artistic processes as a main component of research (McNiff 2008). But such approaches are subject to severe criticism in Portuguese and Spanish-speaking countries, as Aguirre and Araño have expressed. Artistic research and arts-based research are sometimes confusing approaches, embedded in lyrics, poetics and subjectivity that may throw art education away from the academic mainstream of education. For Aguirre and Araño there is a major need for clarification of arts-based approaches in art education research if we are to safeguard our field, which is already at risk and needs solid and recognized research. For José Maria Lema from the University of Coruña, artistic and arts-based research methods are attractive in art education, as a current trend, but do not yet have a substantial research corpus, and are sometimes ambiguous with vague concepts. Very often we see interesting artistic and arts-based biographical studies that are vaguely related to art education, so we must question its impact in the field. Arts-based and artistic methods are not criticized because they are not purposeful or rigorous, but they are questioned in terms of their validity and utility in social and political terms.

Nevertheless, ABR is growing in the field of art education. Under the umbrella we may include arts-based educational research (ABER), a/r/tography, arts-informed research, practice-based and practice-led research, and artistic research. For Pilar Perez from the University Autonoma of Madrid, arts-based research methods have instilled flexibility and interdisciplinary possibilities for researchers in art education (Perez 2015). Joaquin Roldán and Ricardo Marín advocate for photo-essays as a research tool (Marín and Roldán 2010). Moreover, Ángel García-Roldán used video art, José Maria Lema used photography and photoactivism, Marta Madrid used comics and illustration (García-Roldán 2012; Lema 2012; Madrid 2015), Judit Vidiella and Maria Morales used performance as a narrative inquiry tool (Vidiella 2008; Morales 2015), and Ângela Saldanha used community-based art practices as a collaborative research process (Saldanha 2015). Ricardo Marín, among others, believes the number of doctoral theses using artistic and arts-based methods will continue to grow in the years ahead.

Hernández explains the doctoral programme in art education in the University of Barcelona as following three main axes: subjective narratives, narrative inquiry and performance-based pedagogies. For Hernández, the research group in Barcelona approaches ABR as a method where images and artistic practices are used for social research. In the University of Jaen, Isabel Moreno speaks about two main methodological approaches: arts-based and artistic research. For her, arts-based research starts to be 'based' in the way the paradigm or approach will be sustained by research built on the arts as the main media. Artistic research is more about using creative processes to develop the doctoral study. In our correspondence Moreno stated:

> In both cases I try to help the doctoral student by giving him or her advice in terms of organization. I shadow their inquiry process; I help them in looking for the rationale to discuss paths for inquiry and design alternatives, provoking situations. When the student is engaged in artistic research, the process is based on dialogue rather than proposing organizational alternatives.
>
> (2015)

Joaquin Roldán, from the University of Granada, stresses the need for logical design structures that will hold both narrative (discourse) and analysis (systematic) instruments:

> In our group we believe it is necessary to develop and justify not only the sources that justify the methodology, but the instruments themselves to be used. For example, there are some theses that use a series of pictures as a research tool [...] we try to clearly describe these instruments: its nature, its role in research, its relevance, new developments and their instrumental shortcomings in view of the results. Thus, others can use these instruments in the future.
>
> (2015a)

In universities like Porto, Lisboa, Barcelona, Jaén, Girona, Madrid, Santiago de Compostela and Granada, doctoral students in art education programmes come with very different backgrounds, some of them have some knowledge and experience about research methods acquired during master's degrees, others do not. To overcome the discrepancies, some doctoral programmes in art education promote seminars about research methods and a few of them promote seminars about arts-based and artistic research methods. For Paiva and Martins, at the University of Porto, and for Marín and Roldán at the University of Granada, the research centre, that is, the university and the department, plays a major role in defining and shaping research. In the case of Porto, we have a discussion group of graduate students, and in the case of Granada, they have what is called a research incubator. Group dialogue between researchers is essential to discuss alternatives. The main concern across all universities is to be consistent with methodologies, so the research process can be justified in academia. As Roldán stated, to 'keep specific lines of research and encourage research in these lines is the best solution' (2015b).

In the University of Porto, Portugal, the doctoral programme in arts education includes a great array of research methods for studies in dance, museum, drama, visual arts, design and multimedia education. Some graduate students are using specific lenses, like artistic research and arts-based research methods. Many doctoral students and post-doctoral researchers who are trained as artists or designers and working in the field of education are enthusiastic about the a/r/t/ographic approach because they feel this approach respects their interests and ways of working in the arts and in education. A/r/tography recognizes their multifaceted identities as artists, researchers and teachers, and by viewing research as a living inquiry, it is a way of generating theory through praxis. Contemporary art practices in education and practice-based theory are fundamental issues in the University of Santiago de Compostela where Maria Jesus Agra Pardiñas founded the research group C3. C3 advocates for activist research in art education; the group has several members in Portugal and Spain and bases the work on collaborative research based on designing and implementing artistic actions with students in the communities to ground theory about art in education.

For many researchers such as Roldán, studies in art education need to go beyond personal interests. Subjective self narratives, although important to situate the researcher in context, are not per se sufficient to increase the scope, impact and utility of art education research. Cutting-edge collaborative research studies in arts and education following arts-based and a/r/tographic approaches oriented towards community-based actions are now mapping alternative ways to frame arts-based research methods in education (Abad-Molina 2009;

Lema 2012; García-Roldán 2012; Madrid 2014; Saldanha 2015; Morales 2015). As Morales advocates:

> I see ABR as a way for inquiry to make visible things that cannot be made visible by other means, taking into account the aesthetic factor, enabling other forms of looking at and talking about the different experiences of reality of the individual. On the other hand I see ABR as a way to make new connections, questions, opening unexplored places by enabling us to adopt activist positions that blur the boundaries between the personal and the social. It is a method that can be applied in other contexts and spaces of research.
> (2015)

In Spain, and also in Portugal, universities have serious difficulties in maintaining the art education doctoral programmes and research centres. As Marín and Madrid discussed, there are rigorous criteria for publication in indexed academic journals for students and teachers, and the great majority of such journals do not accept articles using artistic or arts-based research methods. This problem requires attention not only in Portugal and Spain but also in other countries. The art education research community does not have enough authors and enough indexed academic journals to have the work published and recognized as mainstream. Universities and professional organizations have to join forces and pool their efforts to create such academic outcomes. In Spain, the universities have joined efforts in a common doctoral programme on arts education. The research centres working in cooperation, namely in Porto and Barcelona, are also making art education and ABR more visible in broader research communities. For example, it is worth mentioning the network Research on Arts Education in the European Educational Research Association, or EERA, created in the EERA 2012 Congress. It is also important to mention the conferences about ABR and artistic research held in Barcelona (2013), Granada (2014) and Porto (2015) that have provoked influential debates with researchers from Iberian and other countries.

ABR and artistic studies are still in a chrysalis stage, and we need to solve epistemological and methodological aspects. In the InSEA Doctoral Award[1] the selection committee reviewed submissions reflecting inquiry that extends a significant line of research, addressing an issue that has been neglected in the field, filling a gap in current knowledge and/or raising significant questions about existing knowledge in art education. One of the main criteria for selection is rigour and coherence. But how can we define it for ABR and artistic research? How can we explain to a jury that an ABR study has rigour and coherence? Does it concern artistic skills in the form, the content, the end product or the process? Although we expect ABR and artistic research to have artistic qualities in terms of form, we do not reduce the scope to researchers with art training. Nevertheless, how can we define exactly the qualities we are looking for in studies using such research methods?

Stokrocki describes the six features of qualitative study listed by Eisner as: (1) field-focused; (2) constructed so that the researcher is an instrument; (3) interpretive in nature; (4) expressive in language; (5) highly detailed; and (6) persuasive (Stokrocki 1997: 34).

Do arts-based and artistic research studies have different features? Can we include them under the umbrella of qualitative research? If so, what are the specific sub-features that can characterize an arts-based research study? Moreno suggests that although arts-based and artistic research can be used by researchers from other fields, arts-based and artistic methods should be framed in the specific research methodology for each. For Marín, researchers can learn how to use art processes and tools as they can learn statistical tools to undertake their studies. From our point of view, researchers do not need to work alone if they want to engage in ABR or artistic research; they can work collaboratively in interdisciplinary teams, with one possible feature, constructing research collaboratively. Roldán sees a distinctive feature in the way images such as photography, video, comics and records of performance are used as a discourse and not as illustration. In this case, images are the most important constituent of the thesis and therefore of the research results. Another possible issue lies in using art, craft, multimedia or design language. It may be that instead of highly detailed ABR and artistic studies, such research is holistic. Instead of being persuasive, such research should be provocative. These questions need further debate. We will need more years of exploration, more studies using arts-based or artistic methods from different geographical and linguistic regions to be able to define the main characteristics of arts-based research methods. Although some possible clues are already emerging for a first tentative definition (Sullivan 2010; McNiff 2008), we do not have a clear mapping of arts-based research all over the world. A great effort needs to be done in that field to be able to list six or seven distinctive features that will help us define the methodological approach.

Acknowledgements

This chapter was written after having asked, through email, for opinions on arts-based research and art education from well-known Iberian art teachers and art education researchers who are shaping the way we see art education and research in Portuguese and Spanish-speaking countries, and from young researchers from Portugal and Spain who finished their PhD dissertations in the last year and used arts-based methods in their studies. We wish to express our deep thanks to all of those who helped us to map the ideas for this manuscript: Maria Jesus Agra Pardiñas, Juan Carlos Araño, Imanol Aguirre, Fernando Hernández, Isabel Moreno, Ricardo Marín, Joaquin Roldán, Pilar Perez, José Maria Lema, Maria Morales and Marta Madrid.

References

Abad-Molina, J. (2009), 'Iniciativas de educación artística a través del Arte Contemporáneo para la Escuela Infantil', PhD thesis, http://eprints.ucm.es/9161/. Accessed 30 March 2017.

Araño, J. C. (2015), personal communication, 22 August.

Bruner, J. (1960), *The Process of Education,* Cambridge: Harvard University Press.
Clandinin, D. J. (2007), *Handbook of Narrative Inquiry: Mapping a Methodology,* Thousand Oaks: Sage.
Clandinin, D. J. and Connoly, F. M. (2000), *Narrative Inquiry: Experience and Story in Qualitative Research,* San Francisco: Jossey-Bass.
Denzin, N. K. and Lincoln, Y. S. (2000), *Handbook of Qualitative Research,* Thousand Oaks: Sage.
Dewey, J. (1934), *Art as Experience,* Rahway: The Barnes Foundation Press.
Eça, T. T. de, Pardiñas, M. J. A. and Trigo, C. (2012), 'Transforming practices and inquiry in-between arts, arts education and research', *International Journal of Education Through Art*, 8:2, pp. 183–90.
Eisner, E. (1991), *The Enlightened Eye: Qualitative Inquiry and the Enhancement of Educational Practice,* New York: Macmillan.
Eisner, E. and Peshkin, A. (eds) (1990), *Qualitative Inquiry in Education: The Continuing Debate,* New York: Teachers College Press.
García-Roldán, Á. (2012), 'Video-arte en contextos educativos', PhD thesis, http://veraiconoproduccion.wix.com/videoimagebasedresearch. Accessed 30 March 2017.
Hernández, F. and Rifà, M. (eds) (2011), *Investigación autobiográfica y cambio social,* Barcelona: Octaedro.
van Leeuwen, T. and Jewitt, C. (eds) (2002), *Handbook of Visual Analysis,* London: Sage.
Lema, J. M. M. (2012), 'Fotografía y educación de las artes visuales: El fotoactivismo educativo como estrategia docente en la formación del profesorado', PhD thesis, http://0-hera.ugr.es.adrastea.ugr.es/tesisugr/21081748.pdf. Accessed 30 March 2017.
Madrid Manrique, M. (2014), 'Creando narrativas audiovisuales participativas: A/r/tografía e inclusividad' ('Creating audiovisual participatory narratives: A/r/tography and inclusivity'), PhD thesis, http://digibug.ugr.es/handle/10481/35191. Accessed 4 February 2019
Madrid, M. (2015), personal communication, 13 July.
Margolis, E. and Luc Pauwel, L. (2011), *Handbook of Visual Research Methods*, London: Sage.
Marín, R. and Roldán, J. (2010), 'Photo essays and photographs in visual arts-based educational research', *International Journal of Education Through Art,* 6:1, pp. 7–23.
McNiff, S. (2008), 'Arts-based research', in G. Knowles and A. Cole (eds), *Handbook of the Arts in Qualitative Inquiry: Perspectives, Methodologies, Examples, and Issues*, Thousand Oaks: Sage, pp. 20–39.
Morales, M. (2014), 'Tejiendo espacios: Intervenciónes artísticas como investigación educativa', *Terciocreciente: Revista de Estudios en Sociedad, Artes y Gestión Cultural,* 5, http://www.terciocreciente.com/index.php/revista-n-5. Accessed 4 February 2019.
——— (2015), email to author, 6 December.
Moreno, I. (2015), personal communication, 23 August.
Pardiñas, M. J. A. and Trigo, C. (2012), personal communication, 13 August.
Perez, P. (2015), personal communication, 30 August.
Roldán, J. (2015a), personal communication, 22 August.
——— (2015b), email to author, 23 August.
Saldanha, Â. (2015), 'No caminho para casa – um estudo a/r/tográfico de recolha de memorias numa comunidade informal', Porto: FBAUP.

Stokrocki, M. (1997), 'Qualitative forms of research methods', in S. D. La Pierre and E. Zimmerman (eds), *Research Methods and Methodologies for Art Education*, Reston: NAEA, pp. 33–56.
Sullivan, G. (2010), *Art Practice as Research: Inquiry in Visual Arts*, Thousand Oaks: Sage.
Vidiella, J. (2008), 'Prácticas de corporización y pedagogías de contacto: Una aportación a los Estudios de Performance', PhD thesis, Barcelona: Universidad de Barcelona.

Note

1 http://www.insea.org/insea/awards. Accessed 30 March 2017.

Chapter 19

Finnish Arts-Based and Artistic Dissertations in Context: Explorations, Interventions and Glocal Interpretations

Mira Kallio-Tavin and Kevin Tavin

An overview

There are three universities in Finland where it is possible to defend a doctoral thesis in visual art education: Aalto University, University of Lapland and University of Jyväskylä. The first two institutions offer art education certification for teachers and provide teaching focusing on artistic research for doctoral students and post-doctoral researchers.[1] In this chapter, we concentrate on artistic and arts-based doctoral dissertations, focusing on art education, through the Department of Art at Aalto University.

In general, the Department of Art focuses on mediating art: techniques, stances, methods, education, curating and so on. This means that researchers are taking part in discourse, with a systematic approach, with tools and materials well managed by educated skills, and with a task, to gain something and to add something to the discourse. Some guiding questions for arts-based and artistic research at the doctoral level include: how are art and education related? In what ways can we identify and interpret societal meanings of contemporary art? What is the significance of artistic and pedagogical interventions? And, how do we identify the methodology of artistic and arts-based research?

In terms of structure, at the moment, doctoral studies through the Department of Art require studies of 60 credits in the form of the European Credit Transfer and Accumulation System (ECTS). The studies include, for example, aesthetics, contemporary philosophy, philosophy of science, research methods, courses on academic writing and studies on the specified area of the individual research project, plus studies on the actual research question of the student. In doctoral seminars and symposia, students give presentations alongside professors and other academic speakers. Every doctoral project will have one supervising professor and one or two advisors. If a student chooses to include artistic or arts-based production in the thesis, there are many ways to do so, including having it as a starting point and then writing about it, or having it embedded into the ongoing dissertation process itself and unfolding as research. It can also be given different forms and varied sites for exhibiting. However, if the doctoral candidate decides that the artistic production should be evaluated as an independent part of the thesis, the project needs to be presented in public and evaluated by two pre-examiners. Documentation is an important part of the artistic production, since in some cases the overall assessment might be done based on the documentation. When the supervising professor and advisor(s) so decide, and the author so wishes, the entire thesis will be proposed to the Doctoral Studies Committee for pre-examination, meaning that the dissertation and documentation of the artistic production are sent out to two outside examiners for approval and for comments. The feedback from the external pre-examiners addresses the next step: the thesis either is approved with minor or major revisions or it requires more work under supervision. If and when the pre-examiners so decide, and when the revisions are made, the *public* defence that usually includes one opponent (although it may include two) will take place. The opponent is someone whose task is to make public declarations and ask critical questions at the defence, based on a careful reading of the dissertation. The defence itself is a very formal process, an academic tradition and ritual, and an important public event, lasting from two to six hours. However, at this point no more changes are done in the dissertation, which is already published and for sale as a book at the event.

In general, through the Department of Art, research is essentially 'free'. There is no tuition. Besides the lack of tuition, every researcher is free to follow their interest, skills, intellect and motivation when they decide what and how to research. This sense of freedom is, of course, framed within the larger aim of both new methodological thinking (artistic research) and challenging the status quo in art research, the discourse on visual culture and art education and the situation of art in society and ideological contexts.

In the broader picture, conducting research within an academic context using art and visual practices is a relatively new approach in Finland. Artistic, visual, multi-sensorial and practice-based knowledge are difficult to articulate, especially in terms of what sort of knowledge they introduce to the research. Traditionally, this kind of knowledge was left outside of scientific definitions of research, considered as something, for example, too vague to pin down. This kind of indeterminate knowledge has become a focus of interest in Finland since the beginning of the twenty-first century, based on increased discourse and institutional support, although there is still a need to articulate and advocate for a more profound shift in the dominant world of 'scientific research'. However, arts-based and artistic research is an officially approved research method in the aforementioned universities in Finland.

The first doctoral dissertation in art education in Finland was defended in 1997 (Räsänen 1997). From 1997 through 2015, many doctoral dissertations have been defended in art education in Aalto University, and nine of them have used arts-based or artistic methodologies. In addition, there have been a few artistic dissertations within the last couple of years which are not related to art education but still use arts-based or artistic methodologies.

For this chapter, we discuss two dissertations that, taken together, represent recent and ongoing projects that emphasize artistic processes, and are related to the field of art education. When discussing the characteristics of the dissertations, we focus on the knowledge the dissertation aims to achieve, and the societal, political, critical and educational perspectives embedded in the research. In both cases, the researchers adopted arts-based approaches. In arts-based research, the researcher is investigating an issue by/through an artmaking process, using artmaking as an instrument. Typically, arts-based research is concerned with social, societal, cultural, educational, philosophical or psychological issues, which are explored through art practice (Kallio 2008, 2009, 2010; Suominen et al. 2017). Artistic research, on the other hand, aims to learn more about the artistic process and the artist's artmaking, to strengthen her/his artist identity and deepen her/his artistic views, and to produce high-quality art *objects* (Hannula et al. 2014; Rinne 2016).

Arts-based and artistic dissertations in art education

While there are some similarities to the North American arts-based educational research methodology, the academic territory in Finland has included quite different combinations of academic influences, and has mainly been informed by artistic research done in the art academy. In addition, within Finland, there are parallel and different methodological artistic research discourses, including fine art research discourse, research done by philosophers and international discourse, especially European. The differences between the different discourses have to do with the dissimilar institutional traditions in different universities and art academies, and differences in artmaking paradigms between different art forms. One influential discourse is based on the series of theoretical publications by Juha Varto (2009) and Mika Hannula, Juha Suoranta and Tere Vadén, who have been interested in articulating the essence of knowledge within artistic research from quite theoretical perspectives (Hannula et al. 2003, 2005, 2014). Another discourse comes from the more contemporary university collaboration between the arts universities: University of the Arts Helsinki and Aalto University, where faculty and students are exploring artistic practices, thinking and observation.[2] Related publications can be found in *Studies in Artistic Research Ruukku*.[3] The name *Ruukku* means a jar (as a container) in Finnish and hence also refers to the *Journal for Artistic Research* (JAR),[4] which is the journal of the Society for Artistic Research, a European network for artistic research. A third discourse concerns the research done in the field of art education, which this chapter concentrates on. Some of the methodological approaches come from the discourses in arts-based educational research from Europe, especially Spain and Portugal, and from North America. All of these discourses have influenced doctoral dissertations in Aalto University, although quite differently, and although the influence of research from outside Finland on doctoral dissertations is still quite small.

Most of the arts-based and artistic dissertations defended within the past two decades in art education in Aalto University have focused on artmaking processes, and claim to be artistic research rather than arts-based research. They are closer to artistic research made in fine arts than in art education, even though the students' research field is art education. Research questions have focused on the origin of an artwork, such as where the idea for an artwork came from or how an artwork evolved (Houessou 2010; Mäkikoskela 2015), and often, these dissertations have to do with a dialogue with an artwork (Erkkilä 2012; Pullinen 2003; Valkeapää 2011). Other social and cultural questions might be included.

For example, Leena Valkeapää's thesis (2011) focuses on Sámi reindeer herding culture and living in nature. Another doctoral student, Tapio Tuominen was interested in exploring art as a ritual behaviour (Tuominen 2013). Three dissertations define themselves as arts-based and art educational research (Erkkilä 2012; Kallio-Tavin 2013; van Boeckel 2013). Mira Kallio-Tavin's (2013) collaborative arts-based research process explores pedagogical dialogue with a person with autism. Jan van Boeckel's thesis (2013) is about arts-based environmental education. Jaana Erkkilä (2012) explores artistic encounters between artist-teachers and students, with interactions through artworks. In all of these dissertations, there is a significant connection to art education. In the next two sections, we look closely at two examples of dissertation research – one completed and one ongoing (at the time of the writing of this chapter) – that employ arts-based and artistic methodologies.

The author is another

In her dissertation, 'The author is another – how does visual dialogue develop?', Jaana Erkkilä (2012) focuses on the possibilities of artistic production and the interaction between an artist-teacher and her students. The context of the thesis is in schooling, and in appreciation of the different students' cultures. There is concern about stigmatization and the social exclusion of children and young people based on different cultural and societal backgrounds. The study attempts to achieve knowledge between students' and teachers' different and multiple lives and representations in visual culture, and visual art through visual and narrative dialogue. Erkkilä wanted to learn from students and to be inspired by them in her own artistic production, as well as inspire their visual expression. During the teaching period, a large selection of contemporary and historical artwork was explored to represent varied ways of existing, and hence the differences between different people and the cultures they represent came to the fore of discussion. One artwork was given a primary position in the teaching and in the entire research project: Pieter Bruegel the Elder's *The Donkey in the School* (1556), which, although a historical image, functioned as a critical mirror to the contemporary schooling. For Erkkilä, this particular artwork served as a thread for the entire research, art working and thinking, and a tool to criticize school, education and its practices.

As a starting point to cultural diversity, Erkkilä explores the school's assumptions of different learners and different students, and how the term 'special student' rarely refers to an especially successful student. Analysing Bruegel's artwork with students, she builds a link between contemporary school issues and *The Donkey in the School*, which seems to suggest that a donkey does not become a horse in school. She asked the meaning of education and the future for students who seem to be predetermined by the school institution and society. The diversity between the students' cultures in Finland, in addition to ethnic diversity, often comes from different family backgrounds, such as different health and wealth potential. Erkkilä points out how the Finnish school system has tried to convince students, and society at large, of equal study opportunities for everybody. At the same time the school has remained oblivious to teachers' racist behaviours, for example. Many issues in successful school attendance seem to depend on the teacher's ability to tolerate and teach different learners, and so-called special students. While the curriculum includes learning from different foreign and geographically distant cultures – which are studied namely through cultural and art history – other cultural diversities are often excluded from the Finnish school system, such as gender, minorities, different religious groups or even popular culture phenomena from the perspectives of students. In this dissertation, the students' visual culture is recognized as being as foreign as any other foreign culture is to the teacher. Erkkilä approaches visual cultures as an interesting field to learn from students. Perhaps, Erkkilä could have approached the students' living cultures also through the selected art media, including more contemporary and more student-centred media.

In addition to the theories of art education, Erkkilä used literature from philosophy (Heidegger 2000; Blanchot 2001), religious studies, sociology, radical pedagogy, art history and fictive literature (Proust 2007). An important source she names is Mikhail Bakhtin's (1991) thinking about Dostojevski's structure of the polyphonic novel, which she applies in her visual production. Her artistic work is based on the visual analysis between students' artworks and art historical examples, and between students' artworks and her own artwork. Some themes she explores with students are the differences between imagination and truth, gender, discipline and control, and the question of moral good and bad. She explored similar themes in her visual and essayist artistic work. She wrote, and asked her students to write, fictional narratives. Following the idea of Bakhtin's polyphonic novel, she wanted to explore how a singular authorship becomes a group voice of different authors and interpretations. Through associative fiction writing and visual artmaking, Erkkilä dealt with issues of marginalization, poverty, prejudices, control and discipline and social responsibility.

Although Erkkilä describes how her own artistic process is not the focus of the research project, she explains how she has found a new way of artmaking: one she would not have found without collaborating with students in a research project. She mentions that one of the aims of the research is to utilize the fact that she is an artist making a study located in the field of art education. Interestingly, Erkkilä identifies herself as an artist who teaches art, not as an art educator. As a researcher, she identifies herself as an artist-researcher, whose research is done in the context of art education. This is a typical situation within almost all of the nine dissertations mentioned earlier in this chapter. Typically, students with a strong art education identity have used methods other than artistic or arts-based. Erkkilä has a master's degree in fine arts in addition to art education, and therefore her identification as an artist is understandable. However, while completing a dissertation in art education and while researching in a school context, she unfortunately wants to distinguish her professional identity from art education as a field. This is somewhat odd, although not uncommon with art education students (even on a more global level), since in her methodology chapter she participates in the Finnish and international conversation on arts-based methodology, and hence expands the field of arts-based research in Finnish art education. In fact, Erkkilä's thesis is an example of how research projects add to methodological diversity, and how this plays a role in developing new research methodologies.

Believing is feeling: Performing the politics of false hope

Lisa Erdman's ongoing dissertation, 'Performing false hope: Ethical outcomes of fictitious pharmaceutical advertising as public art intervention', addresses the ethical challenges and dialogical outcomes of her satirical, public performance intervention entitled Finnexia®. Presented in 2012 in the Helsinki Railway Station, the project consisted of a multimedia advertisement campaign for Finnexia®, a (fictitious) medication that enhances the process of learning the Finnish language.[5] Erdman developed the project based in part on her own relationship to the Finnish language, the cultural pressures within Finland about language acquisition, and her previous work using appropriation and satire to market fictitious drugs to cure racism, lack of patriotism, lack of consumption and so on. Finnexia® was also built on artistic methods from the performative, subversive and absurdist traditions of artists and cultural jammers, and visual methods from artists such as Dana Wyse, Damien Hirst and Justine Cooper. For Finnexia® in general, the target audience was primarily foreigners living in Finland, and newly arrived immigrants. However, the dissertation, which includes the performative intervention as art and the doctoral research as a post-performance investigation, is not meant to research immigrants per se. Instead, it is in part a critique of the medicalization of society and a deconstruction of the process of para-fictional art intervention.

In addition to still and video images, a product promotion booth and dialogue table were created that served as centrepieces for her intervention. The Finnexia® intervention was meant to evoke an alternate reality that offered an innovative space for conversation among individuals who wanted to acquire the ability to use Finnish language about issues surrounding cultural integration and immigration in Finland. The visual format of pharmaceutical advertising in Finnexia® presents a commentary on the increasingly popular pill-popping approaches for treating a widening array of physical and mental ailments. In addition, the fictitious pharmacy and medical advertisements offered a double-edged investigation of medical aesthetics: a celebration of its characteristic professional slickness, clinical precision and soothing colours, as well as a critique of the limits created by the homogeneity of its form. This tension between medical aesthetics and the ethics of offering false hope is a major component of the post-performance research and part of the entire dissertation. Of course, there are many other tensions that drive the dissertation research, post-performance, including the ethical relationship between a subversive cultural jam, fictional pharmaceuticals, and open and dialogical engagement. Some key questions for Erdman's dissertation include, what is the role and responsibility of the artist-researcher in society? What are the ethical considerations when intervening through cultural jamming?

And, to what extent is dialogue achieved or denuded when discussions are based upon performative satire that may mislead participants to believe in the promise of the fictional medication?

As an arts-based intervention, the performance of Finnexia® is situated within the medical realm where the neo-liberal discourse associated with this industry is now familiar to many people on a personal and global level. For example, prescriptions and pharmacy visits have a place in everyday life, and direct-to-consumer medical advertising is taking on an increasingly international presence within the media landscape. In general, the pharmaceutical discourse reveals a cultural desire for instant relief from ailments, as well as our intimate relationship to the consumerist framework, which drives such desires. While pharmaceutical developments offer cures, health benefits and the possibility to improve quality of life, the excess consumption of drugs raises many other societal concerns.

Another part of the dissertation includes researching what it means to open a space from which public dialogue can emerge in Finland regarding language acquisition and cultural integration. With the internationalization of Finnish culture, there is a need for new spaces and platforms that offer both Finns and non-Finns the opportunity to share concerns and discussion regarding such sociopolitical topics. Traditionally, these venues take the form of commentary in news media, online forums, panel discussions on television or through multicultural venues. However, most of these formats require certain levels of competency in the Finnish language, and thus may exclude a significant portion of the non-Finnish population from the discussion table.

The methodological approach to Erdman's research is multidisciplinary, as it combines methodologies and uses a systematic set of theoretical and philosophical frameworks for analysis of public pedagogy. These frameworks include Foucault's (1977, 1980) discourse on normality and deviance, Bakhtin's (2004) concept of dialogical art practice and Sandlin and Milam's (2008) analysis of culture jamming as critical public pedagogy. In a sense, Erdman's dissertation project is 'defined through its performative functions, its ongoing work of mediation and its attentiveness to the interconnections and struggles that take place over knowledge, language, spatial relations, and history' (Giroux 2000: 354).

Developing areas in art education

Arts-based and artistic research methodologies are developing areas in art education in Finland. Doctoral students are pursuing them as a personal and societal research method to challenge the boundaries of knowing and gaining research knowledge. This approach has enabled an intriguing interplay between art, education, research and its social function. The focus, situated between art and education, reaches society within and outside of institutions, whether it is a school context or a more general audience in the society where the research project takes place. Although the general structure of arts-based and artistic dissertation work is consistent across the few Finnish universities that embrace this type of work, different methodologies and theories influence the direction of content, including fine-art research discourse, research done by philosophers and international discourse. For a relatively small country, Finland has a diverse range of approaches. We chose to focus on work from Aalto University, where we both work and supervise doctoral candidates. While for some, artistic research from Aalto University can be seen in the context of fine arts rather than art education, even though the students' research field is art education, we have provided examples specifically focusing on art education – or public pedagogy – in one way or another. Both examples try to connect individual artwork with research, art working and critical thinking, and offer tools and methods to critique society, education and hegemonic culture and its practices.

References

Bakhtin, M. (1991), *Dostojevskin poetiikan ongelmia*, Helsinki: Kustannus Oy Orient Express.

——— (2004), *The Dialogic Imagination: Four Essays* (trans. C. Emerson and M. Holquist), Austin: University of Texas Press.

Blanchot, M. (2001), *Kirjallinen avaruus*, Helsinki: ai-ai.

van Boeckel, J. (2013), 'At the heart of art and earth: An exploration of practices in arts-based environmental education', PhD thesis, Helsinki: Aalto University.

Erkkilä, J. (2012), 'Tekijä on toinen: Kuinka kuvallinen dialogi syntyy', PhD thesis, Helsinki: Aalto University.

Foucault, M. (1977), *Discipline and Punish: The Birth of the Prison* (trans. A. Sheridan), New York: Random House.

——— (1980), *Power/Knowledge: Selected Interviews and Other Writings 1972–1977* (ed. C. Gordon), Brighton: Harvester.

Giroux, H. (2000), 'Public pedagogy as cultural politics: Stuart Hall and the "crisis" of culture', *Cultural Studies*, 14:2, pp. 341–60.

Hannula, M., Suoranta, J. and Vadén, T. (2003), *Otsikko uusiksi: Taiteellisen tutkimuksen suuntaviivat,* Tampere: niin & näin.

——— (2005), *Artistic Research: Theories, Methods and Practices,* Helsinki: Academy of Fine Arts.

——— (2014), *Artistic Research Methodology: Narrative, Power and the Public,* New York: Peter Lang.

Heidegger, M. (2000), *Oleminen ja aika*, Tampere: Vastapaino.

Houessou, J. (2010), 'Teoksen synty: Kuvataiteellista prosessia sanallistamassa', PhD thesis, Helsinki: University of Art and Design.

Kallio, M. (2008), 'Taideperustaisen tutkimusparadigman muodostuminen', *Synnyt: Taiteen Tiedonala*, 2, pp. 106–15, https://wiki.aalto.fi/display/Synnyt/Home. Accessed 30 March 2017.

——— (2009), 'Confronting (inter) subjectivities through arts-based research', *The International Journal of the Arts in Society*, 4:3, pp. 1–8.

——— (2010), 'Taideperustainen tutkimusparadigma taidekasvatuksen sosiokulttuurisia ulottuvuuksia rakentamassa: PARADIgMA', *Synnyt: Taiteen Tiedonala*, 4, pp. 15–25, https://wiki.aalto.fi/display/Synnyt/Home. Accessed 30 March 2017.

Kallio-Tavin, M. (2013), 'Encountering self, other and the third: Researching the crossroads of art pedagogy, Levinasian ethics and disability studies', PhD thesis, Helsinki: Aalto University.

Mäkikoskela, R. (2015), 'Ympäri, sisällä: Kolmiulotteinen työskenteleminen kuvataiteessa', PhD thesis, Helsinki: Aalto University.

Proust, M. (2007), *Kadonnutta aikaa etsimässä: Jälleenlöydetty aika*, Keuruu: Otava.

Pullinen, J. (2003), 'Mestarin käden jäljillä: Kuvallinen dialogi filosofisen hermeneutiikan näkökulmasta', PhD thesis, Helsinki: University of Art and Design.

Räsänen, M. (1997), 'Building bridges: Experimental art understanding: A work of art as a means of understanding and constructing self', PhD thesis, Helsinki: University of Art and Design.

Rinne, K. (2016), 'Investigating Doctoral studies in two Finnish art universities', PhD thesis, Helsinki: Aalto University.

Sandlin, J. and Milam, J. (2008), '"Mixing pop (culture) and politics": Cultural resistance, culture jamming, and anti-consumption activism as critical public pedagogy', *Curriculum Inquiry*, 38:3, pp. 323–50.

Suominen, A., Kallio-Tavin, M. and Hernández, F. (2017), 'Arts based research traditions and orientations in Europe: Perspectives from Finland and Spain', in P. Leavy (ed.), *Handbook of Arts-Based Research*, New York: Guilford, pp. 101–20.

Tuominen, T. (2013), 'Maaginen kuva: Rituaalinen käyttäytyminen kuvataiteessa', PhD thesis, Helsinki: Aalto University.

Valkeapää, L. (2011), 'Luonnossa: Vuoropuhelua Nils-Aslak Valkeapään tuotannon kanssa', PhD thesis, Helsinki: Aalto University.

Varto, J. (2009), *Basics of Artistic Research*, Helsinki: University of Art and Design.

Notes

1 The University of the Arts, Helsinki, also engages students in artistic research.
2 http://www.artisticresearch.fi/tahto/. Accessed 30 March 2017.
3 http://ruukku-journal.fi/en. Accessed 30 March 2017.
4 http://www.jar-online.net/. Accessed 30 March 2017.
5 See http://www.finnexia.fi. Accessed 30 March 2017.

Chapter 20

Barrier or Catalyst: Cross-Cultural and Language Issues for Doctoral Researchers in Japan

Toshio Naoe

Overview of the doctoral programme in art and design at the University of Tsukuba

Today, there are several options to attend doctoral programmes to study art education in Japan, including programmes offered at universities, teacher education colleges and art colleges. Among them, the University of Tsukuba was one of the first institutes to offer such a programme; it can be used as an example to discuss the historical changes of doctoral dissertations in visual arts education. It is also notable, in the sense that it is offered in the programme of art and design, not in the programme of education. Since the doctoral programme was established by professionals including artists, designers, art historians and art educators, it may be a suitable case for the topic of this chapter, which discusses the perspectives of artists, researchers and teachers in doctoral research in visual arts education.

The doctoral programme in art and design at the University of Tsukuba was established in 1976, and it admitted only two students in the first year (Tomie 1996). In that period, the typical conventions in humanities and social studies programmes scarcely allowed students to get doctoral degrees. The doctoral degree was considered to be the final goal of academic life after long years of dedication.

The field of art education was opened in the doctoral programme in art and design in 1984, and the first doctoral degree on art education was awarded in 1991. Table 1 shows the titles of doctoral dissertations on art education awarded in the doctoral programme in art and design. One tendency in these dissertation topics is towards the study of art education in foreign countries. Japanese students in the programme tend to be interested in European and American studies partly because their experiences in art education have been formed under the influences of those cultures. It may also be argued that investigating subjects in different societies using foreign languages and deep knowledge about the culture tends to be considered proof of academic ability because in one sense, Japanese academia has developed through conflicts between new knowledge from the outer world and the responses to it through the leadership of scholars who could communicate with foreign countries. Foreign students, mainly from Asian countries, tend to choose topics related to their own countries. Those tendencies show two ways in which cross-cultural interest has led the doctoral research on art education in the programme, although we should not ignore the fact that some research is focused on Japan.

What kinds of research are conducted in the doctoral programme in art and design in fields other than art education? Since there is not enough space to review the entire history, I will share a brief overview of recent research topics. As of the beginning of 2016, we were judging eleven

	Year	Title
1.	1991	'Historical study on art education in the concept of nature as indicator'
2.	1992	'Education as handicraft'
3.	1992	'Theory and methods of art education of Franz Cizek'
4.	1993	'Study on Sloyd education'
5.	1994	'Study on Mamoru Seki (1889–1939)'
6.	1994	'Comparative study between Taiwan and Japan on curriculum of art appreciation education in lower secondary school'
7.	1996	'Curriculum development of art education in the United States of America today'
8.	1996	'Drawing and painting education in primary school in China'
9.	1996	'Study on Bauhaus'
10.	1997	'Art education theory of V. Lowenfeld'
11.	1999	'Infants' developmental change in drawing humans and variations of head-feet representation'
12.	2000	'Reform in art education in the first half of the twentieth century in the United Kingdom'
13.	2000	'Formation of art education associations in South Korea'
14.	2001	'Basic study on the usage of the Internet in school art education'
15.	2001	'Native art education in primary and lower secondary schools in Taiwan'
16.	2002	'Contribution of the National Taiwan Arts Education Centre to art education'
17.	2002	'Experimental study on assessment of art appreciation by Abigail Housen's theory of aesthetic development'
18.	2002	'Change of art education in modernization in South Korea'
19.	2005	'Historical study on the theory of art appreciation education in the twentieth century in the United States of America'
20.	2006	'Developmental stage and diversity of children's aesthetics'
21.	2009	'Design education movements in South Korea'
22.	2011	'Interaction analysis in art education'
23.	2011	'Methodology of art appreciation education in the United States of America'
24.	2012	'Drawing education in Kindergarten in the Meiji period'
25.	2016	'Primary art education in the Republic of Maldives and Islam'

Table 1: Doctoral dissertations on art education approved at the doctoral programme in art and design, University of Tsukuba. Titles were roughly translated from Japanese by the author based on the information in the University of Tsukuba Repository (https://tsukuba.repo.nii.ac.jp).

	Title
1.	'Japanese embroidery in the modern age'
2.	'Study on Taro Okamoto'
3.	'Art education in the Islamic world'
4.	'Lithograph and print art of Eikyu'
5.	'Multi-colour and multiple copperplate prints of Jörg Schmeisser'
6.	'Composition in the works of Caspar David Friedrich'
7.	'Line drawing in the abstract painting of Insho Domoto'
8.	'Artistic view of sculptor Takezo Shinkai'
9.	'A proposal for conservation and utilization of scenery of Tokyo towers based on surveys in Manga and in actual scenes'
10.	'Planning of village space based on shared understanding by residents about disaster and climate change'
11.	'Expressions that contain stories in picture books without words'

Table 2: Dissertations under review in the doctoral programme in art and design, University of Tsukuba, 2016. Titles were roughly translated from Japanese by the author based on the programme on open review day of doctoral dissertations on 7 January 2016.

doctoral dissertations in art and design (Table 2). In contrast with the narrow windows of opportunity in the 1980s, it is now common to earn a degree during the course programme. Another change is the increase of research based on the students' own practices of making artworks. Typically, they investigate artists whose works are related to their own works and experiment with the application of the research outcomes.

The open review day for dissertations in the doctoral programme in art and design, which is both part of the oral examinations and an occasion to invite the public to see the presentations, is certainly exciting. A variety of doctoral dissertations with different topics and methodologies in the fields of art education, art history, graphic design, environmental design and practices of artworks in painting and sculpture are presented to the public, and we discuss them with the audience. The only things the people have in common as participants in the open review day would be our interest in visual investigation and our questions about how that investigation is approved for a doctoral degree.

Study on creative curriculum

Let us move to my own research in the graduate school. My career consists of a mixture of identities as artist, teacher and researcher. I studied painting at undergraduate level, taught art at a lower secondary school in Tokyo for three years, and then entered a master's programme to further study painting. At that time, the field of art education at my university was taught only in the doctoral programme and not in the master's programme. Although I was enrolled in the field of painting in the master's programme, I had an ambition to do research in art education, so I asked the professor of art education in the doctoral programme to personally advise me on my thesis. Usually students in painting wrote theses on their own artworks. However, I wrote a thesis on art education as well as making my own artworks, using oil painting. Professors of painting must have been puzzled to judge my thesis on art education, but they made an exception and awarded me a master's degree. After that, I formally enrolled in the doctoral programme in art and design in the University of Tsukuba to study art education.

My interest in research at that time was to investigate the collective tendencies for implementing art curricula by ordinary art teachers in lower secondary schools. From my own experience of teaching art in these lower secondary schools, I focused on the range of discretion permitted to art teachers for exploring new ideas in the contents of their teaching. In Japan, we have national standards for curriculum and authorized textbooks. However, those official documents do not reflect the actuality of teaching. There should be as many curricula as there are individual teachers, from my perspective. Those curricula practically implemented by teachers are not officially recorded; therefore, they have not been serious subjects of educational research. Nevertheless, the lives of students are certainly influenced by the whole movement of these teachings.

I tackled the issue by sending a questionnaire survey to all of the art teachers in lower secondary schools in eight districts of Tokyo Metropolis. I found two contradictory tendencies that attracted my attention. One was the unexpected conformity between the curricula implemented by teachers and the teaching examples in the authorized textbooks. To my regret, I had to admit that the majority of art teachers were not creative about developing their own curricula. On the other hand, I noticed particular tendencies about how to spend time within the implemented curricula. While time allocations in the teaching examples in the authorized textbooks tend to emphasize drawing and painting, teachers actually spent much more time on design and handicrafts (Naoe 1996).

Examining the background factors behind this phenomenon, I discovered that although more than half of art teachers majored in painting in college, they had difficulty teaching drawing and painting in a lower secondary school. Instead, the teachers willingly adopted handicrafts, which typically involve making things to use in daily life out of wood or ceramic; they did so in response to the students' enthusiasm for it, despite handicrafts being outside of their expertise. I also explained that teachers used design and handicrafts to maintain order against the storm of school violence occurring at that time, because these activities are suitable for step-by-step instruction to restore order and communication in the class. Lower secondary schools in Japan in the 1980s and 1990s suffered from what was then referred to as juvenile delinquency, and the teachers' main concerns tended to be how to save the class from the chaos caused by student gangs. Several teachers also mentioned the effect of woodworking to calm students' aggressive thoughts, for example, by rubbing and polishing the surface of wood. In addition, the value of handicrafts may have its root in people's subconscious minds through a respect for craftsmanship and an affinity with natural materials. These tendencies might be interpreted as a manifestation of collective creativity in practically implemented art curricula.

After entering the doctoral programme, I got a scholarship to study abroad for one year. I decided to conduct research in the United Kingdom to develop the approach discussed in my completed master's thesis in a foreign country. I took this step just after the first national curriculum for art had been introduced into the educational system in England in 1992. I tried to investigate the relationship between the national education systems and the collective creativity in practical curriculum in art classes in the two societies of Japan and the United Kingdom. After I returned to Japan, I did not have enough time to develop these results into a doctoral dissertation before getting a job at a university, but the preliminary work completed proved to be an opening for ongoing interest in the comparative study in the two countries.

Studying the art educator

I completed my doctoral dissertation in five years, and afterwards I started to teach in a university. The research topic of my dissertation was different from what I pursued when I was a graduate student. A comparative study of the ongoing collective tendencies of curriculum implementations in two countries was not suitable for achieving results in a short period of time. Although I did not shape this approach into a doctoral dissertation, I have continued the study in both countries to this day (Naoe 1997, 2014). After I set aside that dissertation topic, what then was my new topic for the degree?

I found a new subject for research during my year of study in the United Kingdom: the theory and practice of Marion Richardson (1892–1946), a teacher who led the reform in art education in the first half of the twentieth century in the United Kingdom. Richardson taught at a local secondary school for girls, where she developed her innovative teaching style. Later she dedicated herself to spreading her thoughts as an inspector of art in London and ultimately abroad, travelling to many countries to share her approach to art education. The institute where I studied, now called Birmingham City University, was the successor of the Birmingham School of Art, from which Richardson graduated. It has an archive of more than ten thousand items related to her educational works. This Marion Richardson Archive contains students' works, syllabuses and teaching materials, typewritten lecture scripts, letters and other documents, and so on, in many boxes piled up in the staff room. I was not interested in historical study at that time, but the supervisor at Birmingham encouraged me to look into the items.

At the beginning, I frequently developed headaches from reading so many items in a foreign language, but soon I was fascinated. This was probably because her work as a secondary art teacher had something in common with my research interest related to the creativity in the curriculum implemented in a local ordinary school. I knew that Richardson's 1948 book

Art and the Child was translated and published in Japanese in 1958. This collection of essays on her positive memories from teaching art lessons gave me the impression that she was just a loving and good teacher. In later readings of the items in the archive, I came to understand that she wrote the book during a chaotic situation in the Second World War when she fell seriously ill. The archive materials showed me entirely new aspects of her clear thought processes and practical activities that differed from the previous impressions I had gained from her book. British researchers had already published some papers from the archive, but I thought that I would be able to make a new contribution when I developed my experience of curriculum study.

I paid attention to the following groups of items. First, I reviewed several versions of Richardson's art syllabuses from different years. This supported my view that the art curriculum is always changing according to the relationship between teacher and student, and that the variations give clues to understanding the nature of art teaching.

Second, I read the typed scripts that Richardson prepared for lectures, mainly to other teachers. I thought that reading through all the scripts chronologically enabled me to follow the changes in her thoughts and teaching.

Third, I viewed around 1500 fascinating student artworks. Especially curious were the artworks known as 'mind pictures'. They are pictures of mental images that students saw when they closed their eyes. Mind pictures have some mysterious aspects. Looking into the items in the archive, I found that Richardson collected these pictures systematically. In a lecture, she emphasized that drawing mind pictures was the core of her teaching. However, her book *Art and the Child* contains only a very obscure reference to mind pictures, and includes no illustrations of them (Richardson 1948). Read (1943) showed the results of his psychological investigation of mind pictures in his book *Education Through Art*, but he does not mention Richardson's name with regard to them. Nevertheless, in other parts of the book, he praises Richardson as a respectable teacher. Analysis of the whole collection of student works and syllabuses and lectures might yield a key to the mystery.

Fourth, I read Richardson's correspondence with others in letters, articles, books and related documents. Among other correspondence, I paid attention to her interactions with two art critics, Roger Fry (1866–1934) and Herbert Read (1893–1968), about the development of new theories of art education. In reading the documents, I gradually found that the relationship with Fry resulted in the mutual development of ideas, whereas Richardson sometimes had disagreements with Read. This may be a good historical case for considering the relationship between practical art teaching and theoretical work.

Fifth, the role of criticism and verbal and writing activities in teaching art came to my mind for the future development of art education in Japan. I was concerned that, especially in Japan, what is called learner-centred art education, based on the philosophy of modern art supported by a hidden curriculum that fosters affinity with craftsmanship, tended to ignore verbal thinking and knowledge, and to educate children only as silent craftspeople. However, Richardson's syllabus for the local secondary school in the 1910s had already placed art criticism as one of the important activities. In her lecture script to the teachers, she stressed that it was indispensable for her students to learn the art of the past and learn how to criticize it in order to understand the value of individual expression.

I completed my doctoral dissertation on this new topic in 2000, five years after I had left the doctoral programme. In Japan, there is a system of awarding PhDs without being enrolled in the doctoral programme. Candidates who are not in the programme and are yet judged to have enough quality and achievement in their academic work are allowed to submit their completed dissertations to the university for examination. This system is called 'dissertation doctor', while the system that awards a doctorate as the final accomplishment of a doctoral programme is called 'programme doctor'. Today, since the system of doctoral programmes has developed, 'programme doctor' is much more commonly used than 'dissertation doctor' for obtaining a doctoral degree.

I also published part of my dissertation as a book (Naoe 2002) and donated it to the archive in the United Kingdom. I am proud of this work as a unique contribution that researchers in the United Kingdom had not covered. However, since the dissertation and the book were both written in Japanese, British researchers cannot understand them unless they learn that foreign language. I confess that I do not have enough ability to accurately translate the massive volume of complicated discussions into English. This creates another language barrier in terms of dissertation research in art education.

References

Naoe, T. (1996), '中学校美術科における教科書指導計画案と実態との関係について' ('Syllabus examples of textbooks and the reality in lower secondary art education'), *藝術教育學* ('Bulletin of the study on art and design education in the University of Tsukuba'), 8, pp. 43–56.

——— (1997), 'イングランド中西部の中等学校における美術カリキュラムの編成動向II–公的試験制度との協力体制' ('On a current situation of secondary art curriculum in schools in West Midlands, England II: Partnership with the formal examination system'), *大学美術教育学会誌* ('Journal of university art education'), 29, pp. 77–86.

——— (2002), *20世紀前半の英国における美術教育改革の研究–マリオン・リチャードソンの理論と実践* ('Reform in art education in the first half of the twentieth century in the United Kingdom: Theory and practice of Marion Richardson'), Tokyo: Kenpakusha.

——— (2014), '英国の中等教育における美術カリキュラムの編成・実施動向—イングランド中西部の学校における調査から（1994年・2010年）' ('Trend analysis of art curricula implementation in secondary education in the United Kingdom: Surveys conducted in schools in West Midlands Region, England, in 1994 and 2010'), *芸術研究報* ('Bulletin of the faculty of art and design, University of Tsukaba'), 34, pp. 13–22.

Read, H. (1943), *Education Through Art*, London: Faber & Faber.

Richardson, M. (1948), *Art and the Child*, London: University of London Press.

Tomie, S. (1996), '芸術研究科の誕生と経緯' ('Establishment and development of the doctoral programme in art and design'), in A. Harada (ed.), *筑波大学芸術20周年記念誌* ('The twentieth anniversary of art and design, University of Tsukaba'), Ibaraki: University of Tsukuba, pp. 30–33.

Yamazaki, H., Fukudome, H., Yamanoi, A., Murasawa, M., Watanabe, T. and Katsuragi, K. (2003), '博士課程における教育と学位授与に関する研究' ('Education and degree awarding in doctoral programmes'), *日本教育社会学会大会発表要旨集録* ('Proceedings of conference of the Japan Society of Educational Sociology'), 22:9, 55, pp. 96–99.

Chapter 21

A Research Profile of Visual Arts Theses in Education in Turkey

Suzan Duygu Bedir Erişti

An overview of PhD theses in Turkey

In reviewing art and design education PhD theses in Turkey, it is apparent that the majority are designed through quantitative methodologies and include a literature review and descriptive surveys (Kucukoglu and Ozan 2013; Ozer et al. 2013; Fazlıogullari and Kurul 2012; Erdogan et al. 2009; Kirisoglu 2009; Altinkurt 2007; Sen 2005). There are several applied experimental studies that include comparisons of control and experimental groups concerning academic success and motivation for research. However, some of the problems with these theses include a lack of some criteria for research samples, problems with measurement tools in terms of reliability and validity, and the effective interpretation of results and conclusions (Simsek et al. 2008; Altinkurt 2007). Another striking point related to the PhD theses in Turkey is the lack of practice-based methodologies. It is possible for a thesis to focus on plastic arts and on art applications while not within the framework of art-based methodologies (Ozsoy 2001).

When postgraduate studies carried out within art education programmes are examined in Turkey, it becomes obvious that many studies were not based on methodologically practice-based or arts-based backgrounds, but rather focused on artistic practices such as interpreting artefacts. Several studies included experimental applications yet the processes did not focus on gathering outcomes of art practices.

At some Turkish universities, theses are grounded in detailed theoretical frameworks with the conceptual framework determining the activities or artmaking designed to reach a level of practice-based information, yet they do not achieve this potential. Basically, this thesis structure involves the interactions of different disciplines (art, technology, education, sociology and so on) alongside art practice, but not necessarily using art-based approaches (Furlong and Oancea 2005). In the process of practice-based research, each study develops its own specific method within a conceptual framework. The reason is that practice-based research is founded on processes of obtaining new information via an art method.

The role of practice-based research

When we talk about art and design education programmes in Turkey, there is a general lack of awareness beyond traditional research design. Instead, PhD programmes have classes that focus on statistical methods in education, quantitative research methods, ethics of related quantitative research methods, social science qualitative research, scientific research and report preparation and qualitative data analysis. None of the programmes include practice-based research or art-based research methodologies, or visual research methodologies such as interpreting, collecting, documenting, creating and presenting visuals.

Another important point related to PhD programmes in art and design education is the lack of creative approaches for presenting outcomes drawn from art practices. For instance, there are several theses that include art practices in fine arts institutes; however, most of these focus on the interpretation of artefacts, such as painting exhibitions, only. There may be performances based on art but the lack of associating art processes with research methodologies causes gaps in research when interpreting the outcomes that should be gathered from production. Unfortunately, this process does not produce creative outcomes through visual arts, performances or exhibitions in the manner of researching. Moreover, doctoral students seldom focus on drawing from artistic practices as part of the research process (as a way of examining research data, questions or solutions). From my perspective, there are several problems with the current approaches to research when it comes to methods and results. An examination of doctoral theses in the records of the Council of Higher Education (CoHE) of the Republic of Turkey for the themes 'fine arts' and 'art education' reveals that the theses have mostly focused on subjects related to art production. Yet, there is insufficient discussion of the process of artmaking, the experiences of researchers and the meaning of the art production to establish this discourse as a body of emergent research.

It could be argued that most of the theses examined reflect different paradigms that are contextualized within the university where they were conducted. In some universities, experimental designs or descriptive surveys based on quantitative paradigms are prominent, while in other universities there are more quantitative, qualitative and mixed-design paradigms, along with art practice. This difference in paradigm might occur due to the viewpoints of the faculty members who supervised the theses because the supervisors encouraged graduate students to take up new paradigms.

In most of the theses, methods and approaches that do not allow for an in-depth research process, such as a descriptive survey or literature review, were common in Turkey. There may be references to arts-based research methods and approaches based on visual research methods, yet due to lack of awareness, the theses do not include any further information. In other words, the researcher did not use practice-based, arts-based or visual research methods consciously, and therefore failed to explain these methods from a scientific perspective. This is quite an important deficiency, especially in the fields of art education and fine arts. Most of the theses focused on repetitive or similar topics using traditional methods and approaches, and thus lacked artistic and research depth. However, when arts-based methods and approaches and especially practice-based research methods were used, the researcher inevitably provided an in-depth discussion of the research process. This was a key finding in a review of doctoral research. Within the framework of practice-based research, the process of data collection is quite important. However, a lack of awareness on the use of art within the context of practice-based research is among the most important gaps demonstrated in the field of art and design. Indeed, students tend to carry out several applied studies relating to their thesis topics in fine arts faculties, yet overall they fail to integrate these applications into their research processes. In Turkey, our graduate students refer to and report the related literature on their topic and conduct a topic-based study. However, they do not interrogate or examine the methodology they apply, nor do they focus on the educational processes or on the reflections of the problems and/or limitations related to their thesis topic. As a result, in my view, this does not demonstrate an expected level of scientific quality. Absent is the integration of an original creative artefact in the research process. The most important reason for this is the fact that in Turkey, art, design and education programmes reside in institutes of fine arts, educational sciences and social sciences and do not include any courses beyond traditional research, yet.

Looking to the future in Turkey

As discussed by Eisner (2006), the use of traditional research methods brings about several challenges, and in this respect, there is a need for alternate methods and approaches that can be associated with the fields of art and design. Practice-based research methodologies allow graduate students to approach the research problem within the framework of different components and situations, and under a variety of special conditions. Researchers interrogate their creativity with respect to their experiences, viewpoints, their development in the application process and their reflections on the process. They then interact directly with the research problem accordingly.

In recent years, we have seen an increase in the number of art and design education studies with well-constructed action research or qualitative approaches. This increase could be due to an awareness of the importance of interactive processes in practical research. Yet, there are still limited detailed and in-depth examinations of action research and qualitative research based studies conducted within the framework of arts-based methodologies. For example, there are research topics such as visual culture, aesthetics, museum education, analysis of a work of art, interdisciplinary art education and art criticism. On the other hand, there are several theses conducted that theoretically engage with topics related to the field of art and design that were previously investigated in the literature without any attention to a methodological framework. I suggest a shift is underway, albeit slowly.

Another striking point that should be raised in relation to the practice-based research is that there appears to be no awareness of the art-based methods, only qualitative and quantitative data collection processes, data triangulation and interpretation of the data. In this respect, the most common problem in existing theses is the limited detailing of research methods used – for example, unclear research purposes; inadequate criteria for selecting research samples; reliability and validity problems related to the measurement tools of quantitative research; lack of in-depth discussion based on qualitative research; and lack of connection between the research topic and the methodology.

At the same time, it is necessary for doctoral programmes undertaken in art education in Turkey to focus more on different dimensions related to these fields. Thesis supervisors should raise awareness of a range of methods and be knowledgeable about the up-to-date literature, including international perspectives. Confusion regarding the methodological viewpoints that could be used in the fields of art and design can and should be overcome. In this respect, experts may need to work more cooperatively and emphasize the importance of conceptual partnerships, both within these institutions, and beyond, to increasingly address concerns in international scholarship.

In conclusion, it is important to highlight such deficiencies when profiling the body of scholarship, given the lack of conceptual sub-structure. To be fair, these applications were not evident in my review. The practice-based results were not presented on the grounds of artistic practices. From my point of view, the results of artistic practices cannot be presented without a discussion of the processes of designing and reporting the research. Within the framework of practice-based research methods, practice-based reflection needs to be underlined in doctoral studies. Aspects and details related to the research purpose, that could contribute to the literature and openness to accessibility with respect to practice-based approaches, are all of great importance. For this reason, especially at the graduate level in Turkey, there is a need for content development studies grounded in alternate methodologies. In addition, future studies will need to be conducted with practice-based research methods based on these preliminary results. It is possible then for alternate approaches to fill the gap to a great extent in relation to the structuring of scientific studies in the fields of art and design in Turkey. It is also important to enhance and revise the art and design education programmes for graduate students in Turkey. In this respect, research grounded in practice-based methods needs to grow in importance, in prevalence and in acceptance within the academy in Turkey.

References

Altinkurt, L. (2007), 'Sanat egitimi ile ilgili lisansüstü tezlerin incelenmesi', *Milli Egitim*, 173, pp. 105–13.

Eisner, E. (2006), 'Does arts-based research have a future?', *Studies in Art Education*, 48:1, pp. 9–18.

Erdogan, M., Marcinkowski, T. and Ok, A. (2009), 'Content analysis of selected features of K-8 environmental education research studies in Turkey, 1997-2007', *Environmental Education Research*, 15:5, pp. 525–48.

Fazliogullari, O. and Kurul, N. (2012), 'Türkiye'deki egitim bilimleri doktora tezlerinin ozellikleri', *Mehmet Akif Ersoy Üniversitesi Egitim Fakültesi Dergisi*, 12:24, pp. 43–75.

Furlong, J. and Oancea, A. (2005), *Assessing Quality in Applied and Practice-Based Educational Research: A Framework for Discussion*, Oxford: Oxford University Department of Educational Studies.

Kirisoglu, O. (2009), *Sanat Kultur Yaraticilik,* Ankara: Pegem.

Kucukoglu, A. and Ozan, C. (2013), 'Sınıf ogretmenligi alanındaki lisansüstü tezlere yonelik bir icerik analizi', *Uluslararası Avrasya Sosyal Bilimler Dergisi*, 4:12, pp. 27–47.

Ozer, B., Yazar, T. and Eren, A. (2013), 'Analysis of graduate thesis papers in Turkey in the field of fine arts education between 1992 and 2012', *Journal of Theory and Practice in Education,* 9:4, pp. 497–510.

Ozsoy, V. (2001), 'Scientific research in fine arts education', *Education and Science,* 26:121, pp. 51–58.

Sen, U. S. (2005), 'Sanat egitiminde bilimsel arastırma yontemlerinin kullanilmasi', *Journal of Ataturk University Social Sciences Institute*, 5:1, pp. 343–60.

Simsek, A., Ozdamar, N., Becit, G., Kilicer, K., Akbulut, Y. and Yildirim, Y. (2008), 'Current trends in educational technology research in Turkey', *Selcuk University Journal of Social Sciences Institute,* 19, pp. 439–58.

Chapter 22

Qualities of Artmaking in Arts-Based Educational Research Dissertations

Alison Shields and Rita L. Irwin

A review of dissertations

This chapter reviews art education dissertations employing forms of arts-based educational research over the past decade within visual arts education at the University of British Columbia (UBC), Canada. We focus our discussion on qualities of artmaking and consider how artmaking functions within educational research. In doing so, we resist tendencies to fit arts-based research into social science research and instead propose that arts-based research has its own methods, qualities and outcomes that are drawn from artmaking practices. We specifically look at the language used to describe the qualities, goals and outcomes of artmaking within these arts-based research dissertations in order to examine what arts-based research is and where it may go within the context of the larger educational research community. Through this examination, we seek to draw out the goals and intentions of arts-based research and the possibilities within these methodologies, and open up a discussion of future possibilities.

To begin, we provide a brief overview of the dissertations examined, highlighting the participants and the types of artistic mediums and processes employed. Of the sixteen dissertations reviewed from that period,[1] eleven dissertations in visual arts education employed arts-based research.[2] While several others drew upon some artistic approaches within other qualitative research methods, we do not address those dissertations within this paper.[3] Of the eleven dissertations using arts-based research, seven describe their methodology as a/r/tography. Most of those, however, explain how a/r/tography allowed them to employ several other methodologies including narrative, autobiography, action research, auto-ethnography and phenomenology and often described their methodology as a 'mash-up' or assemblage of these various methodologies. The three that did not use a/r/tography either describe their work as arts-based or practice-led research. Although the PhD candidates participated in artmaking in all of the arts-based research, four of the PhD candidates were the only participants making art, four worked with teachers or teacher candidates, one worked with contemporary artists, two worked in a community setting and one worked with secondary school art students.

A/r/tography emphasizes the holistic relationship between artist/teacher/researcher, and several artist researchers examined their own artmaking practices for their dissertation research. Sylvia Kind (2006), for example, used knitting and textile art as a way of exploring her own experiences with bereavement and loss as a way of examining how our personal histories shape our teaching practice. Shaya Golparian (2013) similarly draws from her own art practices to explore themes of identity. As an immigrant to Canada, she uses photography, video and performance work to explore themes of unbelonging and unhomedness. Belidson Dias (2006) explores queer gender and sexuality in film representations and uses a bricolage of text and image to reveal his exploration of artmaking as a form of research. Finally, Natalie LeBlanc (2015) describes her research as practice-led research, and the dissertation as an exegesis, as she demonstrates how artmaking generates understanding. Her photographic work of closed schools explores abandonment and her photographic process examines artmaking as a form of inquiry.

Arts-based methods also provide ways for researchers to work with teachers and teacher candidates as they explore their own teaching practices: in doing so they realize how artistic inquiry generates insights into teaching practices. For example, Nadine Kalin (2007) employed a/r/tography and action research methods to explore non-art specialist teachers' perceptions of drawing through a series of drawing workshops and discussions. Through this process, Kalin learned that participants' perceptions of their drawing abilities came from their personal historical experiences with drawing, and that through this arts-based action research, teachers reconsidered and changed their perceptions of drawing. Anita Sinner (2008) worked with teacher candidates to explore their experience of becoming teachers. Through the creation of contemporary triptychs, and drawing from personal narratives, personal images and visual journals, her research examines their identities as they develop as teachers. Adrienne Boulton-Funke (2015) similarly explored teachers' identities as they were becoming teachers. Working with pre-service teachers, they made films of their experiences returning to their old schools. Boulton-Funke explored how their affective and sensory responses to the spaces triggered memories and allowed participants to reconsider their perceptions of teaching.

The remainder of the dissertations surveyed had unique aspects worth noting. Only one dissertation involved an artist working with professional artists, and in particular, whose art addresses their relationship with the land. Patti Pente (2008) had three artists place pieces of cotton into a site of significance to the artist. Through this work, she reconsidered contemporary approaches to landscape and positioned landscape art as a socially critical and embodied form of learning. Moreover, Daniel Barney (2009) was the only artist/researcher during this period who used arts-based research with secondary aged students.[4] Through an investigation of the relationship between dress and visual culture, secondary art students created work that responded to their concept of dress. His dissertation was unique, in that he proposed a/r/tography as not simply a research methodology but also a pedagogical approach to working with secondary students. Lastly, two dissertations involved artmaking with members of the community. Barbara Bickel (2008) worked with a collective of fourteen women from eleven different spiritual and/or religious backgrounds. Through various artmaking approaches, Bickel explores how a/r/tography as ritual allows for both personal and collective change. Valerie Triggs (2012) wrote a manuscript style of dissertation compiling several published articles in addition to original work. The dissertation examines the work of two a/r/tographic research teams as they examine the epistemological paradigms of art and pedagogy. As a result, she calls for a shift in teacher education research and practice from being instrumental or interpretive, towards one that emphasizes movement and interrelationality.

Qualities of artmaking within arts-based research

To examine the way arts-based researchers viewed the role of artmaking in their research, we began by looking for common words used to describe artistic processes within the dissertations. Several descriptive words include: disjunctive, poetic, metaphor/metonymy, hybrid, ambiguous, multiple, embodied, performative, intentionally incomplete, missing pieces, reassembling, relational, uncertain, exploratory, lived, emotional, sensual, affective non-linear thinking, indeterminacy, unpredictable, complexity thinking, emergent; multiple, living inquiry, transformative. Furthermore, words that describe what art does are drawn directly from these qualities and reveal the distinct intentions of artmaking that may differ from intentions of other qualitative methods. In terms of their intention, words used to describe what the art does include: resist, transform, destabilize, interconnect, affect, dialogue, propose, complexify, question, generate. Drawing from this vocabulary and how it is applied to the research process, we highlight three qualities of arts-based research emphasized within these definitions. First, arts-based research is experiential in order to examine the personal, subjective and lived experiences of the participants. Second, it emphasizes emergence, incompletion, non-linearity, multiple meanings and 'not knowing'. And third, it provokes, disrupts and resists traditional ways of doing research in order to examine alternative perspectives. Within this section, we examine a selection of the dissertations to explore how the language used to describe artmaking within these dissertations reveals the intentions of arts-based research.

Several arts-based researchers emphasize the experiential quality of artmaking with emphasis on personal and subjective lived experience. Kalin argues for 'artmaking not [only] as a mode of representation, but also a mode of narrative inquiry that evokes self-understanding and attempts to express experience' (2007: 17–18). Kind (2006) similarly uses material explorations and sensual engagements as a way of examining personal experience. Through her textile work she explores how artmaking becomes intimate and autobiographic as she examines her personal experience with loss. She describes this process with poetic language: 'As I trace my fingers over the openings in my textile pieces and remember the cutting I find my art resonating into my teaching and into my research. So in a circling back through my art I set out to discover what it means to deliberately and actively create holds and openings for the personal, the difficult, and each of our stories of woundings and mendings exploring what it means to open up to loss' (2006: 111).

Patti Pente's work specifically worked to challenge objective representations of the landscape within art education, as she had artists place pieces of cloth in the landscape. Through this process, Pente examines how artmaking becomes an embodied and sensual engagement with our surroundings, and examines how we may use our personal interaction with the land, drawing from our own experiences to examine social issues. Pente explains this perspective: 'One of the contributions of my aesthetic inquiry to the field of art education is in the positioning of a socially critical practice in landscape art as an example of this form of embodied learning through process' (2008: 206). Because of the subjective quality of artmaking, Pente argues that uncertainty is essential to artmaking, research and learning: 'artists' creative processes inspire a pedagogical threshold between the known and unknown' (2008: 206). Sinner similarly describes how arts inquiry creates a space to develop an understanding of the lived experiences of becoming teachers: 'Arts research rendered as a triptych installation, a conversation flowing across and between processes, practices and products, creates alternate constructs of *doing*, unfolding the unexpectedness of uncertainty' (2008: 265, original emphasis). Through this work, Sinner argues that art allows for a necessary ambiguity and emergence of meanings that echoes the process of becoming a teacher.

Through the emphasis on uncertainty and ambiguity, the examined dissertations demonstrate that artmaking is a generative approach to research that allows questions and connections to emerge through the research process. As an emergent form of research, artmaking becomes a mechanism through which research directions become activated. Daniel Barney, for example, began his research examining the relationship between concepts of dress in visual culture and the adolescent as consumer, artist, researcher and activist, but his research evolved into a relational conversation with research methodology and teaching/learning strategies. Kalin similarly argues that through artmaking with the participants she sought to complicate rather than conclude, and generate multiple understandings of drawings through challenging preconceptions. Through the process of working with teachers to address their conceptions of drawing, rather than moving towards a fixed conclusion, she argues that she wants to 'complexify' (2007: 18) their understandings of drawing. Finally artmaking functions to bring affect and emotional responses into the research process in order to generate new meanings and understandings. Boulton-Funke argues that the arts-based research methodology allows for an intuitive, sensory and affective experience to emerge through artmaking. She states that having her participants film an environment from their past, their old secondary school, activates memories and experiences and triggers an affective response that may not have been activated through other research methods.

Through the emphasis on emergent research methods, the research process often becomes non-linear, hybrid and multiple. Through this process, several researchers sought to disrupt and question traditional, objective approaches to research. Dias argues:

> The key argument for arts-based forms of research is that they disrupt the 'standard' methods through which research is shaped, performed, conducted and understood. Arts-based forms of research intentionally displace established modes of research and knowledge making, while allowing a polystemic research and its multiple meanings,

and emphasizing uncertainty, artistry, imagination, illusion, insight, visualization and dynamism.

(2008: 116–17)

Dias' a/r/tographic dissertation is described as a bricolage, as he describes his process of continuously combining disparate and pre-existing elements from other images into new visual representations, through collecting imagery and then distorting and juxtaposing them to continually re-evaluate 'notions of identity, representation, pedagogy, queerness, visuality, spectatorship, and cultural borders' (2008: 3). Through the process of working with text and image brought together as an assemblage, Dias came to realize 'how knowing through a creative process disrupts the concept of a coherent, projected, and safe knowledge within a formal educational setting' and that 'the creative ways of knowing found within a/r/tography inherently disrupt knowledge through the sheer juxtapositions, interactions and disjunctures that happen between textual and visual elements within a visual narrative body' (2008: 118).

Drawing from these descriptions of artmaking, it is apparent that because of the subjective and emergent qualities of artmaking inherent in all of these researchers' processes, it is the intention of the artmaking to provoke, generate, disrupt and complicate. The artistic processes disrupt conceptions of art practices, pedagogy, research and of the self. This occurs through provoking affective responses, multiple interpretations and more questions than answers.

Using artmaking to investigate educational issues

How are arts-based researchers using artmaking to investigate educational issues? While the qualities and intentions of artmaking within the context of contemporary fine arts practices and arts-based research appear to follow similar approaches, arts-based research is intended to provide insights into education. The research from the past years at UBC does this in several ways.

First, the researchers exemplify ways of learning and thinking through artmaking. Golparian (2013) examines experiences of unbelonging and unhomedness through a postcolonial framework. She shares the personal experiences of an artist, researcher and teacher through the lens of an immigrant (born in Iran, where she lived through a national revolution and years of the chaos and air raids of the Iran–Iraq war, she immigrated to Quebec at the age of 19 and then moved to Vancouver), exploring themes of home, memory, language, Otherness, exoticism, invisibility and pain through art, research and life. She asks: 'How does an immigrant negotiate the struggles she goes through as a result of having to live in-between (in my case often contradictory) cultures (including ways of being and communicating with/in the world, knowings, and value systems)?' (2013: 5). She explores this question through her artistic process that draws from her lived experience, but argues that the pedagogical process of un/becoming is not just of personal value as the personal is always engaged with all other relational aspects of life. Therefore, through this self-study, Golparian offers ways that artmaking helps one to make sense of the world and offers ways of approaching issues related to cultures, race, languages and immigration through a '*sensitive* pedagogy of representation' (2013: 206, original emphasis). 'I open up the possibility for a being together, with pain, by exposing myself, my experiences, my memories and by remembering them together with others in the pedagogical spaces of an a/r/tographic living inquiry' (2013: 191).

Similarly, through the autobiographical arts-based approaches, the dissertations reveal how art allows the researcher to develop understandings about their teaching practice. Through the personal narratives that emerged through her art practice, Kind (2006) addresses her experience with loss and bereavement as a way of challenging artists/researchers/teachers to 'consider meanings beyond self and beyond individuals as rational and autonomous beings' (ii). Through doing so she encourages a consideration of how the intimacies and difficulties of teachers' lives affect their understandings and approaches to pedagogy through interrupting a desire for control, certainty and stability.

Second, dissertations provide insights into how arts-based research, specifically a/r/tography, may be not only a research method, but also a pedagogical approach. In Barney's research for example, students become the researchers and a/r/tography becomes a pedagogical model for inquiry. Throughout the research process, the secondary school students became not just participants but also arts-based researchers. He describes the implications for this research in that it provides a redescription of the teacher and learner, demonstrates a/r/tography as a pedagogical strategy, provokes a re/presentation of knowledge, shows divergent interactions of students and research, and demonstrates how classroom practices can enter into discourse with contemporary artistic practices.

Next, researchers explore expanded approaches to understanding content through arts-based research. Pente expands approaches to educational approaches to landscape through performing personally and socially engaged approaches. Through doing so, she also challenges and disrupts traditional hierarchies in the field of landscape that emphasize western perspectives, and in turn also questions traditional approaches to research. She states: 'Landscape art is a site of power that can challenge embedded assumptions regarding national identity within tensions among local, national, and global scales. This research ruptures the Canadian myth of wilderness nation through the creation of an alternative landscape art that is informed by a theoretical discourse on the threshold as a site of difference and of learning' (2008: ii). Furthermore, she examines how through a critical landscape art can educate students about their relationship to community in the land.

In arts-based research where the participants are teachers employing artistic practices, the teachers gain a more thorough understanding of art education that may transform their approaches to teaching. Rather than simply learning about art education by being told how to do it, or watching their students, teachers are led through the challenging process of making. Through the process of (re)learning to draw, Kalin's research participants gained a more contemporary, critical and expanded perspective of drawing education. Kalin described how the participant teachers felt burdened and ill-trained to teach art and found that this developed from their early childhood experiences with art. Through arts-based and action research, and through drawing workshops, the teachers were able to reframe and demystify their relationship with drawing and open up to alternative ways of understanding drawing. Kalin describes this intention:

> Taking my cues from the evolving position drawing holds within art education (historical and current), contemporary art, and art history, as well as the elementary classrooms with which I have become familiar, this dissertation will focus on disclosing the tensions, resistances, practices, media, and understandings of drawing that are enabled through an action research group.
>
> (2007: 5)

Contemporary art, if embraced, could be incorporated directly into art drawing units.

Several dissertations propose ways of learning and researching that may challenge and question traditional/standard approaches to learning and research. As discussed earlier, as an experiential approach to learning, artmaking allows for learning to emerge through the process of making. This process is modelled within the dissertations as artist researchers reflect on their own ways of learning. Regarding this process, Dias states: 'I ask you to welcome my provocations to disturb notions of scholarship and knowledge making in art education, and mingle with the dialogical and pedagogical possibilities that they incite' (2008: 11). Dias argues that 'a/r/tography and queer theory are processes of dynamic flow that denormalize regimes such as gender, sexuality, theory, practice and disciplinarity' (2008: 18). In addition, he argues that his role as a bricoleur, drawing together visual representations and provoking a visual awareness of transdisciplinary practices through a/r/tography, is to refuse standardized models of producing knowledge.

Lastly, through pursuing arts-based research, the researchers further develop and expand approaches to arts-based research and provide further insights into ways that artmaking is a form of academic inquiry, thus expanding methods of research in education. Through performing arts-based research, every dissertation does this in some way. However, LeBlanc's dissertation most explicitly demonstrates how one may analyse artmaking as a form of research. Through her photographic work of abandoned schools, LeBlanc describes her work as practice-led and exemplifies how art practice becomes research that is 'reflection *in* and *through* practice' (2015: 4, original emphasis). Through this process, she explains that questions arise through the research process and allow for uncertainty and ambiguity. Emphasizing the role of the artist, through the dissertation, she explains how through creating, reviewing, analysing and sorting photographs, unexpected associations, narratives and connections emerge that evoke an ambiguous sense of longing or loss.

Arts-based research as reflected in the structure of the dissertation

We now turn to examining: how is the artistic inquiry reflected within the structure of the dissertation? This is an essential question in addressing how arts-based research may be evaluated in a way that values artistic qualities and wherein artistic qualities are not lost due to restrictive parameters, or lost due to overvaluing the text while undervaluing the academic rigour and meaningful contributions to knowledge production of visual art and image based work. For this reason, it is important to recognize how the artistic process is reflected in the construction of the thesis so that the dissertation performs the artmaking rather than just representing it.

Several approaches are used throughout all of the dissertations. Photographs are often used as evidence of the artistic process. The use of personal narratives allows the authors to reflect on the artmaking process (for themselves and their participants). Here, rather than simply show the final art product, the artmaking process is emphasized through narrative. Furthermore, through the personal narrative, they describe their thinking process, therefore making the learning that occurs through artmaking explicit, and thus connecting it to educational discourse. Second, poetic language is used for its experiential, affective quality and its ability to generate multiple meanings, making it complementary to visual artmaking. Several writers employ poetic language as a way of allowing the artmaking qualities to also come out in the written text.

Most of the dissertations used various approaches to achieve an open-ended and non-linear quality to their research, and through doing so often challenged the dissertation format. As described earlier, Dias' (2008) thesis is an assemblage made of visual artefacts of everyday life, a 'metissage' of words, texts and images, references to paintings, collages and photographs, photographs of other visual artists' work and visual imagery from Almodovar's films. Beginning his dissertation with the phrase '[u]nder construction' (2008: vi), Dias' dissertation is an example of this disruption of traditional conceptions of a complete and unified dissertation.

In the introduction to his thesis, Barney highlights the non-linear nature of his research process, thus aligning the document with his arts-based research methods and resisting standardized dissertation methods. He describes it as not standard but rather a disruption that creates possible openings and states: 'The readers of this dissertation are encouraged to choose their own course through this document. I did not sit down and write these chapters in a chronological order, but I did so in relation to my interpretation of the data' (Barney: 2009: 16). The format of this dissertation is significant as it explicitly highlights the emergent quality of art research and presents the research processes and products as an unfolding.

LeBlanc similarly creates a dissertation structure that aligns with her artistic inquiry approach. Calling her dissertation an exegesis, she uses several of the approaches mentioned above to develop an artistic reflection of her practice-led process. Describing it as an exegesis deliberately challenges and sets it apart from traditional dissertation structures: rather than answering or advancing a hypothesis, or providing an explanation of the work, she provokes shifts in thought. LeBlanc also provides a wealth of images throughout the dissertation to highlight the unfolding of themes. She describes how the images are meant to provoke rather than represent and encourages meandering or invention. Thus, she sets up the dissertation as an open-ended, ambiguous and imaginative space of research.

Areas for further consideration

While there has been significant development and proliferation of arts-based research over the course of the past decade, there still remain several challenges. One thing worth noting is that every dissertation reviewed here, to some extent, examined its chosen arts-based research methodology itself. This tendency suggests two things. First, it suggests that arts-based research is a reflexive research method, one that encourages each researcher to self-examine the role of artmaking within the development of their research methodology. Second, it suggests that researchers continue to examine and define arts-based research and how it is situated in relation to other research models. Indeed, several researchers describe attempts to resist and disrupt traditional academic methods, suggesting that arts-based research may continue to remain in a defensive position describing itself in relation to other qualitative research methodologies. While this position is productive in asserting how it differs from traditionally employed educational research, this chapter posits that arts-based research is always in relation to artistic methods, thus highlighting the unique trajectory of research that follows from arts-based forms of inquiry. It is our hope that such discussions of PhD research can open up more ways of emphasizing and valuing the artistic components within arts-based educational research.

Acknowledgement

We would like to thank the Social Sciences and Humanities Research Council of Canada for funding our research.

References

Barney, D. (2009), 'A study of dress through artistic inquiry: Provoking understandings of artist, researcher, and teacher identities', PhD thesis, Vancouver: The University of British Columbia.

Bickel, B. (2008), 'Living the divine spiritually and politically: Art, ritual and performative/pedagogy in women's multi-faith leadership', PhD thesis, Vancouver: The University of British Columbia.

Boulton-Funke, A. (2015), 'An arts-based methodology of intuition: Secondary visual art teacher becomings and encounters with schooling', PhD thesis, Vancouver: The University of British Columbia.

Dias, B. (2006), 'Border epistemologies: Looking at Almodovar's queer genders and their implications for visual culture education', PhD thesis, Vancouver: The University of British Columbia.

Golparian, S. (2013), 'Displaced displacement: An a/r/tographic performance of experiences of being unhomed', PhD thesis, Vancouver: The University of British Columbia.

Kalin, N. (2007), 'Conversations on teaching and learning drawing: Drawn toward transformation', PhD thesis, Vancouver: The University of British Columbia.

Kind, S. (2006), 'Of stones and silences: Storytelling the trace of the other in the autobiographical and textile text of art/teaching', PhD thesis, Vancouver: The University of British Columbia.

LeBlanc, N. (2015), 'In/visibility of the abandoned school: Beyond representations of school closure', PhD thesis, Vancouver: The University of British Columbia.

Pente, P. (2008), 'Being at the edge of landscape: Sense of place and pedagogy', PhD thesis, Vancouver: The University of British Columbia.

Sinner, A. (2008), 'Unfolding the unexpectedness of uncertainty: Arts research as a triptych installation: A conversation of processes, practices, products', PhD thesis, Vancouver: The University of British Columbia.

Sinner, A., Leggo, C., Irwin, R. L., Gouzouasis, P. and Grauer, K. (2006), 'Arts-based educational research dissertations: Reviewing the practices of new scholars', *Canadian Review of Art Education*, 29:4, pp. 1223–70.

Triggs, V. (2012), 'Art as ecological practice: A curriculum of movement for teacher education methods', PhD thesis, Vancouver: The University of British Columbia.

Notes

1 The a/r/tography website contains weblinks to all dissertations discussed here as well as other art(s) education dissertations that may be of interest. See http://artography.edcp.educ.ubc.ca. Accessed 2 February 2019.

2 A complete list can be found in the references.

3 These dissertations employed philosophical inquiry steeped in discourse analysis, historical analysis or other forms of qualitative research.

4 An earlier review of dissertations completed between 1995 and 2005 in the same Faculty reveals further work in arts-based research and a/r/tography (see Sinner et al. 2006).

Notes on Contributors

Jeff ADAMS is Professor of Education at the University of Chester, leader of the EdD programme, and co-director of RECAP, a centre for research into creativity. He is Principal Editor of the *International Journal of Art & Design Education*; his most recent book is *Creativity and Democracy in Education* (with Allan Owens, 2016, Routledge).

Emma ARYA-MANESH is a researcher at the University of Chester, where she is writing up her PhD entitled 'Occupied: A critical ethnography of peacebuilding in formal education in the West Bank'. She a coordinator for RECAP, a centre for Research into Education, Creativity and Arts through Practice, and the administrator for the *International Journal of Art & Design Education*.

Estelle BARRETT is an Honorary Professorial Fellow of the Victorian College of the Arts at the University of Melbourne and Casual Senior Research Fellow at the Institute of Koorie Education, Deakin University. She is widely published in the fields of creative arts research, aesthetics and new materialist perspectives relating to art and knowledge production. She is a Research Fellow of the International Centre for Fine Arts Research, Birmingham University.

Michael BIGGS is Emeritus Professor of Aesthetics at the University of Hertfordshire and Adjunct Professor at the University of Canberra, and is a leading figure in arts research. He is a member of the Board of the National Research School in Architecture, Sweden and Chair of the interdisciplinary expert panel of the Belgian Research Council.

Lorrie BLAIR is Professor of Art Education at Concordia University in Montreal, Quebec. She is the author of *Writing a Graduate Thesis or Dissertation* (2016, Sense Publishers). She is an active supervisor of MA and PhD students and is the 2017 recipient of the Concordia University Award for Graduate Mentoring.

Barbara BOLT is a practising artist and art theorist, and Professor in Contemporary Arts and Culture at the Faculty of Fine Art and Music, University of Melbourne. She has written extensively on artistic research and research ethics. She is the author of *Art Beyond*

Representation: The Performative Power of the Image (2004) and *Heidegger Reframed: Interpreting Key Thinkers for the Arts* (2011) and has co-edited four books.

Natalia CALDERÓN is a researcher and Professor of Artistic Research at the Universidad Veracruzana, México. She completed a PhD in arts and education at the University of Barcelona, Spain and an MA at the Utrecht Graduate School of Visual Art and Design, the Netherlands. Her work has focused on generating and exploring pedagogical experiences through art practices and research.

Jo Chiung Hua CHEN, EdD, is a Professor of the Fine Arts Department and ex-Vice President of National Taiwan Normal University. She was honoured with the 2014 Ziegfield Award of the United States Society for Education through Art. She serves on the Board of Arts Education Committee of Ministry of Education, R.O.C.

Belidson DIAS is an Associate Professor at the Visual Art Department of the Art Institute of Universidade de Brasília, UnB, Brazil. He is a specialist in critical studies of sexuality and queer theory. His research interest includes education and visuality, curriculum studies, transculturalism, multiculturalism, postcolonialism, cultural pedagogies, sexuality and gender.

Suzan Duygu Bedir ERIŞTI is Associate Professor of Art Education at Anadolu University in Eskisehir, Turkey. In 2016 she won the Turkey Visual Arts Education Association Academician of the Year Award for consistent contributions through published literature and her outstanding contribution to national art education.

Tatiana FERNÁNDEZ is an Assistant Professor at the Visual Art Department of the Art Institute of Universidade de Brasília, UnB, Brazil. Her work and research is centred on artistic events as cultural pedagogies. Her interest includes decolonial aesthetics, identity politics, pictorial turn in education and pedagogical turn in art.

Kathryn GRUSHKA is a Senior Lecturer at the University of Newcastle's School of Education. She is a nationally recognized artist and visual/design teacher educator, curriculum writer and practising artist. Her research interests span learning, cognition, embodied visual knowing and subjectivity insights, visual pedagogies, multi-modal learning, narrative and arts health.

Fernando HERNÁNDEZ-HERNÁNDEZ is a Professor in the Unit of Cultural Pedagogies in the Fine Arts Faculty of the University of Barcelona. He is the director of the master's programme on 'Visual arts and education: A constructionist perspective' and doctoral programme on arts and education. He is the co-coordinator of the quality research group

ESBRINA – Contemporary Subjectivities, Visualities and Educational Environments and a member of REUNI+D – University Network for Educational Research and Innovation.

Mirja HILTUNEN is Professor of Art Education and Head of the Department of Art Education at the Faculty of Art and Design, University of Lapland, Rovaniemi, Finland. Her research focuses on socially engaged arts in the North and she has published widely on community-based art education.

Brooke HOFSESS, PhD, is an Associate Professor of Art Education at Appalachian State University immersed in aesthetic and poetic approaches to inquiry, contemplating teacher education and renewal.

Allyson HOLBROOK is a Professor in the Faculty of Education and Arts at the University of Newcastle, NSW Australia, and member of the Australian Research Council College of Experts in the Social Sciences. She is Director of the centre for the Study of Research Training and Impact (SORTI) and a leading academic in the field of postgraduate learning and assessment with internationally recognized expertise in the study of research student learning and examination across disciplines.

Maria HUHMARNIEMI is a lecturer of art education and applied visual arts at the Faculty of Art and Design, University of Lapland, Rovaniemi, Finland. She engages with questions concerning the North, multiculturalism and communality.

Rita L. IRWIN is a Distinguished University Scholar and Professor of Art Education at the University of British Columbia, Canada. While her research interests include arts teacher education, artist-in-schools programmes and sociocultural issues, she is best known for her work in expanding how we might enact arts practice-based research methodologies through collaborative collectives.

Timo JOKELA is Professor of Art Education in the Faculty of Art and Design, University of Lapland, Finland. He is also the leader of the University of the Arctic's thematic network on Arctic sustainable art and design. He has been responsible for several international and regional action research projects in the field of art education and published several articles and books. He works actively as an environmental artist.

Mira KALLIO-TAVIN is Professor of Arts-Based Research and Pedagogy, Head of Research, and Director of the master's programme in the Department of Art, Aalto University, Finland. Her research area focuses on arts-based research, disability studies in art education and animal studies in contemporary art.

Justin B. MAKEMSON is Assistant Professor of Art Education at the University of New Mexico. Makemson's research explores teacher and student-artist identities, place-based technologies, material studies, folklore in curriculum and neuroaesthetics.

April MANDRONA is an Assistant Professor in the Division of Art History and Contemporary Culture at the Nova Scotia College of Art and Design. Her art education practice focuses on rurality and spatial justice, ethical approaches to research and teaching, the social potential of artmaking and building transnational solidarity.

Toshio NAOE, PhD, is a Professor at the University of Tsukuba. He is interested in the dynamics of curricula as implemented by art teachers, comparative studies on art education and art writing in education.

Ramya RAVISANKAR is an artist and educator who received an MFA from Pratt Institute; she is currently a PhD candidate in arts, administration, education and policy at The Ohio State University. Her research investigates shifting notions of materiality through art-making. She is also an instructor of art at Capital University in Columbus, Ohio.

Karinna RIDDETT, PhD, currently works in the field of visual analytics and data visualization as a trainer with Tableau software. She previously taught visual arts for sixteen years in primary and secondary schools in Georgia.

Verónica SAHAGÚN SÁNCHEZ is an artist/teacher/researcher specialized in feminist epistemologies applied to contemporary art/craft in the context of community education. Her research interests include equity in art education and sustainability of vernacular textile traditions, as well as the fusion of digital media with craft processes in art practice.

Ângela SALDANHA, PhD, is a researcher at CIAC, the Center for Research in Arts and Communication, Aberta University. She is a member of i2ADS at the University of Porto, and she is a graduate in design, with a master's degree in visual arts from the University of Aveiro.

Alison SHIELDS is an artist and art educator living in Victoria, British Columbia. She received an MFA at the University of Waterloo and a PhD from the University of British Columbia. She is currently an Assistant Professor of Art Education at the University of Victoria. Through her doctoral research, she explores creative processes, artistic research and the relationship between thinking and making through studio work.

Richard SIEGESMUND is Professor of Art and Design Education at Northern Illinois University. He has received Fulbright awards for arts-based research in both Ireland and Belgium. His publications include *Arts-Based Research in Education: Foundations for Practice* (2008), with a second edition in 2018.

Anita SINNER is an Associate Professor in the Department of Art Education at Concordia University. Her interests include arts research methods, life writing, teacher education, international art education and community art education.

Darlene ST. GEORGES is a Métis artist, poet, Assistant Professor of Art Education, University of Lethbridge and PhD candidate, Concordia University. She embraces the unfolding metamorphosis of scholarship by harnessing multiple lines of inquiry through visual imagery and poetics. 'My creation-research endeavours to explore, through an evolving ontological process, my deepening connection with All My Relations'. She explores complex issues of identity and politicized memory to create spaces in which alternative histories can emerge.

Kevin TAVIN is Professor of International Art Education, and head of the Department of Art, Aalto University, Finland. He holds a BFA, MEd and PhD in art education and has taught K–12 and post-secondary courses since 1990. His research focuses on visual culture, critical pedagogy, cultural studies and psychoanalytic theory.

Teresa TORRES DE EÇA, PhD, works as an art teacher in secondary education (Portugal). Her research interests are focused on participatory research, socially engaged arts, transcultural educational projects and art education activism.

Marnee WATKINS, PhD, lectures in visual arts education at the University of Melbourne. Her teaching and research interests are in teachers' professional learning for arts-rich teaching, and exploring the role artful collaborations between the university and schools play in facilitating this support.

Boyd WHITE is Associate Professor in the Department of Integrated Studies in Education, McGill University. His current teaching and research interests are in the areas of philosophy, aesthetics and art education. Dr. White is the author of numerous journal articles, text chapters and three texts.

Jennifer WICKS is a PhD candidate in art education at Concordia University. She is interested in collaborative and arts-based methodologies, pedagogy and post-qualitative research.

Julie WREN is a PhD candidate at the University of Melbourne. She is an educator with interest in early childhood visual arts education and currently lectures at Edith Cowan University in Western Australia.

Susan WRIGHT is Chair of Arts Education at the University of Melbourne and the Director of the Melbourne UNESCO Observatory of Arts Education. Her teaching and research interests are semiotics, young children's first literacies and multimodal learning through the arts.

Index

www.ingramcontent.com/pod-product-compliance
Lightning Source LLC
LaVergne TN
LVHW080831240826
846232LV00015B/53
* 9 7 8 1 7 8 3 2 0 9 9 1 0 *